D1474680

Parashah Sheleimah

on SEFER BEREISHIS

MOSAICA PRESS

Parashah Sheleimah

on SEFER BEREISHIS

Applying the weekly
Torah reading to life's
events and celebrations

RABBI ALLEN SCHWARTZ

Published by Mosaica Press, Inc.
www.mosaicapress.com
info@mosaicapress.com

In loving memory of

Elizabeth Kent
פיגא בת אהרן ז״ל

Steve Kent
ישראל יעקב בן קאפל הלוי ז״ל

Linda Kent
רבקה מאטל בת ישראל יעקב ז״ל

Milton Schwartz
צבי מנחם מענדל בן מיכאל ז״ל

Sarah Schwartz
חיה שרה בת ר׳ משה ז״ל

MICHAEL AND MICHELLE SCHWARTZ
AND FAMILY

In memory of

Mr. Azriel Feiner

עזריאל בן יעקב ז״ל

and

Mr. Norbert Sternberg

שמואל משה בן שמשון אברהם הכהן ז״ל

לז״נ

משה בן שמואל הכהן

שמשון אברהם בן משה הכהן ואסתר שטרנברג

העושע בת שמואל ואסתר שטרנברג

ולזכר קדושי השואה הי״ד אשר נהרגו על קידוש השם

משה בן שמשון אברהם ומרים שטרנברג

שמואל בן שמשון אברהם ומרים שטרנברג

מרדכי חיים מייזנר

רחל נואמן בת משה ואסתר

מלכה רוזנבאום בת משה ואסתר

חוה וואלוואוויץ בת משה ואסתר

אסתר שטרנברג-מייזנר

מרים בת שלמה זלמן פוקס

שמואל בן יעקב פארקאס

אסתר בת דוד והעושע פארקאס

סימה בת שמואל ואסתר פארקאס

יחזקאל אריה בן יהודה וסימה קעסנער

דוד בן יהודה וסימה קעסנער

בריינדל בת שמואל ואסתר פארקאס

שרה בת מנחם ובריינדל פערל

In memory of

Mort Kaufman

משה בן יעקב ז״ל

Anne Kaufman

דבורה בת יוסף ז״ל

לעילוי נשמת

רבקה בתיה ב״ר מרדכי ע״ה

נלב״ע ג׳ שבט תשס״ה

ת.נ.צ.ב.ה.

הונצח ע״י

זכריה דוד פרנסקי שיח׳

In memory of my dear mother

Dr. Riva Prensky ע״ה

DEDICATED BY ZACHARY PRENSKY

Dedicated by

Rebecca and Randy Modell

and

Jodi and Adam Weinstein

in memory of their departed loved ones

May the insights in this special *sefer*
be a source of inspiration for future generations.

לעילוי נשמת

עטא בת אברהם משה, ז״ל

Joan Schoen Bortnick, z"l

A friend to all God's creations

ויעש אלקים את חית הארץ למינה ואת הבהמה למינה
ואת כל רמש האדמה למנהו וירא אלקים כי טוב
ויאמר אלקים נעשה אדם בצלמנו כדמותנו...
ויברך אותם אלקים ויאמר להם אלקים פרו ורבו ומלאו את הארץ

From her loving and devoted children and grandchildren
THE SCHOEN FAMILY

Rabbi Hershel Schachter
24 Bennett Avenue
New York, New York 10033
(212) 795-0630

הרב צבי שכטר
ראש ישיבה וראש כולל
שיבת רבינו יצחק אלחנן

ברכת מזל טוב

כי יכירו ויודיעו הרה"ג מזליק שליט"א,
ה"ה, נואם כאש להלהיב לבבות של
הבחורים, וכן מארגן על תלמודות סיפרי
התורה, כלומר, אוצרה אוצר - השם ה' לרחת
מכל פרשה, תמינה, ברספמהה, ודרה
ואלף על, בלימת תלמות הפל, וכל
אתאמתי בזכל כל אתאמתי קהילות ספרין
הקל למת, ותהלות שים - הכם ה' דנין
הקהל, אימין, ואמל ואת כן ונהל.
הכתב והחותם לכמד התורה,
הרב צבי שכטר
ת"שא

בס"ד

Table of Contents

Acknowledgments

I thank my life partner, Alisa, who has commented over the years on many of these thoughts and worked with me studiously through the entire project. This work was also considerably enhanced by the editing and careful reading of my son Ellie, whose scholarship and advice were indispensable. I also thank my children, Shonnie and Yoni, Chani and Joel, Moshe and Renee, Ellie and Carly, Esti and Aaron, and Mindy and Yoni, and their families, who have kept our Shabbos table alive with Torah, *zemiros*, and Shabbos spirit. I also thank the multitude of guests we've had over the years who have contributed Shabbos ideas to our table.

My thirty-plus years at Congregation Ohab Zedek have been a time of great growth for my family, and I dedicate this work to all those who have made Shabbos such a glorious experience. At the end of Friday night services, right after my weekly Mussar Moment, I bless the congregation with the line from *bentching* that requests: "הרחמן הוא ינחילנו יום שכולו שבת ומנוחה לחיי העולמים—May the Merciful One bring us the day which will be totally Shabbos and rest, in eternal life." After this I say, "May the next twenty-four hours be 'מעין עולם הבא'—May Shabbos bestow upon us a taste of the World to Come." I do hope that this work will enhance Shabbos in the eyes of the reader.

Introduction

The Weekly Torah Portion

The weekly Torah portion is a great unifier of our people. Jews of all stripes read the same words of Torah week after week all over the world. These words serve as inspiration and as a connection to history and current events, as well as to our life events. For this reason, we scour the weekly Torah portion to deliver a message for a *shalom zachor*, a *bris*, *simchas bas*, *pidyon haben*, *upsherin*, bar or bas mitzvah, *aufruf*, wedding, *sheva berachos*, and sadly at a funeral as well. The Torah portion can connect to current events just as it can connect to a graduation ceremony, a special anniversary or birthday, or any commemorative event.

The purpose of this work is to offer the reader a multifaceted approach to the weekly Torah portion. For the purpose of brevity, I will refer to the weekly *parashah*, even though, technically, this is a misnomer. The custom of breaking up the Torah into weekly portions, beginning with *Bereishis* and ending with *V'Zos Haberachah*, was the Babylonian custom, and these portions are known as *sidros*. There are fifty-four[1] *sidros*

---

in the Torah and they are read from the first Shabbos after Simchas Torah until Simchas Torah the next year.[2] The older custom, practiced in Israel, was to read the Torah over a period of three years, beginning with the first of Nissan.[3] These portions are more correctly called *parashiyos*[4] and the Torah is divided into approximately 154 of these.[5] By the twelfth century, this custom of a triennial cycle of Torah completion was no longer in practice with few exceptions.[6] Based on this, it is more correct to speak of the *sidrah* of the week than the *parashah* of the week, but I will refer to the language commonly used and call our weekly portion "the *parashah*."[7]

---

the same numerical value of the word גן. See *Sefer Hagan*, edited by M. Orlian (Jerusalem: Mossad Harav Kook, 2009), pp. 22–23, Introduction.

2   *Megillah* 31b. *Rambam, Mishneh Torah, Hilchos Tefillah* 13:1, refers to the completion of the Torah taking place on Sukkos. See Avraham Yaari, *Toldos Chag Simchas Torah* (Jerusalem: Mossad Harav Kook, 1998), especially chaps. 3 and 4, to trace the connection of Torah completion to this holiday.

3   *Megillah* 29b. *Rambam, Mishneh Torah, Hilchos Tefillah* 13:1, refers to this as a "custom that is not widespread."

4   If the line of text ends and is open to the end of the line, it is known as a *parashah pesuchah*, an "open-ended *parashah*." If the line continues after a space of at least nine letters, it is known as *parashah setumah*, a "closed-ended *parashah*." *Rambam* disqualifies a Torah that doesn't close a *parashah* line according to tradition, and he lists all the correct closings in *Hilchos Sefer Torah*, chap. 8.

5   There are varying traditions of this total. The *parashah* numbers can be found in the margins of the *Koren Tanach*, as follows: *Bereishis*: 43, *Shemos*: 29, *Vayikra*: 23, *Bamidbar*: 32, *Devarim*: 27. For a complete three-year listing of the breakdown of the Torah reading by *parashah*, see *Encyclopedia Judaica*, 1st ed., vol. 15, pp. 1386–1390, "Triennial Cycle."

6   See n. 2, above.

7   In addition, the entire Bible is broken into chapters. This is the work of medieval Christians and is usually included in our Bibles, Concordances, and reference guides for the sake of convenience and expedience. The only Biblical book where Chazal refer to chapter numbers is *Tehillim*, which has its own natural chapter headings. *Berachos* 9b considers *Tehillim* chapters 1 and 2 to be the same chapter, which throws off subsequent chapters by one. *Megillah* 17b similarly numbers *Tehillim* chapters one less than our Masoretic text for the same reason. In addition to *Tehillim* chapter 2, chapters 10 and 33 also have no natural chapter headings, and they also blend into the chapter preceding them. This would leave Tehillim with 147 chapters, and a number of sources connect this number to the years of Yaakov Avinu. See *Yerushalmi, Shabbos* 16:1, based on *Tehillim* 22:4, which refers to "תהילות ישראל," one for each year of his life. See also *Midrash Tehillim*, chap. 22, *Maseches Sofrim* 16:11, *Baal Haturim, Bereishis* 47:29, and *Tosafos, Pesachim* 117a, ד"ה שעומדים.

The Four Shabbos Amidahs

Each *parashah* will include four selections, each of which connects to a key phrase from one of the four *Amidahs* of Shabbos.

Maariv

אַתָּה קִדַּשְׁתָּ אֶת יוֹם הַשְּׁבִיעִי לִשְׁמֶךָ תַּכְלִית מַעֲשֵׂה שָׁמַיִם וָאָרֶץ.

You sanctified the seventh day for Your Name's sake, the conclusion of the creation of heaven and earth.

We pray four times over Shabbos, and these prayers traverse history, taking the Shabbos observer on a whirlwind journey beginning with Creation. The first prayer, *Maariv*, refers directly to the verses in *parashas Bereishis* that speak of God's creation and cessation of creative activity, *melachah*, on Shabbos. *Melachah*, related to the word *malach*, meaning "angel," is not a function of labor, but of creativity. This is a very spiritual time in which we invite angels to begin Shabbos with us as we contemplate the peacefulness of our transition from the six days of activity to the day of rest.[8]

Shacharis

יִשְׂמַח מֹשֶׁה בְּמַתְּנַת חֶלְקוֹ כִּי עֶבֶד נֶאֱמָן קָרָאתָ לּוֹ כְּלִיל תִּפְאֶרֶת בְּרֹאשׁוֹ
נָתַתָּ בְּעָמְדוֹ לְפָנֶיךָ עַל הַר סִינַי.

Moses rejoiced in the gift of his portion that You called him a faithful servant. A crown of splendor You placed on his head when he stood before You on Mount Sinai.

The second prayer takes us to *Matan Torah*, the giving of the Torah on Mount Sinai, seven weeks after we attained our freedom from Egyptian slavery. We had been turned into beasts of burden, performing numerous backbreaking tasks and building great edifices and towering

---

8   There is a custom to sing about Shabbos angels on Friday night, based on *Shabbos* 119b. Perhaps the angels (מַלְאָכִים) are invited to replace (מְלָאכָה), which is eschewed for Shabbos. In the end, we send them away from the table as angels do not eat; they therefore leave before we start the meal.

structures for others. The redemption from Egypt made it possible for us to break the yoke of Pharaoh's servitude so that we could serve God. Shortly afterward, we put our considerable latent talents to work in the construction of God's sanctuary, the *Mishkan*. The common juxtaposition of this construction with the observance of Shabbos teaches that the halachic definition of *melachah* on Shabbos is precisely that which went into the construction of the *Mishkan*.[9] The forbidden labors of Shabbos total thirty-nine activities, and these fall into four categories of *melachah* that underscore the connection of Shabbos—not only to the *Mishkan* and Creation—but also to *yetzias Mitzrayim*, the redemption from Egypt.

The first category, comprising the first eleven *melachos*, is connected to the processing of food. The second category, comprising thirteen *melachos*, is connected to the processing of clothing. The third category, comprising seven *melachos*, is connected to the processing of leather works, and the final eight, to building structures. While all thirty-nine were necessary for the construction of the *Mishkan*, they are also essential activities that underscore the building blocks of human dignity, insofar as we differ from animals. Animals do not process food, weave threads into clothes, form leather into shoes, or build structures within which to live. *Yetzias Mitzrayim* gave us the humanity necessary to be *Mishkan* builders and Shabbos observers.

Musaf

וְשָׁם נַעֲשֶׂה לְפָנֶיךָ אֶת קָרְבְּנוֹת חוֹבוֹתֵינוּ תְּמִידִים כְּסִדְרָם וּמוּסָפִים כְּהִלְכָתָם.

There we will perform before you the rite of our required offerings, the continual offerings in their order and the musaf offerings according to their laws.

The third prayer takes us to the Messianic era and makes reference to the Temple service. This will usher a redemptive age that we call

---

9   *Shemos* 31:12–17 and 35:23 both reference Shabbos observance and are embedded within larger Torah instructions for the construction of the *Mishkan*. This is understood by our Sages to teach that the *Mishkan* is not to be constructed on Shabbos. *Vayikra* 26:2 also juxtaposes Shabbos observance with God's *Mikdash*.

"יום שכולו שבת," the time period in which we will perpetually enjoy the blessings that Shabbos offers us. *Ramban* divided history into six one-thousand-year epochs, each one connected to a day of Creation.[10]

On the first two days, says *Ramban*, the world was still in a confounded state where the land masses and waters were not yet fully separated. This corresponds to the first two thousand years, traversing the time of Adam HaRishon to the age of Avraham when he discovered God.[11] This was when the message of a living, unseen, single God—to the exclusion of any other power—began to spread, likened to the spreading of vegetation throughout the earth on Day Three.

Day Four, when the luminaries were created, corresponded to the shining light of the Temple, which would be the conduit between Heaven and Earth. The luminaries, however, are not always visible—they appear and disappear, waxing and waning. This is exemplified by the construction and destruction of the two Temples during the fourth millennium, which takes us to the creation of beasts on Days Five and Six. This was a very dark period of history—for the world and for us.

The creation and perfection of man, sometime on Day Six, which would correspond to somewhere between the years 5000 and 6000, signifies the Messianic arrival for which we still await.

The year 6000, as we enter the seventh millennium, begins the יום שכולו שבת. This will take us to a perfected world, on the way to the realization of the eschatological prophecy of Zechariah that is part of our daily liturgy. Zechariah refers to a day in the future when "ביום ההוא יהיה ה' אחד ושמו אחד—On that day God will be One and His name One."[12] The Talmud asks: "אטו האידנא לאו אחד הוא—Is He not One today?"[13] The answer to this question appears in *Minchah*.

---

10   *Ramban* to *Bereishis* 2:3, "אשר ברא אלקים לעשות" based on *Tehillim* 90:4, "כי אלף שנים בעיניך כיום אתמול—For even a thousand years in Your eyes are like bygone yesterday."

11   There are different opinions of this age. *Nedarim* 32a puts Avraham's age at finding God at three; *Rambam, Hilchos Avodah Zarah* 1:3, at age forty; and *Ramban*, at age forty-eight (see *Bereishis Rabbah* 64:4). This places Avraham's discovery of God at just before the start of the third millennium.

12   *Zechariah* 14:9.

13   *Pesachim* 50b.

Minchah

אתה אחד ושמך אחד ומי כעמך ישראל גוי אחד בארץ.

You are One and Your name is One, and who is like Your people Israel one nation in the land.

God's very being is impossible for us to grasp. This is why we don't pronounce His name the way it is spelled. The spelling bespeaks a combination of past, present, and future and transcends time, space, and dimension.[14] Today God's name is not one. It is pronounced differently than it is spelled. The Talmud answers that in a time of clarity, after the redemptive age has taken grasp and the blessings of that glorious time will accrue to mankind, we will pronounce God's name as it is spelled, and the full scope of Zechariah's prediction will take hold.[15] For this reason, the *Minchah* prayer begins: "אתה אחד ושמך אחד ומי כעמך ישראל גוי אחד בארץ—You are One and Your name is One, and who is like Your people Israel one nation in the land." The spirit of Shabbos has transformed us into a place that is very close to God and His name. This is why *seudah shelishis* is always a very spiritual time where singing and uplifting and inspiring words of Torah are appropriate.

In this work, each of these four Shabbos prayers will correspond to a section of each *parashah*. We will expound upon the *parashah* using a multifaceted approach based on *p'shat*, *remez*, *d'rash*, and *sod*, which are represented by the acronym פרדס, *pardes*.

- *Maariv*: a brief *d'var Torah* that can be shared at the Shabbos table.
- *Shacharis*: a brief introduction to the Torah reading that encapsulates the message of the *parashah*, mostly in the realm of *p'shat*.[16]

---

14   This is the plain meaning of "אהי-ה אשר אהי-ה," which God told Moshe when he asked for God's name in *Shemos* 3:15.

15   The pronunciation must wait for this time period, which the Gemara calls *Olam Haba*, the "World to Come." (*Pesachim* 50b) The Mishnah considers such a pronunciation before this time to be so severe a dogmatic sin that one who pronounces God's name in this manner would forfeit their share in the World to Come. See *Sanhedrin* 90a; *Avodah Zarah* 18a.

16   The word *p'shat* as a noun stems from the same word as the adjective פשוט, which means

- *Musaf:* The main homiletic exposition of the *parashah* with a more global message in the realm of *d'rash.*[17]
- *Minchah* **(and *Seudah Shelishis*):** The spiritual side of the *sidrah*, often accompanied by a story or *gematria.*[18] *Gematria* (numerology) enters the realm of *remez* or *sod*, the more esoteric levels of Biblical exposition.

In addition, each *parashah* will include an explication of the haftarah and its connection to the *parashah*, and each *parashah* will have what I call a "Mussar Moment." This is a brief aphorism that connects the *parashah* with an ethical lesson through a brief explanation.

The reader will also have the opportunity to connect the *parashah* to three sets of events: (1) birth, *shalom zachor, simchas bas, bris, pidyon haben, upsherin*; (2) bar or bas mitzvah; and (3) *aufruf*, wedding, *sheva berachos.*

Finally, each chapter will contain an exposition of a word in the *parashah* that is either rare, unusual, or deserves special attention. I call this the "Word of the *Parashah.*"

The ten sections of each *parashah* are ordered as follows:

1. Friday Night
2. Introduction to the Torah
3. Introduction to the Haftarah
4. Derashah
5. Mussar Moments
6. Birth
7. B'nei Mitzvah
8. Marriage
9. Seudah Shelishis
10. Word of the Parashah

"extended" and "widespread" (as in *Rambam, Hilchos Tefillah* 13:1, referenced above in n. 3). *P'shat* would therefore refer to an extension of the contextual meaning of the verse. A related connotation is the word להפשיט, which means "to skin [i.e., an animal]." *P'shat* takes the simple, surface-level meaning of the word or storyline, in contrast to the next level, *d'rash.*

17 *D'rash* is a deeper exposition of the text than *p'shat*. It digs beyond the outer-level understanding of the text to deliver its inner message.

18 See "*Lech Lecha*, (9) *Seudah Shelishis*" for an elaboration on the concept of *gematria*.

Parashas Bereishis

—1—
Friday Night
תכלית מעשה שמים וארץ

Rashi opens his Torah commentary with a justification for including the story of Creation in a law code. This is because the nations of the world will always say:

לסטים אתם שכבשתם ארצות שבעה גוים.

You stole this land in your conquest of the seven Canaanite nations.

The nations, *Rashi* says, would begrudge our rights to our land because the Canaanites were there before us. This reason we are told of Creation is, in *Rashi's* words, encapsulated by a verse in *Sefer Tehillim*:

כח מעשיו הגיד לעמו לתת להם נחלת גוים.

The strength of His deeds He revealed to His people, to give them the inheritance of nations. (Tehillim 111:6)

On closer scrutiny we notice that there is an inconsistency in *Rashi*. While he says that the Creation story is told as a message to the nations, the proof text speaks of a message to the Israelites. According to *Rashi's* opening thesis, the verse should read something like:

כח מעשיו הגיד לגוים לתת לעמו את נחלתם.

The strength of His deeds He revealed to the nations, to give His people their inheritance.

We can answer that first and foremost, the message *is* for the Israelites. *We* must first and foremost believe that the land is ours before anyone else accepts that this is so. Historically, the descendants of Shem lived in Israel first, and the Canaanites took it from them. We see when Avraham first arrived in Canaan, the Torah says:

והכנעני אז בארץ.

*The Canaanites were **by then** in the land. (Bereishis 12:6)*

This implies that they were not originally in the land, as *Rashi* states explicitly: "The Canaanites conquered the land of Israel from the descendants of Shem, for the land of Israel fell in the portion of Shem when Noach divided the lands to his sons. As is stated (*Bereishis* 14:18): 'And Malkitzedek king of Shalem.'"

Therefore, God said to Avraham that at a future time, He would return Canaan to Avraham's children, since they are descended from Shem. We can't expect anyone else to accept this unless we are sure of it first.

— 2 —
Introduction to the Torah

ישמח משה במתנת חלקו

Chazal teach that the Torah begins and ends with acts of *chessed* from God.[1] In the beginning, God clothed Adam and Chavah's nakedness,[2]

---

1   See *Sotah* 14a. This idea also appears in Chazal with a third component. The beginning and end of the Torah both record acts of *chessed* from God, and these bookends of *chessed* also encompass acts of *chessed* from God in between, such as God visiting Avraham as he recovered from circumcision (*Bereishis* 18) or protecting the camp of Yaakov in his confrontation with Eisav (*Bereishis* 32). See *Tanchuma* (Buber), *Vayeira* 1:4, *Tanchuma Yashan, Vayeira* 1; *Tanchuma, Vayishlach* 10. See also the introduction of *Abarbanel* to *parashas Vayeira*. As such, this source adds that the Torah encompasses acts of *chessed*, not only at the beginning and end but also in the middle.

2   *Bereishis* 3:21.

and at the end, God buried Moshe.[3] One can note a textual difference between these two acts of *chessed*. While the clothing of Adam and Chavah is attributed to God, the burial of Moshe is not.

ויעש ה׳ אלקים לאדם ולאשתו כתנות עור וילבשם.

And the Lord God made garments of skins for Adam and his wife, and He clothed them. (Bereishis 3:21)

וימת שם משה עבד ה׳ בארץ מואב על פי ה׳. ויקבר אתו בגי.

And Moshe the servant of God died there in the land of Moav at the command of God. And He buried him in the valley. (Devarim 34:5–6)

The closing *chessed* of the Torah is cryptic enough to allow for midrashic opinion, which states that the subject of "He buried" is Moshe himself![4] Surely the plain meaning of the verse is that God buried Moshe, but the absence of the subject is nonetheless noteworthy. Our Sages teach us that the highest form of charity or *chessed* is when the act is done anonymously.[5] This would explain why God's *chessed* to Moshe is anonymous. However, regarding Adam and Chavah, it was important for God to broadcast His role in this *chessed*, in order to relay the message that even though God rebuked and punished man's rebellion, God still loves man, and is concerned with his welfare.[6] This is a powerful message in relationships, in parenting, and in teaching. Early man attempted to eat from a tree and to be like God,[7] as if to say that man doesn't need God. God wanted to inform man that even in rebellion, and even when we think we don't need God, He is there for us, and that the path to repentance is always open.

---

3   *Devarim* 34:6.

4   *Rashi* cites the opinion of Rabbi Yishmael in *Sifri, Naso* 32, that the subject of ויקבר is actually Moshe. This is perhaps because Moshe is the subject of the previous verse.

5   See *Mo'ed Katan* 16b.

6   See Rabbeinu Bachya, *Bereishis* 3:21, ד״ה וילבשם.

7   *Bereishis* 3:5, "והייתם כאלקים."

— 3 —
Introduction to the Haftarah

The Torah's account of Creation has a unique component. Its purpose is not to relate the details or even the order of Creation. *Rashi* points to this in his comment on the very first verse in the Torah, and then again and again in the first two chapters of *Bereishis*. The haftarah of *parashas Bereishis* begins with the same message:

בורא השמים ונטיהם רוקע הארץ וצאצאיה נותן נשמה לעם עליה ורוח
להולכים בה.

Who created the heavens and stretched them, who spread out the earth and what it brings forth, who gave breath to the people upon it and life to those who walk thereon. (Yeshayahu 42:5)

The haftarah immediately continues to describe Israel's duty to pursue justice. *This* is the purpose of Creation. Our Sages, in the second chapter of *Chagigah*, proscribed delving into the secrets of Creation.[8] This *masechta* is dedicated to the laws of pilgrimages to Jerusalem and the requirements of ritual purity and includes tangents on the moral components of Creation. Yeshayahu picks up on this, complaining that Jerusalem has lost its moral component and that the weak have no protection.

היו לבז ואין מציל משסה ואין אמר השב.

Yet it is a people plundered and despoiled: All of them are trapped in holes, imprisoned in dungeons. (Yeshayahu 42:22)

True protection would come in the realization of God as the Creator of all; the One who fashioned the desert and the seas and carved out the mountains and islands would protect His people. Throughout the first two chapters of *Bereishis*, *Rashi* describes a jealous moon, rebellious trees, compliant vegetation, and other midrashic manifestations of Creation that impart the moral component of the entire story rather

---

8   *Chagigah* 11b.

than an account of what actually transpired. To apply scientific cosmic detail to the Creation story misses the point. The *Bereishis* account of Creation is not nearly as creative as Sumerian, Babylonian, or Egyptian accounts of Creation—and there is a good reason for this. Those accounts attempted to explain *how* the world was created. *Maseches Chagigah* warns us not to delve into this question with great depth. Rather, we understand the agenda of *Bereishis* as an attempt to teach us *why* the world was created.

That is made clear in our haftarah:

אני ה׳ קראתיך בצדק ואחזק בידך ואצרך ואתנך לברית עם לאור גוים.

I, the Lord, have summoned you in My grace, and I have grasped you by the hand. I created you, and appointed you a covenant people, a light of nations. (Yeshayahu 42:6)

למען תדעו ותאמינו לי ותבינו כי אני הוא לפני לא נוצר אל ואחרי לא יהיה.

So that you may take thought, and believe in Me, and understand that I am He: Before Me no god was formed, and after Me none shall exist. (Yeshayahu 43:10)

— 4 —
Derashah
ושם נעשה לפניך את קרבנות חובותינו

Adam and Chavah fulfilled their first mitzvah and bore two sons. The past perfect, "והאדם ידע," implies that Kayin was conceived while they were yet in the garden.[9] Chavah's experience in giving life to another, as

---

9 See *Sanhedrin* 38b. The Latin medieval Christian work known as *Elucidarium* is in the format of questions and answers of Church doctrine, from student to teacher. One of the student's questions is to describe Adam and Chavah's first day of existence. The answer, astonishingly, exactly resembles Chazal's list of the breakdown of the first day into twelve hours, with one exception. In the Gemara, the conception of Kayin and Hevel (according to this source, the boys were twins since the text only refers to one conception) precedes their sin, and in the Christian source, the sin precedes the conception. This order stands in line with Christian

God had given to her, was expressed in the name she gave her son Kayin because "I have acquired a man with the help of God." This expression of acquisition stands in sharp contrast to the name of her second child, Hevel, which connotes futility and worthlessness.

A number of commentaries have suggested a correlation between these two names and the occupations they choose.[10] Kayin attaches himself to the material acquisition of earthliness and works the land, while Hevel, realizing, as is written at the beginning of *Sefer Koheles*, that life is limited and we must therefore come to grips with our ultimate futility, works with living creatures that will, like him, one day cease to exist.[11]

The story line begins with the words, "ויהי מקץ ימים—In the course of time." *Kli Yakar*[12] notes that this is a common expression to denote the Messianic age.[13] As such, he writes that Kayin and Hevel were discussing their philosophy of life. What was their end to be? Why were they on earth? What was their relationship with God? The result of this discussion was that Kayin brought a grain offering to God, of the fruits of the ground. Kayin initiated the idea of giving of himself to show gratitude to the Heavenly Power he felt was responsible for his success.[14]

"והבל הביא גם הוא" implies that Hevel's offering came only in reaction to Kayin's. Hevel saw what Kayin brought and exceeded him in two ways: (1) Hevel brought "מבכורות צאנו—from the best of his flocks," while Kayin brought "מפרי האדמה," with no description. The comparable gift on Kayin's part would have been "מראשית פרי האדמה—from the first

---

10   Philo of Alexandria, *Abarbanel*, and *Kli Yakar* to the beginning of *Bereishis* 4.

11   This is not to say Hevel was a fatalist. The first calling of *Koheles* is not to claim that everything in life is futile. "*Havel havelim*" is not saying that nothing in life is worth pursuing; those words are written as a *lashon tzivui*, in the expression of a command. We are commanded to be sure to treat the futile things in life with the appropriate measure of contempt. See *Ibn Ezra, Koheles* 1:2, ד"ה הבל.

12   *Bereishis* 4:3.

13   See *Daniel* 12:13 and consider the next to last line of *Yigdal*: "ישלח לקץ הימין משיחנו."

14   *Shadal* likens Kayin's actions to the common practice of giving a gift in order to maintain a close relationship with another person. Kayin wanted to connect to God by giving to Him.

fruits of the ground." (2) The possessive form צֹאנוֹ implies that Hevel put more of himself into his offering. Some commentaries derive this from "וְהֶבֶל הֵבִיא גַם הוּא," as if "Hevel brought **himself also**," as an offering to God.[15]

For these reasons God accepted Hevel's offering in a way that both he and Kayin could sense. Whatever attention or reward Hevel received, Kayin did not, and Kayin grew angry and became depressed.

Perhaps Kayin had good reason to feel jealous of his brother. After all, Kayin had initiated the idea of giving back to God. Also, in terms of sacrifice, Kayin gave fruits they were eating, while Hevel sacrificed an animal they were *not* eating.[16] We may also wonder why we are told that Hevel offered the first of his flocks and the fat thereof. If the verse had omitted the reference to the fat, would we have wondered whether he would remove it? We would have assumed the fat was included; it's part of the flock. Simple Rabbinic hermeneutics point out that if the Torah records something specific that was brought that there would be no reason to exclude—even if it hadn't been mentioned—it may be alluding to another item that *was* excluded. That item may have been the wool. If Kayin had seen Hevel shearing the wool for himself, that would have *really* angered Kayin, and this anger may have turned to depression.

God then interceded and informed Kayin that He knew what was in his mind, presumably including what Kayin was thinking of doing to his brother. God rendered a "pep talk" to Kayin about personal responsibility and how to succeed, and Kayin immediately proceeded to kill his brother.

If the objective of God's two-verse speech to Kayin was to prevent violence, it is interesting to note He did not render a more coercive

---

15   This message is derived similarly in the beginning of *Sefer Vayikra*: "אָדָם כִּי יַקְרִיב מִכֶּם קָרְבָּן לַה׳" can refer to the imperative that when bringing an offering to God, one must be sure to bring up *oneself* as well. Some have suggested that Hevel's זֶבַח (animal sacrifice) was more acceptable than Kayin's מִנְחָה (grain sacrifice). See the very end of *Menachos* (110a) and *Tehillim* (50), that this is not a worthwhile difference. God accepts all offerings equally from a sincere heart, regardless of their value.

16   Based on the comparison of the food allowed to Adam (*Bereishis* 2:16) and the food allowed to Noach when he left the ark (*Bereishis* 9:2–4), early man did not consume animals.

speech. Surely some kind of rewarding recognition or a brief taste of horrific punishment would have kept Kayin in line. And how can we explain that Kayin utterly ignored God's advice?

The fact is that Kayin did take God's advice. He did not feel he had actually sinned, but that he had to try harder but wasn't sure exactly how. So he swallowed his pride and approached his younger brother.

Any commentary of this conversation notices two glaring points: (1) We are told not once but twice that Kayin and Hevel are brothers,[17] and (2) we are not told what was said.[18]

Kayin asked Hevel what the secret to gaining God's attention was. *Rashi* says they immediately started arguing and the Midrash fills in the gaps with several specific opinions.[19]

Perhaps we can give the simplest explanation for why nothing is recorded: because nothing was said. And, in explaining the Torah's silence, we can also come to learn about what Kayin's initial sin actually was.

Kayin came to Hevel in brotherhood to make amends. He realized he had done something wrong, not only with respect to God, but with respect to his brother. This explains the two expressions of "הבל אחיו." Kayin's sin was *before* he brought his offering, in that he brought it alone. Kayin sought to gain God's favor alone. He came up with an excellent idea and didn't share it with his brother. Kayin essentially introduced competition into the world, and Hevel quickly caught on. In fact, he improved on Kayin's product. And while competition brings out the best in products, it can also, unchecked, bring out the worst in people.

God informed Kayin that he had it within him to succeed, and Kayin asked Hevel for help, but Hevel was silent. He had been taught well

---

17   This may be to accentuate the profound evil of what is about to transpire, akin to the constant reference of אח and אחות in *Shmuel II*, chapter 13, where Amnon violates his sister, Tamar. See *Kli Yakar, Bereishis* 4:8.

18   Had the verse begun with "וידבר," that Kayin *spoke* to Hevel, this could stand alone, but when the verse begins with "ויאמר," that Kayin *said*, we need to know *what* was said.

19   See Nechama Leibowitz, *Studies on the Parashah, Bereishis* 5, for a deeper treatment of these opinions. The Septuagint's version of the missing phrase is "And Kayin said to Hevel, 'Let's go to the field.'" See *Megillah* 9a for Chazal's approach to the origins of the Septuagint.

by Kayin. Hevel was enjoying being God's favorite and wasn't ready to share that status.

This is not to say that Kayin's behavior was excusable. The moral of the story up to this point is to recognize the crucial need for human cooperation in order to stand alongside healthy competition. God's "pep talk" to Kayin clearly shows that we live in a meritocracy, but the story takes a drastic turn where raw competition turns to man's ruination.

Imagine how different our story would be if the two brothers had agreed *together* to express gratitude to God. Hevel would have made suggestions to Kayin that would have made both brothers be respected simultaneously. *Bereishis* would not have begun with the trend of sibling rivalries between older and more successful younger siblings. Brotherhood itself would have been redefined. Each of the generations of *Sefer Bereishis* will bear its own set of challenges as we grow from a family to a nation.

—5—
Mussar Moments

The scientist wants to know *how* the world was created. The philosopher wants to know *why* the world was created.

Comment

Rashi's commentaries to *Bereishis* 1–2 constantly point out that the Torah is not interested in the details of Creation. Sumerian, Babylonian, and Egyptian creation epics are long on detail but short on morality. In contrast, the Midrash and *Rashi* draw attention to pervasive moral messages throughout the two chapters that comprise the story of Creation, to help us answer the question of our purpose, or why we were created. In this instance, "why" introduces a much more important question than "how."

> The person who knows *how* will always
> have a job. The person who knows *why*
> will always be his boss.

— 6 —

Birth

Our Sages record a series of questions the Roman emperor Turnus Rufus asked Rabbi Akiva about Creation.[20] One was about the mitzvah of *bris milah*. If God wanted males to be circumcised, the Roman asked, why did he create them with a foreskin? Another question was why God created grain, which needs so much work to make into bread. A third question was why man must keep Shabbos if it was God who created and rested.

Rabbi Akiva answered these three questions as one. They all involve man's mission, in which he is charged to be a partner with God in Creation. After God rested on the first Shabbos, the world continued under His constant care. (As we say at the end of the first blessing before the morning *k'rias Shema*: "In His goodness He continually renews the work of Creation each and every day.") The continuation of creativity was left with us.

Animals have no need to process food, wear clothing, or find shelter, but humans do. These are our ways of partnering with God in Creation. The foreskin of a new baby boy is removed to continue the partnership. We clothe our sensitive skin out of a sense of modesty and to protect from the elements. Bread needs to be processed from what is taken from the ground, and the creativity that defines Shabbos labor is connected to the construction of God's holy sanctuary. In this way, we build a house that encompasses not only shelter from the elements, but a place for the sheltering wings of God's presence to reside in our midst.

---

20   See *Bava Basra* 10a, *Tanchuma, Tazria* 5.

It all starts with the partnership we make with God by completing the human form with a *bris milah*.[21]

— 7 —
B'nei Mitzvah

At a *bris* we say, "זה הקטן גדול יהיה—May this little one grow to be a big one." We can understand why we refer to the child as a *katan*—he is only eight days old—but what do we mean by the hope or prediction that he should be a *gadol*? Do we mean a great and influential person?[22] Surely we expect more of this child than simply reaching the age of maturity. Is there nothing in between simply reaching the age of maturity and becoming great that we can hope for this eight-day-old baby?

Perhaps the answer is in the description of the two great luminaries.[23] At first, they are both called "*gedolim*," great luminaries, only to immediately be divided, one called "*gadol*" and one called "*katan*." This is not simply a division based on size. From the standpoint of the earthling, the full moon looks as big as the sun. Rather, the delineation is based on the source of the light.

The Torah calls the sun the *gadol* because it is the source of the light that reflects off of the smaller luminary. To be great is to be a source of giving. A *katan* is mostly a receiver.

We are born extremely helpless, totally dependent on the care of *gedolim*. The job of good parents is to slowly teach a *katan* how to one day be a *gadol*, which is to be a giver; to take the light that shone on him and to use it to one day create his own light for others. This is the *berachah* we extend to every newborn. To be a giver puts us well on the way to becoming a *gadol*, in every sense of the word. *B'nei mitzvah* begin to fulfill that early hope and prediction through the very act of the celebration of reaching the age of mitzvos.

---

21   *Avodah Zarah* 27a; second *berachah* of *Birkas Hamazon*; and see *Minchas Asher, parashas Lech Lecha, siman* 14–16, regarding a woman's share in *bris milah*.
22   As in "לא תהדר פני גדול—Do not show deference to the mighty" in *Vayikra* 19:15.
23   *Bereishis* 1:16.

— 8 —
Marriage

זה ספר תולדת אדם.

This is the book of the generations of man. (Bereishis 5:1)

So begins the fifth chapter of *Sefer Bereishis*, with a list of names from Adam to Noach. This is the simple meaning of *"toldos adam,"* the names of Adam's descendants. *Ramban*, however, understands those words in a much deeper light. To him, the book the verse refers to is not *Bereishis*, chapter 5, but the entire book of the Torah, which is actually the "story of man." God would reveal this book to guide mankind through the moral vicissitudes, ethical dilemmas, and the inevitable twists and turns of daily life. *Ramban* saw the narratives of the Torah, and especially *Sefer Bereishis*, as blueprints for guiding and navigating the rough waves of the human experience.

The first stories of man seem to be fraught with competition. Early man competes for God's attention. It seems the snake desires to compete for Chavah's attention. Brothers compete, early inventors compete, and all man seems to care about is making a great name, becoming mighty, and standing above others—and this inevitably leads to intolerable violence. Rather than allow such violence to destroy the world slowly, God does it all at once in the Great Deluge.

If man is to successfully emerge from this Deluge and build life anew, he must learn to move from a mode of competition to a mode of cooperation. Such seems to be the case in the story of the Tower of Bavel. In *parashas Noach*, we will be curious to see why the cooperation that defined the building of the Tower was not pleasing in God's eyes. In the meantime, if we must compete, let's compete to see who can be most helpful, most understanding, and most caring as we appreciate the unique attributes of every individual. That will lead to the best type of cooperation, which is marriage.

Our Sages considered the task of making a match to be in the realm of the miraculous. That two people from different backgrounds can settle their different habits, tastes, customs, and preferences in peace and harmony requires compromise and magnanimity. The English word "marriage" draws its etymology from the Roman god of war Mars. Judaism knows no such thing. Marriage in Judaism is *kiddushin*, a word whose etymology bespeaks holiness and purity. It requires us to prepare ourselves for a life of giving and growing, and the only competition should be where each one competes to love the other one more.

— 9 —

Seudah Shelishis

אתה אחד ושמך אחד

Chazal say that King David's favorite chapters of *Tehillim* begin and end with the word "*Ashrei*," which generally describes a state of happiness.[24] *Tosafos* point out that the Gemara means to expand upon David's favorite chapters and not to limit the similar beginnings and endings to *Ashrei*, since this is the *only* such example using that word.[25] Rather, David's favorite chapters begin and end with similar words or phrases. The last five chapters all begin and end with the same word, הללוי-ה. Chapter 145, which begins תהילה לדוד, (the chapter we often refer to as *Ashrei*) ends similarly, with תהילת ה'. Chapters 113, 117, and 118 also begin and end with similar phrases.

The Torah's first word is בראשית, which connotes beginnings. Starting something new is always exciting. We feel refreshed and rejuvenated for a new challenge and new horizons. No doubt, there will be many struggles along the way to the completion of our goals, visions, and dreams. The last word of the Torah is ישראל, a name given to Yaakov because he struggled with God and with man.[26] Our role as the descendants of Yaakov is to struggle alongside God in making this the best

---

24 *Berachos* 10a. The Gemara's point is to show that chapters 1 and 2 of *Tehillim* are considered as one unified chapter. While most chapters in *Tehillim* have a defining title, chapter 2 seems to flow directly from chapter 1, and chapter 2 ends the way chapter 1 begins, with the word *Ashrei*.

25 Ibid., ד"ה כל.

26 *Bereishis* 32:25.

of all possible worlds. Yaakov did not struggle *against* God but *with* God. This is our purpose, from בראשית to ישראל, and both words have the letters of אשרי embedded within them. The three additional letters spell לבת—which means "within the heart" or "within the midst of."[27] May we approach every word of the Torah from בראשית to ישראל with happiness and joy from within all our hearts.

— 10 —
Word of the Parashah

אם כל חי—The mother of all the **living**
Bereishis 3:20

Adam named his wife twice. The first time he named her *ishah*, "woman," because she was taken from *ish*, "man."[28] The letter *hei* at the end of a word denotes femininity,[29] signifying the difference between the genders.[30] The second time, he named her "Chavah" because she was "אם כל חי—the mother of all the living."[31] But surely Chavah was not the mother of all living creatures on earth? *Radak* resolves this by translating the mother of all "חי" as the mother of all who speak.[32] In the description of man, "ויהי האדם לנפש חיה—and man became a living being,"[33] *Targum Onkelos* and *Targum Yerushalmi* translate חיה as "ממללא—one who speaks."

---

27   As in *Shemos* 3:2, "בלבת אש."

28   *Bereishis* 2:23.

29   See the commentary to *Mishlei* 18:22 of Rabbi Elazar Rokeach, "מצא אשה מצא טוב," and the ingenious and creative way he uses our verse to reconcile the apparent contradiction between *Mishlei* 18:22 and *Koheles* 7:26, as described in *Berachos* 8a and *Yevamos* 63b.

30   The vowel beneath the first letter is a short vowel for *ishah* (the first syllable rhymes with *wish*) and a long vowel for *ish* (rhymes with *leash*), because of the letter *yud* that follows it. The *yud* falls out for *ishah* so as not to confuse the word for "woman" with "her man." *Bereishis Rabbah*, *Bereishis* 18 uses these two words to prove the primacy of the Hebrew language over other Semitic languages, such as Aramaic, for the similarity of the two words. See also *Ibn Ezra*, *Bereishis* 2:23.

31   *Bereishis* 3:20.

32   *Radak* refers to additional verses referring to "כל בשר," which would normally include both man and beast, yet clearly only refers to man. See *Yeshayahu* 66:23 and *Tehillim* 145:21.

33   *Bereishis* 2:7.

This meaning is confirmed by the following verse:

יום ליום יביע אמר ולילה ללילה יחוה דעת.

Day to day makes utterance; night to night speaks out.
(Tehillim 19:3)

The root of our word appears quite often in Aramaic in the book of *Daniel*, as well as in the book of *Iyov*,[34] meaning to "inform" or "express." This is ironic since the only other speaker in the early *Bereishis* narratives was the snake, which in Aramaic is חויא. The snake used its original gift of speech to deceive Chavah. In one last twist of this word, the Giveonim, who deceived Yehoshua,[35] are also referred to as the Chivi. *Radak* cites the *Yerushalmi* that the Giveonim are so called because they took the path of the snake to deceive Yehoshua.[36] The mouth can deceive and cause man to lose his place in Gan Eden, or it can give life. We get to choose.

---

34 The Hebrew of *Iyov* is very difficult and it has long been suggested that Iyov's narratives were originally spoken in Aramaic. See an exhaustive recent study on this topic by C.G. Rata (2008), "Observations on the Language of the Book of Job."

35 *Yehoshua* 9:7.

36 *Kiddushin* 4:1.

Parashas Noach

— 1 —
Friday Night
תכלית מעשה שמים וארץ

There are two memorable images that signify an end of the destruction brought about by the Great Deluge. One is a dove with an olive branch, and the other is a rainbow. There are two separate violations that led humanity on the path of destruction. One was the sexual exploitation and licentiousness that is described in the beginning of *Bereishis* 6. One gets the sense of mighty men (*b'nei elohim*) taking advantage of vulnerable women (*b'nos ha'adam*). *Rashi*[1] cites the Midrash that the official would violate a new bride on the day of her wedding,[2] a despicable practice that continued into Talmudic times and beyond.[3] The sexual licentiousness crossed over from man to animal, as the Torah speaks of the corruption of all flesh: "כי השחית כל בשר."[4] *Rashi* states that this brings about androlomasia, a Greek word that describes a pandemic

---

1   *Bereishis* 6:2, ד"ה כי טבת הנה.
2   *Bereishis Rabbah* 26:5.
3   See *Kesubos* 9a.
4   *Bereishis* 6:12.

that wipes out everyone in its path.[5] Perhaps humanity was about to be obliterated by a miserable disease spread exponentially by man's behavior, and God mercifully prevented this prolonged misery with the Great Deluge.[6]

The other path to destruction was חמס, "violence." Early man turned on one another. Jealousies, competition for limited resources, and quests for power drove early man to devolve to his worst tendencies. This sealed man's fate, as God told Noach, "I have decided to put an end to all flesh, for the earth is filled with violence."[7]

The two images referenced above were meant to atone for the two sins that caused the Flood. The Jewish people are likened unto a dove. *Shir Hashirim*, a book of *Tanach* that metaphorically describes the undying love between God and His people, refers to the beloved as God's *yonah*, "dove," on several occasions.[8] This prompted our Sages to ask why the Israelites are likened unto a dove. Throughout Rabbinic literature we find numerous explanations of this comparison.[9] The one that fits our image is that once a dove recognizes its mate, it never rejects it for another, even after the mate is no longer there. So too, the Israelites as a people never utterly rejected God for another.[10] The olive branch in

---

5   *Rashi, Bereishis* 6:13, ד"ה קץ כל בשר.

6   God's name in announcing the Flood in *Bereishis* 6 is אלקים, denoting the attribute of justice. God's name in bringing about the Flood in *Bereishis* 7 is יקוק, which denotes the attribute of mercy. See *Ramban, Bereishis* 7:1 and *Rashi, Bereishis* 8:1.

7   *Bereishis* 6:13.

8   *Shir Hashirim* 2:14, 5:2, 6:9.

9   Just as the dove is protected by its wings, so too is Israel protected by its observance of mitzvos. *Berachos* 53b; *Shabbos* 49a; *Tosafos* ibid. ד"ה כנפיה explains that while every bird is protected by its wings, the dove is especially protected by its ability to fly with one wing at a time. This may explain why, when the raven failed to produce any information for Noach, he chose to send a dove, rather than a hawk or an eagle. Also, Noach assumed that when the dove did not return, this signified that it had found dry land and that Noach could soon leave the ark. He did not consider that the dove flew too far to return and drowned, for a dove will always make its way back by flying with one wing. *Shir Hashirim Rabbah* 1:63 and *Tanchuma, Tetzaveh* 5, list a series of comparisons between Israel and the dove.

10   *Tanchuma, Tetzaveh* 5. Prophets throughout *Tanach* rail against the Israelites for rejecting God. See especially *Yirmiyahu* chapters 2 and 3. A careful reading of these chapters indicate that even while rejecting God's Torah, and even while entertaining other belief systems, we always knew where the true source of existence was. See *Daas Sofrim* of C. Rabinowitz,

the mouth of the dove represents a similar image. The *Tanach* refers to the Israelites with the image of the olive branch as well.[11] This prompted our Sages to explain the connection in a similar fashion as the dove above. Just as an olive branch cannot be grafted with any other tree, so too the Israelites would never graft themselves onto another belief system.[12] In addition, our Sages call attention to the fact that olive oil does not mix with other liquids, which makes a similar point.[13] As such, the dove, which stays true to its mate for its entire existence, carrying an olive branch that cannot mix with another, is a powerful image of Israel's loyalty to God. If unbridled promiscuity led to the Flood, then such an image would be a worthwhile atonement. If the intention of the text was simply to inform us that Noach was aware that dry land would soon be spotted, it could have just said a bird was carrying a leaf in its mouth. The specificity of the dove and the olive branch draws our attention to these points.

The rainbow is an image that more readily atones for the second sin. While our Sages discuss the meaning of the appearance of a rainbow,[14] we know that the seven colors of the electromagnetic spectrum all combine to blend into the color white. The symbolism is that we can all acknowledge our differences and our individuality as we strive together through our daily existential challenges. We can move beyond early man's tendencies to violence and lawlessness, applying this symbolism of the rainbow.

Yirmiyahu 3:1–12. See also *Radak*, *Bereishis* 15:9–10, ד"ה ותר וגוזל, regarding the image of the dove at *Bris Bein Habesarim*.

11   See *Yirmiyahu* 11:16, "The Lord called your name, a green olive tree, fair with choice fruit." See also *Hoshea* 14:7, *Tehillim* 52:10.

12   *Yerushalmi*, *Kilayim* 1:7.

13   *Shemos Rabbah* 36:1.

14   See *Kesubos* 77b, *Zohar*, *Shemos* 66, *Bamidbar Rabbah* 2:31 for negative implications of seeing a rainbow. It is a reminder that we may once again deserve the punishment of a deluge, if not for the fact that God promised us this wouldn't happen. See *Bereishis* 9:13–17 and *Yeshayahu* 54:9. See also, *Meiri*, *Chagigah* 16a, for an explanation of these sources to refer to a different type of rainbow with seven shades of blue, imperceptible to the human eye. See also *Shulchan Aruch*, *Orach Chaim* 229:1, that we may glance at a rainbow for a short period to make the appropriate blessing, but we should not stare at it.

These two images, the dove with an olive branch and the rainbow, serve as eternal reminders of man's first covenant with God after the Great Deluge, and the endowment of our ability to rebound after destruction.

—2—
Introduction to the Torah
ישמח משה במתנת חלקו

The Midrash renders a sharp critique of Noach regarding his entry into the ark. The Torah records:

ויבא נח ובניו ואשתו ונשי בניו אתו אל התבה מפני מי המבול.

Noach, with his sons, his wife, and his son's wives went into the ark because of the waters of the Flood. (Bereishis 7:7)

Rav Yochanan considers Noach to have been lacking in faith:

נח מחוסר אמנה היה. אלולי שהגיעו המים עד קרסליו לא נכנס לתיבה.

Noach was lacking in faith. If not for the fact that the water reached his ankles, he would not have entered the ark. (Bereishis Rabbah 32:6)

The extraneous words at the end of the verse are the source of this claim. We are told that Noach entered the ark "מפני מי המבול"—not because God said so, but because the rains forced him to.[15]

Rashi changes two things about Rav Yochanan's *d'rash*. One, instead of referring to Noach as lacking in faith altogether, *Rashi* refers to Noach having a small degree of faith, "מקטני אמונה." This is *Rashi's* version:

אף נח מקטני אמונה היה. מאמין ואינו מאמין שיבא המבול ולא נכנס לתיבה עד שדחקוהו המים.

---

15   We already learned that Noach did as God had commanded (*Bereishis* 7:5) and *Rashi* writes that this refers to entering the ark. The repetition of verse 7 that he did so, given the extra three words at the end of the verse, teaches that Noach lacked in faith. *Rashi* indicates that the repetitive nature of our verse also teaches that marital relations were forbidden in the ark "because of the waters of the Flood."

*Even Noach was of those who had little faith. He believed and
did not believe that the Flood would come and he did not enter
the ark until the waters forced him.*

The second thing *Rashi* changed is the expression by which Noach
doubted that the Flood would come. After all, verse 5 indicates that
Noach did as commanded and *Rashi* writes that this refers to entering
the ark! Perhaps we can blunt the effect of Noach's deficit of faith by
rearranging the punctuation of *Rashi's* statement to the following:

אף נח מקטני אמנה היה מאמין.

Even Noach had faith in those of little faith.

Noach believed they would repent and gain God's mercies.

ואינו מאמין שיבא המבול.

He didn't believe the flood would ever come.

Because Noach believed the people's repentance would cancel
the decree.

ולא נכנס לתיבה עד שדחקוהו המים.

He didn't enter the ark until he was forced to.

Even as the rains began to fall, Noach thought the decree might still
be avoided because of his faith in the people.

Perhaps Noach miscalculated the extent of the evil of the people of his
generation, but from here we see that he had great faith in them—and
Rashi had great faith in Noach.

—3—
Introduction to the Haftarah

This week's haftarah makes reference to the "waters of Noach," which
the prophet Yeshayahu invokes to comfort the Israelites into believ-
ing that they could rebuild their lives after destruction, just as Noach

had done.[16] The Israelites had felt barren, with no hope for the future, bereft of offspring and possessions, facing nothing but desolation. Who could blame these people for their pessimism? Of all the images for Yeshayahu to conjure to raise the spirits of his people, he chose the waters of Noach. Imagine the desolation that Noach witnessed upon leaving the ark. The challenge of carrying on humanity must have been daunting, yet that is exactly what Noach, his three sons, and their wives did.

Yeshayahu is not the only one of our later prophets who mentions Noach. Yechezkel refers to Noach alongside two other characters in a message of survival. "These three men, Noach, Daniel, and Iyov, by their righteousness, saved themselves."[17]

On this basis, the Midrash connects these three men as having lived through three worlds: first in *"yishuv,"* a surrounding that is inhabited and in peace; then in destruction; and then rebuilt again.[18] This can equally characterize the amazing generation of survivors of the destruction of European Jewry in the Holocaust. How they carried on to build productive lives and to help create a better world for their children is incredible. It represents the indomitable spirit that helps us overcome adversity and strengthens our faith that the words of Yeshayahu in this week's haftarah can sustain us in our own ability to build our lives after tragedy.

A self-published memoir of my father's Holocaust experiences describes his arrival in the United States after the war.

> *In February 1949, I set sail for America on the steamship Marine Shark. I do not have words to describe the emotions I experienced when I saw for the first time, on March 3, 1949, the incredible sight of the Statue of Liberty—America's symbol of liberty and freedom—after having survived the atrocities that I had witnessed. It wasn't a picture, it wasn't*

---

16   *Yeshayahu* 54:9.

17   *Yechezkel* 14:14.

18   *Tanchuma, Noach* 5.

a photograph, but the real statue that I was seeing in New York harbor with my open eyes. The words to describe the feelings have not been invented yet.

If words cannot describe the feelings, they can certainly describe the waters beneath his ship. They were the "waters of Noach," which inspired a heroic generation to quickly build a world that faced destruction similar to what faced Noach. May we build on their stoic heroism, and may we be strengthened by the assurances of our prophets. The better world this generation bequeathed to us is a fulfillment of the promises of this haftarah.

— 4 —

Derashah

ושם נעשה לפניך את קרבנות חובותינו

There is so much human failure in the early stories of mankind. Man's proclivity for power, might, and fame led to violence that culminated in the Great Deluge. Noach and his family emerge from the ark and one of the first stories to follow that emergence is the Tower of Bavel.[19]

Man seems to have moved from a mode of competition to a mode of cooperation. This should have been considered a good thing. Yet in God's eyes, these workings deserved to be disrupted and confounded.

What was it about the builders of the tower that warranted disruption? What was wrong with the unity of spirit and purpose that this group entailed? While unity is surely a good thing for a group, it is *not* good when such unity is forced upon everyone to the exclusion of any contrary opinion whatsoever. Our Sages tell us that anyone who disagreed with the mode of building for the great tower was thrown into the brick mortar. The Midrash describes that if a brick fell from a scaffold, the builders would mourn; but if a person fell, it was not considered such a loss. The Midrash concludes that when Avraham (who at

---

19   *Bereishis* 11.

first thought the attempt at unity was noble) saw this, he asked God to confound their plans.[20]

The problem with the builders of the Tower was that all dissent and individuality was quashed. There is no greater tyranny than for the masses to be forced into conformity and into a single line of agreement. *Bereishis* is filled with stories that point to this message. While a number of trends emerge in the book, a number of contrasts are demonstrated as well:

- Avraham leaves Israel in the time of famine; Yitzchak is told not to.
- Yitzchak's marriage was set up for him; Yaakov made his own arrangement.
- Avraham and Yaakov dealt with infertility by taking additional wives; Yitzchak resorted only to prayer.

The message is that there is often more than one way to understand a particular issue or solve a particular problem. Many other examples besides these abound in *Sefer Bereishis*. The generation of the Tower of Bavel is known as "דור הפלגה—the generation of disunity." A society that puts equality before freedom will have little of both and will end up with confusion and separation. The Torah rewards merit but tries to level the playing field with many mitzvos that are meant to teach us to be generous and magnanimous toward those who are less fortunate. Avraham, by personal example, leads the way toward this goal.

—5—
Mussar Moments

You need both rain and sunshine to make a rainbow.

---

20 *Bereishis Rabbah* 38:6; *Pirkei D'Rabi Eliezer* 24.

Comment

The rain and the sunshine represent two extremes in our expectations. We usually prefer sunshine to rain, but without either we would all soon perish. The rainbow, as a thing of beauty, is a reminder of God's covenant with mankind to never again allow the rain to cause such utter destruction as in *parashas Noach*. God informed Noach how to survive with specific instructions and directions.

A number of years ago, Robert Flugman wrote a poignant list of life's instructions that we all learn in our early youth, which he titled, "All I Really Need to Know I Learned in Kindergarten." I ran across a similar list titled, "Everything I Need to Know About Life, I Learned from Noach's Ark." Here are the points with a bit of commentary:

1. Don't miss the boat.

Our Sages say that Noach spent 120 years trying to get people to join him, but no one was interested.

2. Remember that we are all in the same boat.

A woodpecker would probably do serious damage to the boat. Let's concentrate more on our similarities than our differences.

3. Plan ahead. It wasn't raining when Noach built the ark.

Our Sages declare: "Who is wise? The one who looks ahead and anticipates what is to be."[21] The time to fix a leaky roof is when the sun is still shining.

4. Stay fit. When you're six hundred years old, someone may ask you to do something really big.

Life is filled with surprises. Let's accustom ourselves to roll with the punches. The greatest prophet of all time (Moshe) didn't receive his Divine Mission until he was eighty.[22]

5. Don't listen to critics; just get on with the job that needs to be done.

Noach suffered all manner of derision and calumny but none of that deterred him from what he knew was the right thing to do.

---

21   *Tamid* 32a.
22   *Shemos* 7:7.

6. Build your future on high ground.

Always take the high road. We'll survive any flood if we do.

7. We should prefer to travel in pairs.

It's safer that way.

8. Speed isn't always an advantage. The snails were on board with the cheetahs.

Moving along with consistency and conviction is a sure recipe for completing our goals no matter how long they take.

9. When you're stressed, float a while.

Let us refrain from acting on impulse and think things over to a greater extent.

10. Remember, the ark was built by amateurs; the *Titanic* by professionals.

Let's all try our best at whatever we do and rely on God's help for success in any endeavor.

11. No matter the storm, when you are with God, there's always a rainbow waiting.

Chazal actually tell us that a rainbow is a sign that the world deserves destruction again. The *Meiri* claims that the rainbow that is a reminder of destruction is one with seven shades of blue and cannot be seen except by very perceptive people.[23] The rainbow we often see in the sky, of seven different colors, is a sign of great beauty and warrants a blessing.

ברוך אתה ה' אלקינו מלך העולם זוכר הברית ונאמן בבריתו וקיים במאמרו.

Blessed are you our God, King of the universe, who remembers the covenant and is trustworthy of the covenant and fulfills His word.

Sefer Bereishis will continue to take this covenantal theme to even higher levels.

---

23   See above, n. 14.

—6—
Birth

Some modern commentaries to the story of Noach call attention to the fact that the dimensions of the ark Noach built could never contain all the animals he would take aboard. It is inconceivable, they say, for a three-story 300×50×30-*amah* structure[24] to contain all the provisions they would need for a full year. They are missing the point. They have no concept that if God could make it rain for forty days and forty nights, He could also make all those animals fit in the structure described above. God could have also started all over some other way that wouldn't involve so much trouble on the part of Noach. In reality, God wanted a partner in saving the world, just as Chavah felt God was a partner in her first birth.[25]

In *Tanach*, the number forty represents metamorphosis. It took three sets of forty days at Mount Sinai to fully transform the people of Israel to a faith-centric people. It took forty years in the desert to transform a nation with a slave mentality to finally be ready to enter their Promised Land. Yonah gave the inhabitants of Ninveh forty days to save themselves,[26] just as we all hope that the forty days from Rosh Chodesh Elul until Yom Kippur will change us to be worthy of a successful year ahead. Forty days is also the time our Sages set for *yetziras ha'velad*, the stage by which the child begins to recognizably develop inside its mother. And the Flood lasted forty days, as Noach prepared the world for its own new rebirth.

The mystery of how all those animals could fit in the ark is the same as the mystery of birth—it was a miracle, and when you believe in miracles, *everything* is possible.

---

24   *Bereishis* 6:15–16.
25   See *Bereishis* 4:1.
26   *Yonah* 3:4.

—7—
B'nei Mitzvah

The Flood started on the seventeenth day of the second month,[27] and it rained for forty days and forty nights. There is a dispute in Chazal over whether this is the second month from Tishrei, which would be Marcheshvan, or the second month from Nissan, which would be Iyar. Some commentaries prefer the former opinion because it places the Flood in the proper rainy season. This, in and of itself, is not enough of a reason to prefer Marcheshvan over Iyar.[28] If God could make it rain for forty days and forty nights, He could start the rain in any month He chooses. There is another reason to prefer Marcheshvan over Iyar, namely the word for "flood" itself, מבול.

Between the redemption from Egypt and the Babylonian exile, the months of the year were designated by the proximity to the month we were freed, Nissan. In the post-exilic books of the Bible, such as *Esther*, *Zechariah*, *Ezra*, and *Nechemiah*, names of months begin to appear. While the first letter of the word מבול has the numerical value of 40—the days of the Flood—the rest of the word, בול, is a rare early Biblical name for the month of Marcheshvan.[29] Therefore, the מ for forty days, and בול for the month the Flood started, render the word מבול.

The first letter of the Torah is ב of בראשית. The last letter of the Torah is ל of ישראל. The middle letter of the Torah is the ו of the word גחון.[30] As such, the beginning, middle, and end of the Torah spells בול. The word בול means a "stamp." The challenge of *b'nei mitzvah* is to begin to demonstrate how the Torah stamps its impression upon them.

There is a calling for the Jew to be "קובע עתים לתורה,"[31] which is usually understood to mean to set aside time for the study of Torah. The challenge of *b'nei mitzvah*, especially in the month of בול, coming off the heels of the intensity of the holidays of Tishrei, is to assure that

---

27 *Bereishis* 7:11.
28 *Rosh Hashanah* 11b–12a.
29 *Melachim I* 6:38.
30 *Vayikra* 11:42.
31 See *Bamidbar Rabbah* 10:21, *Shabbos* 31a.

we establish our approach to our time using Torah ideals—literally to be קובע the עתים according to the Torah and not vice versa. In this way, we connect to the beginning and the end of Torah, and everything in between.

—8—
Marriage

A bride wears a white dress and a groom covers himself in a white *kittel* to denote the purity of the new couple beginning their lives anew. *Parashas Noach* presents us with another aspect of the symbolism of wearing white at a wedding.

The rainbow after the Flood represents various shades and colors that find themselves on the same spectrum. When combined, they are white, because white denotes not only purity but a beautiful synthesis between the particularism of each color and the universalism of all the colors. A healthy marriage allows each partner to maintain some level of individualism, even as they both build their lives together.

This is the message of the Gemara that states that when love is great, a couple can reside together on the sharp side of a sword.[32] Of course, there isn't room for one person in such a small space, but there is room for two. When each one nullifies themselves to the needs of the other, they will separately take up room—but together take up no room. As above, each one may maintain individuality, but only insofar as it fits in the will of the other. This represents the colors of the rainbow, all melding together into the color white.

—9—
Seudah Shelishis
אתה אחד ושמך אחד

Man's original diet was delineated right after Creation. God said, "See, I have given you every seed-bearing plant that is upon the earth, and

---

32   *Sanhedrin* 7a.

every tree that has seed-bearing fruit. They shall be yours for food."[33] The previous verse, which mentions man's dominion over animals, does not mention them as food and they were not included in man's diet until Noach left the ark with his family. At that point, God repeats the message that man shall have dominion over animals,[34] and then includes animals as food in the next verse: "Every creature that lives shall be yours to eat, as with the green grasses, I give you all these."[35] Our Sages say that six of the seven Noachide Laws were actually given to Adam as he entered the Gan Eden.[36] The seventh prohibition—against eating the limb of an animal cut off before it dies—was not revealed to Adam because he was not eating meat at all. Since the final law was revealed to Noach, we refer to all seven laws as "שבע מצוות בני נח—the seven Noachide laws."

Kli Yakar posits that the order of Creation serves as a hint to a hierarchy of man's nutritional needs.[37] Air, water, and minerals were created on the first two days, followed by the spread of vegetation on day three. Even the creation of day four serves man's nutritional needs, as the sun strengthens our healing powers. On days five and six we see the emergence of fish, fowl, and land animals. These too are presented in the order of health needs for man. Ostensibly, the least healthy food for man to eat is the flesh of the land animals. For this reason, while the vast majority of fish and fowl on the planet are kosher, there are only ten land animals that the Torah allows.[38]

There is, of course, one more creation—even after all the land animals were created—that we should certainly consider last on this list, and that is the human being.[39]

---

33   *Bereishis* 1:29.
34   *Bereishis* 9:2.
35   *Bereishis* 9:3.
36   *Sanhedrin* 56b, based on *Bereishis* 2:16.
37   *Bereishis* 1:26.
38   See *Devarim* 14:4–5.
39   There is an exhaustive responsa of the *Rashba* on the question of whether human flesh is considered kosher or not. See *Teshuvos HaRashba*, sect. 1, 364. See also *Minchas Chinuch*, mitzvah 3(2).

— 10 —
Word of the Parashah

צהר תעשה לתיבה—Make an **opening for daylight** in the ark
Bereishis 6:16

Noach was instructed to make a צהר for the ark within a cubit of the top of the ark.[40] *Rashi* cites two opinions that appear in Chazal,[41] one that the צהר was a window, and the other, that the צהר was an array of bright gems that would brighten the ark like midday (צהרים). The first opinion is perhaps guided by the expression, "צהר תעשה לתיבה." Noach was instructed to *make* a צהר. If the צהר was an array of gems, the verse should have read, "צהר תביא לתיבה," to "bring," not to "make." In defense of the second opinion, תעשה can mean to "prepare" as in "ובן הבקר אשר עשה."[42] Avraham surely did not make the food; he prepared it. The second opinion is perhaps guided by the specific reference to a window that Noach opened, "ויפתח נח את חלון התבה אשר עשה."[43] If this reference is to a window, and the common word, חלון is used, then צהר must mean something else. Perhaps the first opinion doesn't read the text so closely and allows *Bereishis 8:6* to shed light on the meaning of 6:16.

Either way, the word implies some type of brightness, related to the word צהרים, "midday," the brightest time of the day, and to יצהר, "oil," which is fuel for light. The word is related to the similar sounding זהר, which appears in the mystical prophecies of *Yechezkel*[44] and *Daniel*,[45] and is of course, the source of the name of the fundamental work of Jewish mysticism, the *Zohar*, which means to "radiate."[46] The two opinions may reflect two different approaches to the purpose the צהר served. According to Rav Saadiah Gaon and *Ibn Ezra*, צהר is actually

---

40   *Bereishis 6:16.*
41   *Bereishis Rabbah* 31:11. See also *Sanhedrin* 108b.
42   *Bereishis 18:8.*
43   *Bereishis 8:6.*
44   8:2.
45   12:3.
46   צהר also seems to be related to the root צחר, in *Shoftim* 5:10 and *Yechezkel* 27:18, to connote brightness or whiteness.

plural.[47] Noach was told to build many windows across the ark (as is usually depicted in pictures). Noach was meant to connect with what was happening outside the ark and not to hide from all the destruction. According to the second opinion, Noach was to concentrate on his own survival and the renewal of the world after the Flood would end. God did not want Noach to see the destruction, perhaps akin to the survivors of Sodom not looking back at the destruction[48] or the Israelites not leaving their homes during the tenth plague in Egypt.[49]

The word צהר in its singular form is a hapax legomenon, which is a word that appears only once in a full body of literature, in our case, the entire *Tanach*. As such we can only tell what it means from its context. In ancient Akkadian, the language of Akkad, a nation mentioned in *Bereishis* 10:10, "tzehru" means a top cover placed over an object.[50] If so, the singular צהר may also refer to the cover of the ark that Noach removed: "ויסר נח את מכסה התבה."[51]

The Midrash prefers the connotation of light, perhaps as a sign of the light that Noach and his family would be tasked to bring to a new world. It is the same task we have always assumed as a people in the direct aftermath of tragedy and catastrophe.

---

47   Such as, "ויהי לי שור וחמור—I have oxen and donkeys" (*Bereishis* 32:6), even though the words are singular.

48   *Bereishis* 19:17.

49   *Shemos* 12:22.

50   See Prof. Hayim ben Yosef Tawil, *An Akkadian Lexical Companion for Biblical Hebrew* (Ktav Publishing House, 2009), p. 318.

51   *Bereishis* 8:13.

Parashas Lech Lecha

—1—
Friday Night
תכלית מעשה שמים וארץ

When Moshe was tasked with the mission of redeeming his people and revealing the Torah to them, his first reaction was to wonder why he was chosen.[1] This was an expression of Moshe's characteristic humility. The reader already knows Moshe as a man of conviction, action, integrity, spirituality, and compassion.[2] When Noach was tasked to build an ark to save mankind, the reader knows him as righteous and perfect.[3] But when Avraham was told to relocate from Mesopotamia to Canaan, the reader has no inkling as to why. All we know of Avraham is that he had accompanied his father with some other family members to make the trek to Canaan even before God told him to.

Our Sages say that Avraham had God in his heart for many years before he left for Canaan. This is based on a tradition embedded in the text to *Yeshayahu* 40–41, found in *Targum Yonasan*.[4] Avraham's heart moved him to travel west even before God's command as he began to

---

1   *Shemos* 3:11.
2   See *Shemos Rabbah*, and *Rashi* and *Seforno* on *Shemos* 3:1.
3   *Bereishis* 6:9.
4   See especially *Targum Yonasan* to *Yeshayahu* 41:2.

spread the word of ethical monotheism. *Maharal* explains that the Torah purposely omitted all references to Avraham's past in order to indicate that the status of Avraham's descendants as God's chosen people is unequivocal and will never change.[5] If Noach had not been righteous and perfect, he could not have been tasked to build the ark. If Moshe had not demonstrated his characteristics of humility, integrity, and conviction, God would not have appeared to him at the burning bush. But God's appearance to Avraham is without condition. The cherished and treasured nation status of his descendants is without condition. Even as God came very close to considering rejecting us in the third chapter of *Yirmiyahu*, He relented, "כי חסיד אני," because God is a *chassid*.[6] Avraham exemplifies the characteristic of *chessed*, "kindness," and thus assured that God would demonstrate this characteristic with us and always maintain an everlasting connection.

— 2 —
Introduction to the Torah
ישמח משה במתנת חלקו

Avraham grew up in a world where people attributed various powers to different gods, each of whom had to be addressed to help the worshipper with a particular need. The sun and the six visible moving celestial objects were each granted a particular power. The sun was endowed with the power of healing. Mercury was the god of safe travel, because it moved so quickly across the sky in its short circuit around the sun. Venus was the goddess of love, and of the human aspiration for reaching full potential. Mars was the god of war, and Jupiter was the god who promulgated justice. Saturn represented power and might, and the moon represents the ability for renewal and rejuvenation. In the ancient world, if any of these attributes were required, the worshipper directed prayers to these figures.

---

5 See *Maharal, Netzach Yisrael*, chap. 11 (Yahadus edition, 1980), pp. 65–74.

6 *Yirmiyahu* 3:12.

Avraham realized that all these powers must be sourced within the same being. We reflect this sentiment in our daily prayers in the first morning blessing before *k'rias Shema*. *K'rias Shema* itself begins with an affirmation of God's uniqueness. In the first blessing before *k'rias Shema*, we stress a similar affirmation by saying, "כי הוא לבדו—God alone is…"

- "פועל גבורות—He does mighty deeds." This takes the place of Saturn.
- "עושה חדשות—He rejuvenates." This replaces the moon.
- "בעל מלחמות—He is the Master of battles." This replaces Mars.
- "זורע צדקות—He sows righteousness." This replaces Jupiter.
- "מצמיח ישועות—He makes salvation grow." This is our own planet where we can consider God's salvation.
- "בורא רפואות—He creates cures." This replaces the sun.
- "נורא תהלות—He is revered in praises." This represents the traveling message of Mercury, to spread God's praises across the cosmos.
- "אדון הנפלאות—The Master of Wonders." This represents the love that is indicative of Venus, as our Sages considered finding true love to be the greatest of miracles.[7]

Avraham saw all these things in God alone, "כי הוא לבדו."

—3—
Introduction to the Haftarah

Each of the first three Torah portions of the year all find their haftarah within a short range of chapters in *Yeshayahu* and all connect thematically. The common theme is that God is not aloof from man, as Aristotle taught, but is profoundly concerned with mankind. In the haftarah of *Bereishis*, Yeshayahu posits that God's purpose of Creation is to connect morally to man, and for all men to realize this and thus connect to one another. In the haftarah of *Noach*, Yeshayahu posits that God cares enough to goad man into changing his ways and will alter nature and

---

7   See *Sotah* 2a.

events to teach man that He cares. In light of man's rebelliousness, God will choose among the righteous to teach His ways.

In *parashas Lech Lecha*, that choice goes one step further. One man awakened the East to the morally monotheistic ideal, and he and his descendants alone would heretofore spread God's word. However, we are left with a problem. Selecting someone for a chosen status will awaken the ire of others who may feel left out. Consider, for example, the jealousy of students toward the teacher's pet, or workers toward a favored employee.

Therefore, in the haftarah, Yeshayahu teaches Avraham's descendants how to be sure they will use God's favored status to their advantage. The secret can be gleaned from examining why Yaakov's sons bore jealousy and enmity to Yosef in *parashas Vayeishev* but bore no such sentiment to Binyamin later in *parashas Vayigash*, when they were required to protect him for their father's sake. This was because they saw the favoritism exhibited to Binyamin as something positive for themselves. The Egyptian viceroy's anger toward them would be tempered, in their eyes, because of the favored Binyamin's presence. However, Yosef brought his brother's enmity upon himself.

The message is encapsulated by Yeshayahu's call for the Israelites to be "לְאוֹר גוֹיִם—to enlighten the nations."[8] If the nations would only see how their lives have been enhanced by God's chosen people, their enmity would be replaced by love and adoration. Let the world take note how this tiny percentage of the population has enhanced the world with medical, scientific, and social advances, and with high technological achievements and biotechnological prowess. The tiny state of Israel has by far and away the highest per capita level of patents in the entire world. This list can go on and on to prove the many ways in which we have fulfilled our mission as a group.

---

8   *Yeshayahu* 42:6. See also 49:6.

Nevertheless, we mustn't lose sight of our mission as individuals, which Yeshayahu meant for us to embrace as well, as God told Avraham in his opening calling:

ונברכו בך כל משפחות האדמה.

And all the families of the world shall bless themselves by you.
(Bereishis 12:3)

—4—
Derashah

ושם נעשה לפניך את קרבנות חובותינו

Yitzchak Heineman wrote an essential work for students of *d'rash* called *Darkei Ha'Aggadah*, which classifies all midrashim into five categories. The most creative of the five is a category he calls *"milui pe'arim*—filling in the gaps." The Torah is very sparing on some of the details about certain events, and the Aggadah is reliable in filling in these details. If we wondered what Moshe did between fleeing Egypt until he was eighty, the Midrash can enlighten us. If we were curious about the extent of the depravity of early man that they deserved the Great Deluge, the Aggadah does not disappoint. And if we wondered what Avraham's life was like before the age of seventy-five, when we are introduced to him, we have plenty of information on that as well. According to an opinion in Chazal,[9] Avraham was three when he discovered God. *Bereishis* 26:5 says: "עקב אשר שמע אברהם בקולי"—Inasmuch as Avraham heeded My voice," and "עקב," with the numerical value of 172, teaches that Avraham heeded God's voice for 172 of his 175 years. Other opinions in Chazal place Avraham's age of discovery at forty,[10] forty-eight,[11] or fifty-two.[12] There is a parable that captures the essence of Avraham's journey to find God:

---

9   *Nedarim* 32a.

10   See *Rambam, Hilchos Avodah Zarah* 1:3.

11   See *Bereishis Rabbah* 95, and *Hagahos Maimoniyos* ibid.

12   See *Ramban, Bereishis* 2:3. Avraham turned fifty-two in the year 2000 from Creation. *Ramban* considers every day of Creation to be represented by one thousand years of history

A coal miner is chipping away at the bottom of a mountain with his pickax and wondering about his place among the cosmos. He looks around him to consider what appears to be in charge of everything, and after much thought, he concludes that the sun must be the ultimate power. After a considerable amount of contemplation and prayer, he becomes the sun himself. He is so proud of his incredible power, and he shines across the solar system—but especially on earth, where people can bask in his glory. But then he notices that many people are deprived of seeing his glory because of clouds. He surmises that if clouds can block the sun, they must be more powerful, so he quickly transforms into an awesome, huge cloud, proudly blocking the mighty sun. But before he can bask in his position, he finds himself being carried across the sky, and has no control to stop it. He wonders what it is that can move the cloud that can hide the sun. *This* must be the true power, so he wills to become the wind. Now he is so proudly whooshing his way across oceans and land, but before he can bask in his newfound glory, he is once again rebuffed as the wind becomes blocked by a huge impediment and can't get around it. It is inconceivable that anything could possibly thwart the wind that could move the cloud that could block the sun. He wills to become that thing, which is a mountain. Now he's really proud to be the thing that can block the wind that can move the cloud that can block the sun. But within moments of becoming a great mountain, he can feel sharp pains at his base and wonders what could possibly be doing that to a being with such power. He must become *that*—and only then does he realize that the great mountain was being chipped away by a coal miner with a pickax.

The full scope of this story captures the essence of Avraham's mission. Avraham was not the only ancient monotheist. The Egyptians had occasional monotheistic leaders.[13] What set Avraham apart was the notion

---

from *Bereishis*. The first two thousand years were a soupy mess, just as the earth took on no particular form until God spread out the vegetation on Day Three and gave the earth form. This corresponds to Avraham spreading the word of God in the beginning of the third millennium.

13 The most famous of these was the Pharaoh Akhenaten (reigning 1352–1336 BCE), who worshipped one god.

of ethical monotheism. The notion that a man could be in communion with his God—and interrupt that Divine visit to help strangers—is a foreign concept in the ancient world. Avraham's gift to the world is the notion that there is a piece of God in every human, and that the coal miner in the parable comes to realize this very same point after his long journey. This idea would manifest itself in the Torah that Avraham's descendants would receive, which refers to man being created in the image of God.[14] Avraham's behavior reflected this understanding and guided his behavior and actions.

— 5 —
Mussar Moments

The purpose of life is a life of purpose.

Comment

Avraham was born into a troubled world. The generation of the Flood and the building of the Tower of Bavel were not too far in the past. Idolatry, violence, licentiousness, and disorder were raging. The world was on fire! People looked at the flaming world and complained, blaming the conflagration on others who started the fire, until one man took a stand to extinguish it. His name was Avraham, and this was his purpose in life. He did it within the spirit of a monotheistic mindset, guided by *chessed*. He would feed people, and as they finished their meal, he would suggest they show gratitude to the one responsible for the food. When they thanked him, Avraham explained that he had a higher power in mind. In this way Avraham spread the word of God.[15] The ancient world did appreciate justice and charity as important backdrops for a successful society. Avraham slightly changed this formula to pursue charity and justice as the way of God Himself. Avraham put the

---

14   *Bereishis* 1:27.
15   *Bava Metzia* 86b.

emphasis first on charity so that the justice should be charitable. This is why the Torah refers to Avraham as one who would raise his children "לעשות צדקה ומשפט,"[16] in that order.[17]

Kindness is more important than wisdom, and the recognition of this is the beginning of wisdom.

— 6 —
Birth

God informs Avraham that he will finally have a son with Sarah and that he should be named Yitzchak, ostensibly because Avraham laughed with joy upon hearing the wonderful news. "Yitzchak" means "he will laugh" and stands in sharp contrast to Avraham's other son, Yishmael who would be cast from the family home for being a "מצחק."[18] This is curious since the word מצחק stems from the same root as יצחק. Translations of this word vary from "playing" to "mocking" to "scoffing." While *Rashi* connects this word to the most egregious of sins, perhaps we can render the simplest of explanations: that the difference between יצחק and מצחק is the tense. Both words mean to laugh and experience enjoyment; the difference is that the son who will carry on Avraham's legacy puts off his enjoyment for a future time, much like *eishes chayil* of *Mishlei*: "ותשחק ליום אחרון—She laughs at the time to come."[19] In contrast, Yishmael lives for the moment. He is a מצחק; he laughs in the present and doesn't think of the time to come. (It's no wonder that Eisav, who also lived for the moment, sought out the daughter of Yishmael for marriage.[20])

---

16 *Bereishis* 18:19.

17 The Talmud lists an unwavering, rigid pursuit of absolute *din*, "law," as a reason for the destruction of the Second Temple: "לא חרבה ירושלים אלא על שהעמידו דיניהם על דין תורה" (*Bava Metzia* 30b).

18 *Bereishis* 21:9.

19 31:25.

20 *Bereishis* 28:9.

When a new child is born, we actually need to live in the moment. There are many practical concerns to take care of. But when these needs are fulfilled, often with the help of family, community, and friends, it is the time to think of plans for the future; to give this newborn an inextricable connection to Avraham and Sarah, and the privilege of being part of an everlasting covenant. God told Avraham:

ואת בריתי אקים את יצחק.

My covenant, I will establish through Yitzchak. (Bereishis 17:21)

"אקים" is an acronym for what we say at every *bris*: "אשר קדש ידיד מבטן—He made the holy one beloved from the womb." This is true of every child whose parents think of the future while shaping the present.[21]

— 7 —
B'nei Mitzvah

אשריך אברהם אבינו שיצא רבי אלעזר בן עזריה מחלציך.

Avraham our father, you should be happy that Rabbi Elazar ben Azariah descended from you. (Mechilta D'Rabi Yishmael, Bo 13)

There is an exposition of the 612th mitzvah of the Torah by Rabbi Elazar ben Azariah that should especially gladden the heart of Avraham. That mitzvah is known as *hakhel* and commands every member of the community to gather every seven years to hear words of Torah. The Torah specifically includes men, women, and children in this command,[22] and Rabbi Elazar ben Azariah expounds this atypical verbosity.

אם אנשים באים ללמוד ונשים באות לשמוע טף למה באין? ליתן שכר למביאיהם.

---

21   This acronym is found in *Sefer HaGan* of Rabbi Aharon HaKohen to *Bereishis* 17:21.
22   *Devarim* 31:10–13.

If the men come to learn and the women come to listen, why do the children come along? To render reward to those who bring them. (Chagigah 3a)

Rabbi Menachem Mendel of Kotzk wonders about the question regarding the children. If all the men and women make the pilgrimage to perform this mitzvah, of course they will take their children with them. The question is, why does the Torah tell the parents to do something they were going to do anyway? The answer is, says Rabbi Elazar ben Azariah, to reward them for doing so. This seems to be brought down on one side of the Talmudic debate over whether or not it is greater to perform a mitzvah voluntarily, "גדול אינו מצווה ועושה," or to do so after being commanded, "גדול מצווה ועושה."[23] By commanding the parents to bring their children in order to receive the reward for doing so, Rabbi Elazar ben Azariah is proving that "גדול מצווה ועושה," and this is why Avraham should rejoice that he had such a descendant.

The Talmud maintains that Avraham kept the entire Torah, and even the Oral Law.[24] But there was one mitzvah he obviously did not keep for most of his life, and that is *bris milah*. He kept all the other mitzvos without being commanded to do so, but he waited to perform *bris milah* because he knew that he would one day be commanded to do so. Avraham wanted to do the mitzvah only after being commanded, but he never knew if he was right in doing so. It was only after Rabbi Elazar ben Azariah's *derashah* on *hakhel* that we have a Torah proof that Avraham was right in waiting to do *bris milah* until commanded, and this explains his delight at the *derashah*.

Hakhel is the 612th mitzvah of the Torah and is further connected to *bris milah* because the word "*bris*" has the same numerical value, 612. An eight-day-old boy connects to his first mitzvah. Thirteen years later, he connects to the other 612.

When a child reaches the age of obligation of mitzvos, there is reason to rejoice, because now they are "מצווה ועושה." They are on the team and

---

23   *Kiddushin* 31a.
24   *Yoma* 28b.

can come up to bat in the game of Jewish life, which is dedicated to bringing about a better world under God's majesty.

Welcome to our team, we look forward to your contribution!

— 8 —
Marriage

People resist change. We are creatures of habit and we get set in our ways. Adam quickly got set in his ways alone and had to be convinced by God to enter the Gan Eden where he would meet his mate. *Rashi* derives this from that fact that God had to take Adam to place him in the garden.[25] He needed convincing. When it was time for Noach to save the lives of his family, he too needed convincing according to *Rashi*. He only entered the ark when the rain forced him to.[26] And when Avraham was told to leave Mesopotamia for Canaan, God told him, "לֶךְ לְךָ,"[27] and the extraneous "לְךָ—for you" is also understood by *Rashi* to mean that Avraham was told that the move would be good for him.[28] Each of these cases demonstrates the natural tendency to resist change and to favor a status quo.

Marriage involves a profound change in life and affords us the opportunity to reach our full potential as a giver. From birth through infancy we mostly receive, and we are not capable of giving much, outside of being cute. As we grow, good parents and teachers guide us to change from being primarily a taker to being a giver.

Marriage in Hebrew is קידושין, which invokes holiness. It is also called נישואין, which shares a root with the word "to carry." In a truly loving marriage, no burden is too heavy, no task is too cumbersome, and there is no limit to the gifts of giving.

---

25   See *Rashi*, *Bereishis* 2:15, from *Bereishis Rabbah* 16:5.

26   See *Rashi*, *Bereishis* 7:7, ד"ה מפני מי המבול, from *Bereishis Rabbah* 32:6.

27   *Bereishis* 12:1.

28   See *Rashi*, *Bereishis* 12:1.

— 9 —
Seudah Shelishis

אתה אחד ושמך אחד

Upon arriving in his new homeland, Avraham quickly learned that Canaan—at the time of his arrival—was not only a famine zone,[29] it was also a war zone.[30] Subjugations and rebellions were the order of the day as a battle raged that involved Avraham since his nephew, Lot, was taken captive. Emphasis is placed on the strength and might of the captors, in the words of *Rashi*, to underscore Avraham's moral audacity in standing up to such force.[31] Avraham gathers 318 men to free Lot and they successfully return all the captives and their possessions. *Rashi* quotes our Sages who maintain that Avraham did all this alone with his servant Eliezer (who has not yet been mentioned but will be in the next chapter).[32] *Rashi* indicates that the *gematria*, the numerical value, of "Eliezer" equals 318, the number of men listed in the text.[33] *Ibn Ezra* takes the opportunity here to weigh in on his opposition to *gematria*. He states that the Torah never speaks through such coded messages, because if *gematria* was incorporated into our commentaries, we could fabricate any message we want—good or bad—regarding any person or event.

But, surely *Ibn Ezra* knows that the Talmud and Midrash are filled with *gematria*, some even in the realm of halachah! *Ibn Ezra*'s point, however, is that *gematria* has no place in a Torah commentary dedicated to *p'shat*, the plain and simple message the text wishes to convey. If only two men defeated the four armies, the text should have said so instead of listing 318. When the Talmud engages in *gematria*, it is expounding the text from the standpoint of *d'rash*, a deeper exposition of what

---

29   *Bereishis* 12:10.
30   *Bereishis* 14.
31   *Rashi, Bereishis* 14:9.
32   *Rashi, Bereishis* 14:14, from *Nedarim* 32a.
33   Chazal teach that they used magic dust to defeat their enemies. See *Taanis* 21a, *Rashi*, ד"ה
מעפרא דאברהם הוא.

Ibn Ezra agrees is a deep, complicated, and Divine text.[34] Since *Rashi* has already indicated that *p'shat* takes precedence in his commentary,[35] *Ibn Ezra* feels that *gematria* has no place in such a commentary. *Rashi*, however, does indicate that he will pursue *d'rash* if the *p'shat* fails to resolve a problematic text, which is a word, phrase, or concept that stands out of the ordinary textual standards of grammar, syntax, and context, or other similar texts.

The reason *Rashi* wrote that the number 318 actually represented just Eliezer is not only because of the coincidence that this number exactly corresponds to the name of the only identifiable person it could be,[36] who is about to be mentioned,[37] but also the exactitude of the number. It is not the way of the Torah to refer to such precision. We would normally expect the Torah to refer to three hundred men in such a case.[38] *Ibn Ezra* himself at times conceded to the enticements of a neat *gematria*. He had a tradition that Mashiach's name is Menachem.[39] The prophet Zechariah refers to Mashiach's name as Tzemach,[40] and *Ibn Ezra* points out that those two names share a *gematria*. *Ibn Ezra*, in answering how Rus could possibly carry an *eifah* of barley (the bulk of 432 eggs),[41] rattles off a series of *gematria* that can rival anything that appears in

---

34   See *Ibn Ezra*'s introduction to his book on Biblical grammar, *Safah Berurah*: "ועתה בני שים לבבך כי קדמונינו ז״ל מעתיקי המצוות פרשיות גם פסוקים לבדם גם מלות גם אותיות על דרך גם דרש גם במשנה גם בתלמוד ובברייתות ואין ספק שהם ידעו הדרך הישרה כאשר היא על כן אמרו כלל, אין מקרא יוצא מידי פשוטו והדרש הוא תוספת טעם."

35   See especially *Rashi* to *Bereishis* 3:8.

36   There is an unwritten rule in *gematria* that the count can be off by one. The source of this allowance is *Bereishis* 48:5, where Yaakov tells Yosef, "אפרים ומנשה כראובן ושמעון יהיו לי—Ephraim and Menasheh shall be mine no less than Reuven and Shimon." The *gematria* of אפרים ומנשה is 732 and the *gematria* of ראובן ושמעון is 731, and Yaakov equates the two. See *Baal Haturim*, *Bereishis* 48:5 and *B'nei Yissaschar*, months of Kislev to Teves, p. 42.

37   *Bereishis* 15:2.

38   See *Rosh*, the very end of *Pesachim*, where he suggests that 69 people entering Egypt were rounded off to 70 (*Bereishis* 46:27), the 49 days between Pesach and Shavuos were rounded off to 50 (*Vayikra* 23:16), and the 39 lashes were rounded off to 40 (*Devarim* 25:3). Also, Avimelech killed 69 of his brothers, but the text numbers 70 (*Shoftim* 9:5).

39   See *Sanhedrin* 98a for other traditions of Mashiach's name.

40   *Zechariah* 3:8.

41   *Rus* 2:17.

Rashi's commentary. The fact is that the Bible does speak to us through *gematria*, according to all opinions, if we expand its definition.

In the introduction to Rabbi Elazar Rokeach's commentary to the Torah, he reveals no less than seventy-three different types of codes that he incorporates into his commentary. Numerology is a code whereby a word signifies a message that is transferred to a number. This can be done in many ways and it is incontrovertible that we find this in the Bible. When Yirmiyahu wants to extend a hidden message regarding Bavel or Kasdim, he refers to them by substituting the letters of their names with a code known as *At Bash*, which is where the first eleven letters of the Hebrew alphabet are substituted by the last eleven backward and vice versa, so that בבל becomes ששך,[42] and כשדים becomes לב קמי.[43] This is only one of the *Rokeach's* seventy-three codes!

Perhaps when all is said and done, we can read into *Rashi* that these 318 men fought together in such a cohesive group, it was as if they were a single unit fighting as one.[44]

— 10 —
Word of the Parashah

והכנעני אז בארץ—The Canaanites were by **then** in the land
Bereishis 12:10

When Avraham arrived in Canaan from Charan, he found that "והכנעני אז בארץ—the Canaanites were in the land. This translation omits the word "אז" from its rendition.[45] The word appears quite often in *Tanach* and can have several meanings. It can mean:

- **At that time**, as in, "אז הוחל לקרא בשם ה'—At that time men began to call in the name of God" (*Bereishis* 4:26).
- **At a previous time**, as in, "ככחי אז וככחי עתה—As my strength was then, so is my strength now" (*Yehoshua* 14:11).

---

42   *Yirmiyahu* 25:26; 51:41.
43   *Yirmiyahu* 51:1.
44   Or maybe *Rashi* felt that Avraham and Eliezer had the magic dust referenced above, n. 33.
45   This is as if to say that "והכנעני אז בארץ" means the same as "והכנעני בארץ." See below for an explanation of the extra word.

- **Then it will be**, as in, "אז ימלא שחוק פינו—Our mouths will then be filled with laughter" (*Tehillim* 126:2).
- **A consequence of something in the past**, as in, "כי אז תצליח את דרכיך—Only then will you prosper in your ways" (*Yehoshua* 1:8).

Rashi and *Ibn Ezra* dispute the meaning of this tiny Hebrew word, with great ramifications. *Rashi* understands "והכנעני אז בארץ" to mean that by the time Avraham reached his destination, the Canaanites were *already* there. This implies that they were not originally there, because Avraham's ancestor Shem was there first.[46]

In contrast, *Ibn Ezra* understands "והכנעני אז בארץ" to mean that when Avraham arrived, the Canaanites were *still* there. The implication of this rendition is that by the time the Torah was given, they were no longer there, which is of course untenable. This comment of *Ibn Ezra* has garnered some controversy,[47] and we prefer *Rashi's* rendition because it justifies our place in Israel not only on our terms but on objective terms. We were there first.

---

46 See *Bereishis* 1.

47 See *Ibn Ezra*, *Devarim* 1:1, ד"ה בעבר הירדן. See commentary of Rav Yosef Tuv Elem of Bonfils, *Tzafnas Pane'ach* to Ibn Ezra. See also *Ibn Ezra*, *Bereishis* 36:31, and *Igros Moshe*, *Yoreh Deah*, vol. 3, *siman* 114–115.

Parashas Vayeira

—1—
Friday Night
תכלית מעשה שמים וארץ

The founders of our nation underwent name changes at the end of *parashas Lech Lecha* as the letter *hei* was added to both their names. Avram became Avraham and Sarai became Sarah. At the root of these new names is the idea that Avraham and Sarah were each about to undergo a metamorphosis; a name change underscores a change in destiny, as Chazal say, "*Meshaneh shem meshaneh mazal.*"[1]

This would be so for any change in name, but our commentaries take it one step further, by explaining these specific changes.[2] Perhaps the most famous of these explanations is that God added a *hei* from His name to catalyze their ability to bear a child together, solidifying their destiny. Others suggest that the *hei*, which denotes femininity in Hebrew grammar, was an added blessing of fertility to the elderly couple.

---

1   See *Rosh Hashanah* 16b, *Bereishis Rabbah* 44:15, and *Rashi* to *Bereishis* 15:5.
2   The sources in the previous note indicate that any name change can alter the *mazal*, but the custom is to change the name for a specific meaning. For instance, one who is deathly ill might have their name changed to Refael, which connotes recovery. A woman who is having trouble conceiving might have her name changed to Chayah or Chavah, which connote giving life. The prevailing custom today is to add a name to change the *mazal*, rather than changing the name.

55

The Talmud points out that Avram and Sarai are particular names, while Avraham and Sarah connect to the entire world on a universal level.[3] Avraham's new name defines him as an *"av hamon goyim—the father of many nations."*[4]

We see this metamorphosis in Avraham on a practical level between *parashas Lech Lecha* and *parashas Vayeira*. In both, he and Sarah are mistreated by foreign kings, but only in *Vayeira* does he pray for the king. In both *parashiyos* he has dealings with Sodom, but only in *Vayeira* does he pray for them. In both *parashiyos* he casts Hagar from his home, but only in *Vayeira* does he try to intercede on her behalf.

Avraham grows into becoming a *navi* (prophet). God rests His message upon a *navi*, and the *navi*'s job is to intercede on behalf of others, and this is precisely why Avraham would pray for Avimelech, the Philistine king.[5] That is what a *navi* does; he uses his Divine connection to help others.

Furthermore, Avraham was not satisfied for the Divine presence to rest on him alone. He wanted God's presence to descend upon the very mountain where he took Yitzchak, so that others could replicate his prophetic experience. He did this by naming the place "ה' יראה—*Hashem Yir'eh*," so that God would continue to be experienced at this mountain. This could refer to many nations that Yeshayahu predicted would stream to the Temple for Divine instruction:

והלכו עמים רבים ואמרו לכו ונעלה אל הר ה' אל בית אלקי יעקב וירנו מדרכיו ונלכה בארחתיו.

And many people shall go and say: Come let us go up to the Mount of the Lord, to the House of the God of Jacob, that He may instruct us in His ways, and that we may walk in His paths. (Yeshayahu 2:3)[6]

---

3   See *Berachos* 13a.
4   *Bereishis* 17:5.
5   *Bereishis* 20:7. See *Rashi* there for another connection between Avraham's status as a *navi* and the fact that he prayed for Avimelech.
6   See also *Michah* 4:1–2.

It can also refer to the prediction in the book of *Yoel*:

אשפוך את רוחי על כל בשר ונבאו בניכם ובנותיכם זקניכם חלמות יחלמון בחוריכם חזינות יראו.

I will pour out My spirit on all flesh. Your sons and daughters shall give over prophecy. You old men shall dream dreams, and your young men shall see visions. (Yoel 3:1)

— 2 —
Introduction to the Torah
ישמח משה במתנת חלקו

After quite a bit of preparatory activity on Avraham's part for his three guests,[7] they open a dialogue with Avraham by asking where Sarah is. Avraham, ignoring the question of how these strangers knew his wife's name, responds that she is in the tent. The *Chidushei HaRim* wonders why this question and answer precede the message of the birth of Yitzchak, as they seem extraneous. He goes on to show that this short dialogue has monumental ramifications extending all the way to the Messianic persona.

In order to make this point, the *Chidushei HaRim* cites *Rashi's* assertion that the angels, who came to Avraham at the heat of the day, were told to wait until evening to arrive at Sodom to continue their mission.[8] This delay was meant to give Avraham the time needed to argue on behalf of Sodom.[9] This was because among the survivors, due to Avraham's intercession, would be Lot and his daughters: one daughter would give birth to Moav, a nation that would produce Rus, the ancestor of King David,[10] and the other daughter would give birth to Amon, a nation that would produce Naamah, Shlomo's wife, who would give birth to the next king, Rechavam.[11]

---

7   *Bereishis* 18:2–8.
8   *Bereishis* 18:9, ד״ה איה שרה אשתך.
9   *Rashi, Bereishis* 19:1, ד״ה בערב, from *Bereishis Rabbah* 50:1.
10   *Rus* 4:16–17.
11   *Melachim I* 14:21.

The angels pushed back at this suggestion because of the Torah prohibition of allowing converts from these two nations, because they did not meet us with bread and water when we left Egypt.[12] If so, what was the point of saving Lot and his daughters for the sake of Amon and Moav, for two women who would not be allowed to join our *kehillah* anyway? God announced that the women of Amon and Moav are to be treated differently than the men. The angels continued to push back, asking why their women were treated differently than men, whereas in that same section of *Devarim*, the women of Amalek, Egypt, and Edom were treated the same as the men.[13] God responded that the men of Moav and Amon were condemned for not returning the favor of Avraham's intercession on their behalf. But this punishment was never meant to apply to women since it is not the way of women to greet strangers with bread and water. It would not be fair to punish the women of Moav and Amon, for not doing what we wouldn't expect them to do in the first place.

The angels pushed back one last time by telling God, "לא בשמים היא."[14] It is not up to God to determine between two sides of halachah; it can only be done through experience and investigation. God agreed, and therefore the angels would have to test whether it is the way of women to greet strangers with bread and water. That is why they came to Avraham and needed to ask a very crucial question: "Where is Sarah?" Why isn't she greeting us with you, and offering bread and water? Is it because she is away? Avraham answers, "She is in the tent." She is behaving in line with what God said about including the women of Moav and Amon, and as the *Chidushei HaRim* says, this short dialogue has ramifications from Lot to his daughters to Moav and Amon to King David, all the way to the Messianic persona. It also shows that in the Torah, there is no extraneous dialogue.

---

12   *Devarim* 23:4–5.

13   The two sides of this argument are represented in *Yevamos* 76b–77a.

14   See *Bava Metzia* 59b.

—3—
Introduction to the Haftarah

The weekly haftarah, a reading from *Neviim* (the Prophets), is supposed to parallel some facet of that week's Torah portion, or relate to a specific day such as a Yom Tov, Rosh Chodesh, or Chanukah, etc. The haftaros connect to the *parashah* in various ways. Some haftaros parallel a particular mitzvah found in that *parashah*, such as the story of Shimshon, which connects to the mitzvah of *nazir* (*parashas Naso*). A haftarah might pick up one phrase that appears in both Torah and *Neviim*, such as the similar phrasing of the zealousness of both Pinchas and Eliyahu (*parashas Pinchas*). Other haftaros intentionally contrast the Torah portion, like the story of Yehoshua's spies contrasts the story of Moshe's scouts (*parashas Shelach*), while others directly copy large swatches from the Torah portion's narrative, such as Yiftach's conquest of Amon (*parashas Chukas*). Finally, some haftaros are more tenuously connected and just mention the *parashah* in passing, such as Michah's reference to Bilaam (*parashas Balak*), Yeshayahu's reference to Noach (*parashas Noach*), or Malachi's reference to Yaakov and Eisav (*parashas Toldos*).

This brief review is meant to introduce the unprecedented connection between our haftarah and *parashas Vayeira*. The Torah portion has seven parts:

1. Avraham's hospitality to the three strangers
2. The destruction of Sodom
3. The salvation of Lot and his daughters
4. Avraham and Sarah's travels through Philistia and their dealings with Avimelech, the king
5. The birth of Yitzchak to Avraham at age one hundred and Sarah at age ninety
6. The banishment of Yishmael and his near-death experience
7. The binding of Yitzchak

The haftarah begins with a passing reference to a despicable practice that took hold in Israel, wherein parents were forced to sell their children to creditors for unpaid debt. The prophet Amos complains about the same practice in what opens the haftarah of *parashas Vayeishev*, to parallel the sale of Yosef.[15] This abomination loosely connects to (2) the destruction of Sodom, which fell because of that city's horrific social decay. The unnamed woman and her children were saved from their creditors by Elisha's intervention, just as (3) Lot and his daughters were saved because of Avraham's intervention.

The haftarah continues with its main section, which describes a Shunamite woman who prevails upon Elisha to eat, and then to accept her hospitality by spending the night in her home. This clearly parallels (1) Avraham's hospitality in the beginning of the *parashah*. When Elisha asks if she would accept any remuneration for her kindness, such as an audience with the king, she refuses, saying that her lot is cast with all her people and she wants no preferential treatment. This seems to connect to Avraham's travels through Philistia and his dealings with Avimelech (4). Avraham asks God for no preferential treatment in his travels and holds no grievances over the difficulties he faces.

Elisha's attendant points out that the woman is barren and both she and her husband are advanced in age. Elisha, taking a line right out of our *parashah*, gives the old couple hope to finally have a child by announcing that by the same time next year, they will finally have a child. This parallels (5) the birth of Yitzchak to very old parents. Finally, this long-awaited child[16] suffers from heatstroke and is nearly lost to his parents but is revived by paralleling the near-death experience of Yishmael (6) and Yitzchak (7).

This is one of the longest haftaros of the year and surely the one most profoundly connected to the entire Torah reading. Significantly, with all its various thematic connections to the *parashah*, the most important one is the act that makes the Shunamite woman worthy of God's bounty: her hospitality. It was a worthy cause for Avraham to

---

15   *Amos* 2:6.

16   The *Zohar, chelek aleph* 7b, identifies this child as Chavakuk, the prophet who challenged God to give proper recompense for both the righteous and wicked. Elisha told the Shunamite woman, "למועד הזה כעת חיה חיה את חובקת בן‏—About this time next year, you shall embrace a son" (*Melachim II* 4:16). The word for "embrace," חבקת, connects to the name of the prophet חבקוק.

seek—even if it meant interrupting his audience with God—and it led to the fulfillment of the lifelong wishes of two elderly couples.

Think of what it can do for all of us.

— 4 —
Derashah
ושם נעשה לפניך את קרבנות חובותינו

Avraham's sense of justice at first demanded that the righteous of Sodom not be condemned along with the wicked. God readily acceded to this, and Avraham, sensing flexibility on God's part, began to bargain for the sake of the wicked as well. Avraham asked:

אולי יש חמשים צדיקים בתוך העיר?

> *Perhaps there are fifty righteous people in the midst of the city? (Bereishis 18:24)*

Avraham's consideration was that these fifty *tzadikim* could make their presence felt and turn the city toward righteousness. *Ibn Ezra* derives this from the extraneous "בתוך העיר." It would not be enough to have fifty *tzaddikim* to save Sodom—they would have to be in the midst of the city, exerting their influence.[17] Avraham continued to bargain all the way down to ten, but alas, even that number was not to be found, and the city was destroyed.

A similar consideration was made by Yirmiyahu when God told him:

שוטטו בחוצות ירושלים וראו נא ודעו ובקשו ברחובותיה אם תמצאו איש
אם יש עושה משפט מבקש אמונה ואסלח לה.

> *Roam the streets of Jerusalem, search its squares. Look about and take note. If you find even one man who acts justly, who seeks integrity, then I will pardon her [i.e., Jerusalem]. (Yirmiyahu 5:1)*

---

17   *Ibn Ezra to Bereishis* 18:26.

It appears that Yirmiyahu had not managed to find such a person since Jerusalem was destroyed. *Radak*[18] points out that in the rendition of the sacking of Jerusalem we read:

נתנו את נבלת עבדיך מאכל לעוף השמים בשר חסידך לחיתו ארץ.

They have left Your servants' corpses as food for the fowl of heaven, and the flesh of your faithful for the wild beasts. (*Tehillim 79:2*)

Radak wonders why the people, described as עבדיך and חסידך, were not able to save Jerusalem according to Yirmiyahu's calling above. *Radak* answers that Jerusalem must have had many *tzaddikim*, but they were not בחוצות ירושלים or ברחובותיה. They remained in their own domains where their faith and integrity made no impression.

When Rabbi Eliezer lay sick in bed, several of his students came to visit.[19] One by one, they commiserated with their *rebbi*'s suffering. Rabbi Akiva laughed at his *rebbi*'s condition, and when pressed to explain his laughter, Rabbi Akiva claimed that Rabbi Eliezer's considerable successes came with the risk that he was receiving too much reward in this world. Rabbi Eliezer's suffering reassured Rabbi Akiva that ample reward awaited his *rebbi* in the next world. After hearing this explanation of his student's laughter, Rabbi Eliezer asked Rabbi Akiva what he had done to deserve this kind of suffering. Rabbi Akiva replied, "*Rebbi*, you taught us: כי אדם אין צדיק בארץ אשר יעשה טוב ולא יחטא—There is not one righteous man in the land who does only good and doesn't sin."[20]

I have four questions:

1. How could Rabbi Akiva talk to his *rebbi* this way? The Talmud[21] considers drawing attention to the sins of one who is suffering to be a violation of אונאת דברים, "oppression with words."[22]

---

18 *Yirmiyahu* 5:1, ד"ה שוטטו.
19 This story appears in *Sanhedrin* 101a.
20 *Koheles* 7:20.
21 *Bava Metzia* 58b.
22 *Vayikra* 25:17, "ולא תונו איש את עמיתו."

Why wasn't Rabbi Akiva sensitive to this? He spoke to Rabbi Eliezer as Iyov's friends spoke, yet they were rebuked.[23]

2. Rabbi Akiva responded that he was guided by *Koheles* (7:20). If so, he should have said, "שנאמר," not "למדתנו רבינו." The one who taught this verse was *Koheles*, not Rabbi Eliezer.

3. The point of the verse is clear: everyone sins. What is the point of the inclusion of the words "בארץ—in the land"? What does it add to the message?

4. There is a tradition that four Biblical characters never sinned—Binyamin, Amram, Yishai, and Kilav.[24] They only died because death was already decreed upon man. Why didn't Rabbi Akiva simply say that his *rebbi* followed the path of these four righteous people, and that his suffering was not to atone for his own sins, but a similar decree?

Rabbi Akiva did not liken his *rebbi* to these four righteous characters because Rabbi Eliezer's life more readily resembled that of their close relatives: more like Yosef than his brother Binyamin; more like Moshe than his father, Amram; more like David than his father, Yishai; and more like Shlomo than his brother Kilav. The four characters listed in the Gemara lived very passive lives. They were not "בתוך העיר" or "בחוצות ירושלים," as it were. They remained in their own limited domains, not exerting the influence of their more famous, albeit less perfect relatives. This is the way Rabbi Eliezer explained the verse in *Koheles* to his students. It truly *is* possible to live a full life without sinning, but not if you are "בארץ—in the land." Since this was Rabbi Eliezer's exposition of the verse, Rabbi Akiva was paying a compliment to his *rebbi*—that he lived a life like Yosef, Moshe, David, and Shlomo, which was even better than the four who never sinned.[25] All of this is included in the two words that Avraham added to his quest to save Sodom, "בתוך העיר."

---

23   *Iyov* 42:7.

24   *Shabbos* 55b, *Bava Basra* 17a.

25   *Tosafos, Shabbos* 55b, ד"ה ארבעה, notes a contradiction between *Koheles* 7:20 and the contention that four people never sinned. *Tosafos* answers that the Talmud means that most people sin, and some individuals can indeed live a full life without sinning. This exposition agrees, with the caveat of not being "בארץ."

—5—
Mussar Moments

Things turn out best for those who make the best of the way things turn out.

Comment

Avraham was told that his move from Mesopotamia to Canaan would be good for him. In his new home, he would find his destiny. Yet that new home quickly became a famine zone and a war zone. After years of Divine promises of fathering a great nation, he remained childless. He finally fathered a child with Hagar and then with his beloved Sarah as well. Yet he was told to banish Hagar's child, Yishmael, and came very close to losing Sarah's child, Yitzchak as well. Avraham meets trial after trial with magnanimity, resolve, a stiff upper lip, and without losing his moral underpinning. Chazal speak of ten trials of Avraham,[26] and there are different opinions of how to comprise the list of ten.[27] But throughout all this, Avraham always makes the best of the way things turn out.

The believer in God must struggle to explain hardship and suffering—not a small task. But the nonbeliever must explain everything else.

---

26 *Pirkei Avos* 5:3.
27 See *Rashi*; *Rambam, Peirush Hamishnah Avos* 5:3. Most commentaries consider *Akeidas Yitzchak* to be the tenth trial. Rabbeinu Yonah was the first to suggest that the difficulty Avraham encountered in burying Sarah in a land promised to him was the tenth trial.

—6—
Birth

The last story in *parashas Vayeira* is universally known as *Akeidas Yitzchak*, the "binding of Yitzchak." This is a curious point since the fact that Yitzchak was bound[28] seems to be a minor element of the story. We wouldn't call the story "the slaughtering of Yitzchak" because God never asked that of Avraham, and Avraham never got that far in any case. Perhaps the story could have been called the "upbringing of Yitzchak," to fit the command, "והעלהו לעולה," which can literally be understood to mean to bring him up as an "upbringing."[29] We don't see the story referred to as "נסיון אברהם" according to the opening phrase of the chapter, because the main purpose of the story is the effect these events would have on Yitzchak, not Avraham.

If so, the fact that Yitzchak was bound on the altar has a powerful message. Whether we consider *Rashi's* opinion that Yitzchak was thirty-seven at this time,[30] or the opinions of *Rashbam* and *Ibn Ezra* that he was closer to twelve or thirteen,[31] the binding of Yitzchak was to remove any stumbling block to the observance of God's will. Avraham knew he was likely to falter at the last moment, and he wanted to eliminate any excuse for doing so. The binding of Yitzchak would remove this stumbling block. The haftarah of Yom Kippur makes a similar point. It opens with Yeshayahu calling us to clear a path and to remove all obstacles from the road before us, leading to the performance of God's will.[32] This is essentially the job of new parents; to remove the anticipated stumbling blocks before our children and to turn them into stepping-stones. The words אב and בן, "father" and "son" proliferate in our story to indicate that while Avraham was going through the motions of what he felt was the fulfillment of God's will, he never lost sight, hope, or

---

28   *Bereishis* 22:9.

29   An *olah*, however, is a burnt offering and that seems to be how Avraham understood the command.

30   This is implied from *Rashi, Bereishis* 23:2, ד"ה לספוד לשרה ולבכתה.

31   *Bereishis* 22:4, ד"ה ונשובה.

32   *Yeshayahu* 57:14.

anticipation that come what may, God's promise of "כִּי בְיִצְחָק יִקָּרֵא לְךָ זָרַע—For it is through Yitzchak that offspring shall be called for you."[33]

When we name a new child, we confer the same Divine promise of the family's progeny flowing through this name, just as Avraham's destiny flowed through Yitzchak.

—7—
B'nei Mitzvah

The narratives of Avraham portray a man who seeks a universal audience for the word of God. He forges pacts with kings, leaders, and nations. He invites supposed idolaters to his home, and he beseeches God on behalf of the people of Sodom and the king of Philistia. Through these actions it is clear that Avraham fulfills God's prediction of being "אַב הֲמוֹן גּוֹיִם—the father of many nations."[34]

Yet while Avraham's abundant mercies are apparent toward strangers and even foes, they are nowhere to be found for his own sons. Yishmael and his mother, Hagar, are banished from his home with a short supply of bread and water.[35] Yitzchak is placed on the altar ready for sacrifice.[36] Astonishingly, Avraham accepts both decrees from above without protest!

Rabbi Shimshon Raphael Hirsch explains that in the case of Yishmael, Avraham did at first protest, but was convinced by Sarah (and God) that Yishmael had to go.[37] Even the commentaries who find fault with the banishment of Hagar in chapter 16 (such as *Ramban* and *Radak*),[38] agree with the banishment of Yishmael, with his mother, in chapter 21.[39] Yishmael's behavior indicated that he would adversely influence Yitzchak, which did warrant the harsh reaction.

---

33   *Bereishis* 21:12.
34   *Bereishis* 17:5.
35   *Bereishis* 21:14.
36   *Bereishis* 22:9.
37   See S. R. Hirsch, *Bereishis* 21:11.
38   See both commentaries to *Bereishis* 16:6.
39   See both commentaries to *Bereishis* 21:9.

More difficult to reconcile is Avraham's silence in chapter 22. Why was the eloquent defender of Sodom and supplicant on Avimelech's behalf suddenly silent at the prospect of the death of his long-awaited, beloved son?

Rabbi Hirsch claims that Avraham's faith was so profound that he knew the promise of "כי ביצחק יקרא לך זרע—For it is through Yitzchak that offspring shall be called for you,"[40] would somehow prove true regardless of what happened on the mountain. Rabbi Hirsch then posits that the main focus of this narrative is Yitzchak, not Avraham. The story is, after all, called *Akeidas Yitzchak*. The purpose of the *Akeidah* was to jolt Yitzchak into feeling what Avraham felt before God. Conceivably, Yitzchak might have fallen into the complacency of many people born into the fold, failing to express the same burning enthusiasm and drive as Avraham, who found God on his own. Faced with the prospect that his father's God wanted child sacrifice like most other deities at the time, Yitzchak would learn very intimately, through this trial, how God is different. He would learn through the *Akeidah* how to bind himself to the will of God and survive life's greatest tests. This may be why the story is known as *Akeidas Yitzchak* and not *Nisayon Avraham* (the test of Avraham). In addition to the message for Yitzchak, there is also a message for Avraham: Don't forget about your son. You already lost one. Don't lose another. Great men in *Tanach* often concentrated on their universal tasks to such a degree that they forgot their own children. The nation would survive if this happened to Moshe, Eli, or Shmuel, but it wouldn't survive if it happened to Avraham. It's not an easy task to balance our universal concerns of "לתקן עולם במלכות ש-די—Fixing the world under God's dominion"[41] with our own personal needs, but if Avraham had to be taught this message by acting it out in chapter 22, we can be taught the same message by reading this *parashah* carefully and internalizing its lessons.

---

40   *Bereishis* 21:12.
41   *Aleinu* prayer.

Tehillim refers to children as arrows in the hand of the warrior "כחצים ביד גבור כן בני הנעורים."[42]

We try to direct them to reach their target in life, but once those arrows leave the hand across the bow, they may be given to fickle winds or other impediments to reaching their goal. The metaphor has a few additional points. If we never let go of the arrows, they will surely never reach their target, but the best way to assure that they will, is to always hold them close to our hearts. The further back, closer to our hearts, that we pull the arrow, the further it will go when let loose. This is what we do with *b'nei mitzvah* and it is our job to help them navigate life's inevitable challenges and tests.

— 8 —
Marriage

While basking in the glory of a Divine visit, Avraham lifted his eyes and "וירא—he saw" three men in the distance. The Torah then repeats the word "וירא" before he runs to greet them from the entrance of his tent.[43] What is the point of the repetition of וירא? Wasn't it enough to see them once? The answer is that each וירא depicts a specific type of sight. The first וירא describes the data perceivable by Avraham's sense of sight, which anyone could see. The second וירא is a vision shared by insightful people, and it jars Avraham's awareness that the men looked weary, hot, and famished. We all see things. Avraham saw into things.

Our Sages connect the four species of Sukkos to four body parts.[44] We take one *esrog* because we have one heart. We take one *lulav* because we have one spine. We take two *aravos* because we have two lips, and we take three *hadasim* because the Jew must have three eyes—two for sight and a third for vision. A couple endowed with this special insight will be well-positioned to enjoy a successful marriage.

Avraham is often contrasted with Bilaam in Chazal, especially in *Pirkei Avos* (5:22). The most prevailing feature separating the two is

---

42   *Tehillim* 127:4.
43   *Bereishis* 18:2.
44   *Vayikra Rabbah* 30:14.

Avraham's good eye and Bilaam's evil eye. In light of what was written above regarding Avraham's extra eye, it is interesting to note that Chazal say that Bilaam had only one functioning eye.[45] Everything was one-dimensional to him. If Bilaam had had Avraham's extra eye, he might have offered to bless Balak rather than curse the Israelites. Bilaam and Avraham both surely had attendants to saddle animals for them. Yet they both did so themselves, in Avraham's case,[46] because "אהבה מקלקלת את השורה," whereby his love prevails over protocol, and in Bilaam's case,[47] because "שנאה מקלקלת את השורה," his hatred prevailed over protocol. In marriage, love must prevail over every protocol. Love will forge a path before you that will make anything possible. Separately you have nothing. Together you have everything.

— 9 —

Seudah Shelishis

אתה אחד ושמך אחד

Four *Tanach* characters were called twice in a row by God, which is an expression of endearment and love.[48] The four are Avraham,[49] Yaakov,[50] Moshe,[51] and Shmuel.[52] The calling to Avraham and Yaakov was the last time God spoke to them and the calling to Moshe and Shmuel was their initial contact with God. The contact to Avraham stems from an angel who speaks in the name of God, and the contact to Moshe also stems from an angel, as Moshe draws gradually toward the Divine, in stages.[53] This is to say that the last Divine communication to Avraham winds

---

45   *Sanhedrin* 105a.
46   *Bereishis* 22:3.
47   *Bamidbar* 22:21.
48   *Bereishis Rabbah* 56:7; *Toras Kohanim* 1:1.
49   *Bereishis* 22:11.
50   *Bereishis* 46:2.
51   *Shemos* 3:4.
52   *Shmuel I* 3:10.
53   See Rabbeinu Bachya, *Shemos* 3:1 for five stages of Moshe's approach to this Divine encounter.

down through an angel and Moshe's initial communication begins with an angel.

Shmuel's first Divine contact was at a time when prophecy was not widespread and therefore Shmuel mistook the contact for a human voice.[54]

Yaakov, like Avraham, received this expression of endearment as his last communication with God and then faced the challenges of the Diaspora with the assurances of this Divine encounter. Avraham as well, relieved of the burden of the *Akeidah*, faced the challenges of Sarah's burial and Yitzchak's marriage on the strength of the assurances of his last Divine encounter. We never know which goodbye has the potential to be our last. We never know when we won't have another chance to follow up the last conversation. When the conversation with someone you love draws to an end, end it with "I love you." This message of love will linger, empowering us with a sense of well-being and security that will enable us to function at full capacity, fueled by the love we give and receive.

— 10 —
Word of the Parashah

ויטע **אשל** בבאר שבע—He planted an *eshel* in Be'er Sheva

Bereishis 21:33

Avraham distinguishes himself in his dispensation of hospitality to strangers and wayfarers. At the end of *parashas Vayeira*, "Avraham plants an *eshel*...and calls there in the name of the Everlasting God."

A variety of opinions in Chazal attempt to identify this *eshel*. Since Avraham planted it, some consider it a grove of trees to serve guests of its fruits. It could also refer to a specific tree, and is often translated as a tamarisk, a broad leafy and shady tree.[55] Another opinion considers it to be an inn for hospitality.[56] Avraham remembers well

---

54   *Shmuel I* 3:1–9.

55   This reference appears twice in *Shmuel I* (22:6, 31:13) and is preferred for its protective shade.

56   These opinions appear in *Sotah* 10a.

what lengthy travel is like, and he built an inn to offer hospitality to wayfarers. The word for planting, ויטע, has precedence in this context as well, as *Rashi* points out.[57] And insofar as travelers need food and lodgings, they also need to feel safe in their travels. A third opinion, which appears in Chazal but generally does not make its way into the commentaries because it is distant from the simple meaning of the text, is that Avraham set up a Sanhedrin to deal with everyone's questions and to assure that justice prevailed. This appears to be a play on the word אשל to שאל, which means "to ask."[58]

Chazal also saw the word אשל as an acronym for לוייה, שתיה, אכילה, namely food, drink, and an escort.[59] Some acronyms read שכיבה, אכילה, לוייה—food, lodgings, and escort, and some read לינה, שתייה, אכילה—food, drink, and lodgings.[60]

It was through this *eshel* that Avraham taught his guests the ways of God. He taught them to make blessings and to find God in everything we do. Avraham called on the name of the Everlasting God and caused others to hear that call. Perhaps this expression "the Everlasting God" can help us determine the true meaning of the blessing liturgy "אלקינו מלך העולם," which is usually translated, "our God, King of the universe." In light of our verse, and how Avraham used it to teach others to bless God, these words mean "our God, Everlasting King." One way or another, Avraham's hospitality is an everlasting legacy for his descendants. Avraham understood that every action of his would serve as a legacy for future generations.[61] The *eshel* he planted created an everlasting connection between his descendants and God Eternal.

---

57 *Bereishis* 21:33, ד"ה אשל.

58 *Bereishis Rabbah* 54.

59 *Midrash Tehillim* 110.

60 See *Daas Zekeinim, Devarim* 21:7 for five obligations to fulfill the full complement of obligations of hospitality.

61 See *Bereishis Rabbah* 40:8, where God tells Avraham, "צא וכבוש את הדרך לפני בניך—Go out and forge a path before your descendants."

Parashas Chayei Sarah

—1—
Friday Night
תכלית מעשה שמים וארץ

The Torah tells how three couples met and married. They are Yitzchak and Rivkah, Yaakov and Rachel, and Moshe and Tzipporah. We are introduced to all other Biblical couples when they are already married. All three of these couples share a common element regarding their meeting: all took place at wells.[1] There are three types of Biblical water sources: a מעין, "spring," which exists naturally and requires no human input; a בור, "pit," which is constructed fully by human endeavor, to which water is transported; and in between these two, the באר, the "wellspring," which relies on connecting a natural spring of water to a man-made structure. The symbolism of all three matches made at a באר, a well, is to combine a reliance on the concept of "bashert" (destined), together with our own efforts, our hishtadlus. A person's bashert is "the one who is cut out for them," and the source of this concept is Chazal's contention that:

ארבעים יום קודם יצירת הולד בת קול יוצאת ואומרת בת פלוני לפלוני.

---

1   Technically speaking, Yitzchak and Rivkah didn't meet at a well but their match was made at a well.

Forty days before the fetus is formed a Heavenly voice proclaims forth that this girl will marry this boy. (Sotah 2a)[2]

At the same time, the success of *bashert* requires effort on the parts of the couple, as well as their family, friends, and acquaintances. Some people will have their doubts and will need assurances to make the commitments necessary to successfully marry. This effort is what we mean by *hishtadlus*. The well represents the waters of *bashert*, like a spring, that God placed in the earth, together with the human efforts of the pit, to contain the water.

The overarching feature that leads to the success of all three matches are acts of *chessed*, from Rivkah to Avraham's servant, from Yaakov to Rachel, and from Moshe to Yisro's daughters. Perhaps the symbolism of water has an additional message. Water is composed of two highly volatile and explosive gaseous elements: hydrogen and oxygen. It is an amazing miracle of God's world that these two elements can combine to produce soothing, relaxing, calming, tranquil water. The word שידוך is actually an Aramaic word and is the *Targum* to the word שקט in *Tanach*.[3] A good שידוך renders tranquility, as Naomi told Rus and Orpah:

יתן ה' לכם ומצאן מנוחה אשה בית אישה.

*May the Lord grant you that you may find **rest**, each of you in the house of her husband. (Rus 1:9)*

Naomi later told Rus:

הלא אבקש לך מנוח אשר ייטב לך.

*Shall I not seek a **home**, where you may be happy? (Rus 3:1)*

The married home life is referred to as מנוח, a "place of tranquility." Rivkah would soon relieve Yitzchak's unsettled spirit at the loss of his mother and bring him profound tranquility.

---

2   A loose translation.

3   See *Targum Yonasan* to *Shoftim* 3:30, "ותשקוט הארץ" is translated "וישדוכית ארעא."

—2—
Introduction to the Torah
ישמח משה במתנת חלקו

Rav Hai Gaon would read excerpts from *parashas Chayei Sarah* in his shul whenever a *chasan* was called to the Torah for his *aufruf*.[4] He felt that this *parashah* has such powerful lessons for matchmaking that every new couple ought to be enriched with its messages. The overarching message of all comes from the mouth of Lavan who, when asked about the match of his sister Rivkah with Yitzchak said, "מה' יצא הדבר—The thing emanates from God."[5] These words express the idea behind the concept of *bashert*. *Bashert* is a Yiddish word that literally means "the one cut out for us," because everyone has a match somewhere out there. The *Meiri* explains that everyone will casually meet that *bashert* at some point, but the challenge is to be aware at the time that this person will bring out the best in us.[6]

As Avraham's servant was marveling at Rivkah and her hurried actions for him and his camels, one cannot help but notice how much her deeds resemble Avraham's actions for strangers in the beginning of *parashas Vayeira*. He must have said, "What a great match she will make for Avraham's son." We must also wonder what it means to really be a good match. To be cut out for someone means that we make each other better; we complement each other. It doesn't mean we're exactly alike. Perhaps we ought to reorder our priorities when looking for a match. A married person should constantly strive to enhance the life of his or her spouse and contemplate the ways his or her own life is enhanced as a result of the union.

Yitzchak and Rivkah were actually quite different. Their backgrounds were different, and their outlook stressed different priorities regarding their children. Yet they faced the problems of infertility, famine, and

---

4   See *Ritva, Yoma* 70a; *Rashbatz*, vol. 2, *siman* 39.
5   *Bereishis* 24:50.
6   *Sotah* 2a.

rootlessness together, and maintained the legacy of Avraham to pass it over to the next generation.

The question remains why Rivkah felt the need to vouchsafe the blessing for Yaakov with subterfuge instead of just telling Yitzchak that she had heard from God that the younger would prevail. We will discuss this in *parashas Toldos*.

— 3 —
Introduction to the Haftarah

The book of *Melachim* begins with a description taken right out of *parashas Chayei Sarah*. Both Avraham[7] and King David[8] are described in their late years as "זקן בא בימים—old and coming of age." Only one other person in the entire *Tanach* is described this way, and that is Yehoshua,[9] who completed the conquest of Israel at the age of 110. Avraham's virility is manifest well into his second century, while King David seems to be very advanced in age at seventy. In fact, David lived longer than any king of both the Northern and Southern Kingdoms.

The terminology "בא בימים" bespeaks a person who prepared well for his old age. It describes a person who literally has his days coming with him. The events of the past all come together to weave a tapestry that presents itself to the aged Biblical character. And while Avraham and King David may have prepared for the advent of their aging, both are confronted with stark realities pertaining to the next generation. After all Avraham's trials regarding the birth and life of Yitzchak, the fact remains that Yitzchak has not yet forged a path of his own and Avraham realizes the urgency of assuring the future. And after so much turmoil in *Shmuel II*, David's end continues in turmoil as Adoniyahu vies for the throne in his father's lifetime. Batsheva saves the day as she exhorts her husband to fulfill the prophecy that Shlomo would rule after his father.

One has to wonder at the profound contrast between the narrative of this haftarah and the story that is told in *Divrei Hayamim* regarding King

---

7   *Bereishis* 24:1.
8   *Melachim I* 1:1.
9   *Yehoshua* 13:1.

David's final days. In the latter book, David tirelessly prepares for the building of the Temple and establishes the kingdom of Shlomo without a hint of dissent. One could hardly find a greater contrast in theme and content between *Divrei Hayamim* and a parallel *Tanach* narrative. The *Melachim* narrative appears to conclude the punishment of David for the Batsheva saga. Internal family strife would haunt King David to his dying day, but it didn't mean he would submit to such a destiny. In truth, David never ceased to prepare for the future and in the final analysis, while atoning for the grievous sin committed in *Shmuel II*, chapter 11, he paved the way for a successful building of God's Temple that could not be called by his name. The Temple would, however, be built by the very son of Batsheva, as a sign that David's redemption was complete. And although our haftarah continues to recount elements of that redemption, the day is saved because David "took his days" with him to assure that his line would continue, just as Avraham did.

— 4 —
Derashah
ושם נעשה לפניך את קרבנות חובותינו

When Yitzchak met Rivkah for the first time, the Torah says that he was coming from a place called Be'er Lachai Roi.[10] The reader may be curious at the significance of this fact, and is reminded that this place was originally named by Hagar because the angel appeared to her there.[11] Whenever the Torah renders more information than needed, the Midrash will reliably inform us of the significance of this extra information. For instance, the Torah relates that after Rivkah fulfilled Eliezer's plan of finding a wife for Yitzchak by giving him and his camels water, he gave her gifts. The purpose of these gifts was to impress her that he was sent by a very wealthy man. The Torah bothers to relate that Eliezer gave her a gold ring weighing half a shekel, and two bracelets, weighing ten shekels. This is too much information! The text would be missing

---

10   *Bereishis* 25:62.
11   *Bereishis* 16:13–14.

nothing if it had just said that he gave her gold jewelry. *Rashi* explains that these weights and numbers represented great future achievements for her descendants if she would marry Yitzchak.[12]

The half shekel symbolizes the *Mishkan* that her descendants would build in the desert, with half-shekel donations. The two bracelets represent the two Tablets of the Covenant, and the ten shekels represent the *Aseres Hadibros*, contained on those two tablets.

Sometimes, in order to fully understand the true point of a Midrash, we have to give a *d'rash*, a deeper meaning, to the Midrash. The *p'shat*, plain meaning, of this Midrash is that Eliezer was informing Rivkah of a grand future awaiting her if she would accompany him. We will revisit this below.

Let us return to the significance of the place where Yitzchak was when he was preparing to meet Rivkah. Yitzchak remembers that Hagar was cast from his home on his account.[13] He is about to be married, and he therefore wishes to return the favor to his father for arranging for his own happiness. Yitzchak traveled to Be'er Lachai Roi to find Hagar to reconcile with her and to reunite her with his father. According to a broad consensus of midrashim, Keturah, whom Avraham married right after Yitzchak married Rivkah, was actually Hagar.[14] This was Yitzchak's way of assuring that Avraham would find comfort and happiness in his older years. This act of *chessed* on Yitzchak's part comes along with the Rabbinic contention that Yitzchak established the afternoon prayer at this time.[15] Yitzchak spent three years before his marriage in Gan Eden as a buffer to help him return to normal wordly functioning after the *Akeidah*. While in Gan Eden, he engaged in the spiritual pursuits of Torah study.[16] Thus, prior to meeting Rivkah, Yitzchak established his

---

12 *Bereishis* 24:22, from *Bereishis Rabbah* 60:66.

13 *Bereishis* 21.

14 See *Bereishis Rabbah* 61:4; *Tanchuma*, *Chayei Sarah* 8:1.

15 *Berachos* 26a from *Bereishis* 24:63, "ויצא יצחק לשוח בשדה לפנות ערב"—Yitzchak went out to pray in the field before evening."

16 See *Yalkut Reuveni*, *Bereishis* 22:2 and *Pane'ach Raza*, *Bereishis* 24:64.

priorities of Torah, *avodah*, and *gemilus chasadim*, the three pillars of the world.[17]

Now let us ponder the Midrash regarding Rivkah's gifts. The Talmud expresses reservations about the method by which Eliezer found a wife for Yitzchak. One source considers his method an improper test, lest an unsuitable match fulfill his conditions.[18] Another source goes so far as to call his method a violation of divination![19] Yet the test produced the right match because it was founded on *chessed*. Camels drink a significant amount of water after a long trip. To give water to a thirsty stranger is one thing, but to extend the offer to camels as well means the offer is being made by a person with a foundation of kindness that would suit Yitzchak. But *chessed* is only one of the foundations of the world. The other two are Torah and *avodah* (*Pirkei Avos* 1:2). How could Eliezer ensure that Yitzchak's future wife would also appreciate these other two foundations? The Midrash connects Torah and *avodah* to the gifts Rivkah received. This is the deeper meaning of the Midrash mentioned above, and the Torah gives us all the information we need. The weight and numbers of the gifts, representing the *Mishkan* (*avodah*) and the *Aseres Hadibros* (Torah), would assure a perfect match and destiny for this couple and that they would share the same eternal priorities.

— 5 —

Mussar Moments

God made our world round so that
the place that may seem like the end may
also be the beginning.

---

17   *Pirkei Avos* 1:2.
18   *Taanis* 4a.
19   *Chullin* 95b.

Comment

Rivkah is mentioned in the Torah just before Sarah died. Our Sages likened this to a new sun rising just before an old sun sets.[20] Our Sages note a similar connection between Yehoshua and Osniel Ben Kenaz,[21] as well as Eli and Shmuel.[22] Similar statements are made about sages of the Talmud, such as Rabbi Yehudah HaNasi being born the day Rabbi Akiva died.[23] There is a similar tradition regarding Rabbeinu Gershom and *Rashi*.[24] Life is a circle, and this explains the custom of eating round foods, such as eggs or lentils after a funeral,[25] and just before the mournful fast of Tishah B'Av.[26]

Every exit is an entrance to a new place.

— 6 —
Birth

This week's *parashah* is one of two *parashiyos* in the book of *Bereishis* that has the root of the word "life" in the *parashah*'s title. Ours is "*Chayei Sarah*," which tells the story of the passing of our matriarch Sarah; the last *parashah* of *Bereishis* is "*Vayechi*," which describes the passing of our patriarch Yaakov. They both live on in the seeds they planted that have become our nation, and the names of the two *parashiyos* bespeak this immortality as well. These *parashiyos* tell us more about the lives of these great people than about their passing. The first word in both *parashiyos* hint at this very point. Sarah was 90 when Yitzchak

---

20 See *Midrash Hagadol, Chayei Sarah* 23:1, *Pesikta Zutrasa, Chayei Sarah* 23:1.
21 *Bereishis Rabbah* 58:2.
22 *Yoma* 38b, *Bereishis Rabbah* ibid.
23 *Kiddushin* 72b, *Bereishis Rabbah* ibid.
24 The year of *Rashi*'s birth is considered to be 1040, because that is the year Rabbeinu Gershom died.
25 See *Shulchan Aruch, Yoreh Deah* 378:9.
26 See *Shulchan Aruch, Orach Chaim* 552:5.

was born,[27] and she was 127 when she died.[28] That means that she had 37 years with Yitzchak, which is the numerical value of the first word in the *parashah*: "וַיִּהְיוּ." Yosef was 17 when Yaakov was deprived of seeing him for 22 years.[29] Yaakov was 130 at the time they were reunited,[30] and he lived to be 147,[31] which means that Yaakov had 34 years with Yosef, which is the numerical value of the first word in that *parashah*, "וַיְחִי."

What endows these heroes with eternity is that they lived their lives to assure the continuity of the generations that would follow them. Practically everything else is interred with our bones, while what we do for our children lives on to eternity. The secret of Jewish continuity is in the first words of *Chayei Sarah* and *Vayechi* and keeps our people perpetually alive.

— 7 —
B'nei Mitzvah

וַיִּהְיוּ חַיֵּי שָׂרָה, מֵאָה שָׁנָה וְעֶשְׂרִים שָׁנָה וְשֶׁבַע שָׁנִים, שְׁנֵי חַיֵּי שָׂרָה.

Sarah's lifetime came to one hundred years and twenty years and seven years. These were the years of Sarah's life. (Bereishis 23:1)

The opening verse of *parashas Chayei Sarah* is quite verbose and is the source of much *d'rash* on the fullness of Sarah's life. The inclusion at the end of the verse of "שני חיי שרה" is not only extraneous; it's outright repetitive. It can mean "the years of" and it can also mean the number two.[32] This is to say that Sarah lived two lives.[33] She enhanced life to the fullest in this world and ensured that all she lived for would live on when she would pass on to the next world.

---

27   *Bereishis* 17:17.

28   *Bereishis* 23:1.

29   *Bereishis* 37:2.

30   *Bereishis* 47:9.

31   *Bereishis* 47:28.

32   *Bereishis Rabbah* 58:1, "מדצריך לאמר שני חיי שרה באחרונה לאמר לך שחביב חייהם של צדיקים לפני המקום בעולם הזה ובעולם הבא."

33   See *Rokeach, Baal Haturim, Hakesav V'Hakabbalah, Bereishis* 23:1.

Her life was also divided into stages, as all *b'nei mitzvah* encounter. It is a new level of life and a reason to rejoice. A Jewish youth enters a second stage in life upon reaching the age of obligation in mitzvos. The source for celebrating the attainment of such a stage is in the commentary of Rav Shlomo Luria, to a story in the Gemara,[34] about the blind Amora Rav Yosef. Rav Yosef had contemplated two separate concepts regarding his personal religious status as a blind man. One, whether he, as a blind man, is obligated to perform mitzvos, and two, whether there is greater reward for performing mitzvos voluntarily or when commanded. Rav Yosef posited that one's reward for mitzvah performance is indeed greater when commanded,[35] and he offered to throw a party for the rabbis if it could be conclusively shown that a blind man is obligated to perform mitzvos.

Rav Luria writes that Rav Yosef's offer of celebration should apply to anyone who reaches the age of mitzvah obligation. There is no doubt that such an obligation now advances the young child to a second stage of life, and this is the reason why we celebrate.

It is important to note that the two lives of Sarah defined her, the way a bar or bas mitzvah defines a child. A bar mitzvah is not a noun, or a verb. We don't have a "bar mitzvah," but a bar mitzvah celebration. We are not bar mitzvah-ed, but we become a bar mitzvah, because it is an adjective, that defines us for the rest of our lives.

— 8 —
Marriage

Avraham's servant felt confident that he would succeed in his mission to find a wife for Yitzchak, bolstered by Avraham's assertion that God would send an angel before him.[36] Although this servant is never named, Chazal equate him with Eliezer who came from Damascus,[37] which is

---

34   *Yam Shel Shlomo, Kiddushin* 31a.
35   This is known as "גדול מצווה ועושה." See "*Lech Lecha,*" (7) *B'nei Mitzvah.*
36   *Bereishis* 24:7.
37   *Bereishis* 15:2.

the capital of Aram.[38] Eliezer employed a method of choosing a wife through a test that smacked of divination[39] in that the outcome was beyond his control: the first girl who would offer him and his camels to drink would be a worthy mate for Yitzchak. Eliezer relied on the "angel" God would send to make this test a success. In addition, Eliezer knew that divination would impress an Aramean family, as Lavan himself professed that he practices the art.[40]

We might have thought Eliezer would spend some time observing all the "שואבות—women drawing water,"[41] and then judiciously approaching them one by one to see who would include the kindness of watering his camels after a long trip. He did not do this. Instead, he impetuously ran directly to Rivkah as if he saw something extraordinary about her. *Rashi* says this was because he saw the water from the well rise into her pail.[42] The reason for this exposition is seen in the text, in the contrast between Rivkah and the other girls at the well. The others are called שואבות, because they lowered a pail into the well to draw water, but when Eliezer sees Rivkah, this word is absent. All the text says is "ותמלא כדה—she filled her pitcher."[43] She didn't need to be "שואב" because the water came up to her.[44] This is why Eliezer ran straight to her. She worked miracles! Perhaps Eliezer was tempted then to scrap his plan altogether and give Rivkah the gifts right there and then, but he caught himself. He knew that you can't establish a marriage on the expectations of miracles; a much more stable foundation for marriage is *chessed*. When Eliezer saw Rivkah running for a stranger, and when he saw her rushing to perform *chessed*, he was reminded of Avraham's household and knew that only then could he be sure that this was a good match.

---

38   See *Amos* 1:3–5.

39   See *Chullin* 95b.

40   See *Bereishis* 30:27.

41   *Bereishis* 24:11.

42   *Bereishis* 24:17, ד״ה וירץ העבד לקראתה, from *Bereishis Rabbah* 60:5.

43   *Bereishis* 24:16.

44   When Eliezer retells the story (*Bereishis* 24:45), he describes Rivkah as drawing water. Perhaps *Rashi* would answer that Eliezer did not want to refer to the miracle in his version of the story. In fact, after Eliezer puts Rivkah to the test, the story itself has Rivkah performing "שאיבה" (*Bereishis* 24:20).

Perhaps a deeper meaning of this *d'rash* is meant to teach us that even if we find a match that "miraculously" has everything we're looking for, we should not impetuously leap into the commitment of marriage until we're sure that there is a foundation of *chessed*.

Chessed breaks the bounds of expectation. It is limitless and undying. It is magnanimous and flexible. It is optimistic and is the frame for joy and gratitude. These are far more important for a successful marriage than any miracle.

— 9 —

Seudah Shelishis

אתה אחד ושמך אחד

The Torah contains numerous Masoretic anomalies from its very first letter and beyond. Our tradition is to write the first letter of the Torah larger than the other letters of the word, "*Bereishis.*" Another tradition is to write the last letter of the word "*Vayikra*" smaller than the other letters.[45] It is an observable fact that the Torah lacks punctuation and vocalization. The same three letters can be pronounced in numerous different ways. Our Sages approached the Biblical text from the standpoint of infallibility. They were aware of discrepancies between some of their texts,[46] and they resolved them by majority. The Bible that was expounded by the Talmud and Midrash had words spelled one way and pronounced another way (*keri u'kesiv*), numerous open and closed paragraphs right in the middle of a text, inverted letters, hanging letters, dots on top of letters, and more. These anomalies, not to mention deficient and extraneous spelling (*chaseiros and yeseiros*), were not swept away as scribal error, but were built into the system of how our Sages expounded the text (*yesh eim l'mesorah*). For instance, a consistently deficient spelling of the word "*sukkah*" teaches that a sukkah is kosher even if it is lacking in walls.[47] When Moshe cast

45   For a full list of large and small letters in the Bible, see Eliyahu Kitov's *Sefer HaTodaah*, "Sivan."
46   See *Sifri, Devarim* 356; *Radak* on *Shmuel II* 15:21.
47   *Sukkah* 6b.

the two tablets from his hands before the worshippers of the golden calf, the text misspells the word for "hands," as though Moshe cast only one tablet from one hand, מידו, instead of מידיו.[48] Our Sages never thought of correcting this text or any other that looked at first glance to be inconsistent or erroneous. That is because all of these Masoretic phenomena were understood by our Sages to have been embedded into the text by Divine will. So instead of correcting the missing *yud* in מידו, for example, they teach that Moshe's intention was only to smash the first tablet containing the laws between man and God, but God informed Moshe that in the Torah, interpersonal mitzvos and mitzvos that relate to God are intertwined. We can't have one without the other.[49]

This week's *parashah* describes Avraham mourning, eulogizing, and crying for Sarah. The word for "crying" is spelled with a small *kaf*, to the extent that the unprepared Torah reader may skip the letter altogether, and read "ולבתה" instead of "ולבכתה," as if Avraham lost a daughter along with Sarah.[50] Another opinion is that Avraham diminished his crying as an admission of God's justice.[51] If this is indeed the message of the small letter, why was the letter *kaf* changed? Perhaps it is connected to an Aggadah that Avraham sang twenty-two verses of *Mishlei* 31 at Sarah's funeral. This is known as *"Eishes Chayil,"* and Avraham applied the entire poem to Sarah, line by line.[52]

There is a certain feature of this poem that stands out, and it is the word "*kaf*," which pervades the song. It is the part of the body that gives and receives. Verse after verse refers to her *kaf* and her *yad* that are always stretched out to serve her family, her community, the poor, and all who are in need. This was her mission, to be a receptacle of service. *Eishes Chayil* begins by describing the woman's humble origins. She

---

48   *Shemos* 32:19.

49   See M. Kasher's *Torah Sheleimah, Shemos* 32:19, n. 183.

50   The text would be read as: "Avraham eulogized for Sarah and for his daughter."

51   See *Baal Haturim* and *Hadar Zekeinim, Bereishis* 23:2. See a collection of explanations of the small *kaf* in M. Kasher's *Torah Sheleimah, Bereishis* 23:2, and Louis Ginzberg's *The Legends of the Jews*, "The Death and Burial of Sarah," n. 259.

52   *Tanchuma, Chayei Sarah* 4.

starts off making clothing for others, rising before daybreak to ensure there is enough food, always performing her tasks with vigor. Toward the middle of the song, she graduates to owning businesses and surveying land, but throughout, the pervading message is that she is a giver, who is not only clothed in royal purple, but in strength and splendor as well, cheerfully sharing her wisdom and understanding. She is the very epitome of *Toras chessed*. She makes everyone around her better, and all this points to another reason why the letter *kaf* stands out.

This letter in Hebrew is most often used as the *kaf ha'dimyon*, the letter that is used for comparison. The *kaf* is outstanding in describing Avraham's loss, because the *Eishes Chayil* lives a life that others would want to emulate. After 120, someone may encapsulate all our years in an hour-long eulogy, others may spend a week or so talking about us, and then someone will try to epitomize all we did on a four-foot stone. At this point, we hope that people will say, "I want to be like that," which would be a manifestation of Sarah's accentuated *kaf*. That is why the *kaf* stands out. And it may have been more pronounced for the *kaf* to be larger, like the *beis* of *Bereishis* instead of smaller, like the *aleph* of *Vayikra*, but that is just the point: the *Eishes Chayil* does not need to sing her own praises. The poem ends, "Extol her for the fruit of her hand, and let her works praise her in the gates." We should all want to emulate these praises.

— 10 —
Word of the Parashah

עלמה—Young maiden
Bereishis 24:43

When Eliezer recounts the story of how he chose Rivkah, he changes a number of phrases, words, and orders that are all noted by close readers of the text. At first, he referred to a "נערה" who would fulfill his test,[53] and then, when retelling the story, he calls her an "עלמה,"[54] a rare Biblical word also denoting a youthful woman, but perhaps a bit older

---

53 *Bereishis* 24:14.
54 *Bereishis* 24:43.

than a נערה.[55] The word appears five times in the entire Bible and is the source of a significant polemical dispute regarding a prophecy in *Sefer Yeshayahu*.

In chapter 7, the king of Yehudah, Achaz, was being pressured to join a coalition of nations including Aram and the northern tribes against Ashur. Yeshayahu warned Achaz not to join this coalition, as anyone in it would soon be destroyed. Achaz was wicked and not inclined to heed Yeshayahu's warning. Yeshayahu offered Achaz any sign from God to prove that refraining from joining this coalition was the right thing to do. Achaz refused to seek such a sign. Yeshayahu angrily rendered the sign, which also uses the word עלמה. Yeshayahu predicted that salvation from the Assyrians would not come from any coalition but would be realized through:

הנה העלמה הרה וילדת בן.

Behold, the young woman is pregnant and will soon give birth to a son. (Yeshayahu 7:14)

This would be a sign of their salvation. The polemic is that Christianity teaches that this refers to a future virgin birth. According to some commentaries, Jewish responses to this claim changed the landscape of *parshanus* in the Middle Ages.[56] Jews responded first by pointing out that

---

55   *Rashi* says that Rivkah was three years old when she married Yitzchak, see *Bereishis* 25:20, ד"ה בן ארבעים שנה; *Bereishis* 25:26, ד"ה בן ששים שנה. It would seem, however, that *Rashi* was actually of the opinion that she was older than twelve, based on his comment to *Bereishis* 24:57 and his comment to the *Rif*, *Kiddushin* 41a, "אסור לו לאדם שיקדש את בתו כשהיא קטנה עד שתגדל ותאמר בפלוני אני רוצה שנ' נקרא לנערה ונשאלה את פיה." According to *Rashi*, this question could only be asked to a girl who is older than twelve. Perhaps *Rashi*'s contention of her age of three runs along the lines of "(5) Mussar Moments," above.

56   The Jewish response was to show, for many reasons, that this theology was not the *p'shat*, the plain and simple meaning of the text. When Jews were forced into disputations to debate and refute such claims, it sensitized them more to *p'shat parshanut*. The move to *p'shat parshanut* in the Middle Ages coincided with the time that these disputations proliferated. See Elazar Touitou's "*Rashi*'s Commentary on Genesis 1:6 in the Context of Judeo-Christian Controversy," Hebrew Union College Annual 61 (1991). Touitou felt *Rashi* did not let his concern for Christian theology influence his commentary in a noticeable way. See also Sarah Kamin, "*Rashi*'s Commentary on the Song of Songs and the Jewish-Christian Polemic," in *Jews and Christians Interpretation of the Bible* (Magnes Press, 2008). See M.Z. Segol

the Christian interpretation was philologically unsound. The word "עלמה" has no bearing on sexual experience, but upon youth. The word describes Miriam,[57] and youthful women in *Tehillim*[58] and *Shir Hashirim*,[59] and it describes a married woman in *Mishlei*.[60] Furthermore, Jewish debaters pointed out that the Christian interpretation was also grammatically unsound. While the word "הרה" can describe an ongoing situation, in the present ("she is pregnant") or a future situation ("she will be pregnant"),[61] the introduction of the word "הנה—behold" clearly indicates that the birth of this child will come soon, and such a birth immediately fits the context of the story, as this birth is meant to instill in Achaz a reason to rely on God, and not a coalition with Aram for salvation.

According to the context of the story—not to mention, reality—עלמה cannot mean "virgin." The original description of Rivkah[62] refers to her as בתולה, the correct Hebrew word for what Christians attribute to עלמה. The word עלמה has a male form used only twice in the Bible. Once, to describe the youthful David,[63] and once to describe the boy who gathered the arrows shot by Yonasan.[64] Largely using words from *parashas Chayei Sarah*, the Jews argued that philologically (עלמה and בתולה are two different words), grammatically (הרה means "*is* pregnant" not "*will be* pregnant"), contextually (הנה means the things that follow are imminent, not seven hundred years in the future), and realistically (virgins don't give birth),[65] that the Christian interpretation to *Yeshayahu* 7:14 is completely unsound and should surely not be the source of a major dogmatic belief. *Bereishis* 24 and the meaning of the word עלמה fared prominently on the Jewish side of this debate.

הפרשנות הפשטנית Jerusalem, 1944, pages 58–76. Segol suggests that a move to derive the plain meaning of the Talmudic text, even beyond its halachic conclusion, naturally led to a move for such understanding of the Biblical text as well.

57   *Shemos* 2:8.
58   *Tehillim* 68:26.
59   *Shir Hashirim* 1:3; 6:8.
60   *Mishlei* 30:19.
61   See *Ramban* to *Bereishis* 16:11, and *Metzudos* and *Malbim* to *Shoftim* 13:5.
62   *Bereishis* 24:16.
63   *Shmuel I* 17:56.
64   *Shmuel I* 20:22.
65   See *Chagigah* 14b and the Gemara's explanation of the question, "בתולה שעיברה מהו לכהן גדול."

Parashas Toldos

— 1 —
Friday Night
תכלית מעשה שמים וארץ

הקול קול יעקב והידים ידי עשו.

The voice is the voice of Yaakov, but the hands are the hands of Eisav. (Bereishis 27:22)

Yaakov almost blew his cover as he stood before his father. His mother arranged for an elaborate plan involving a number of her husband's senses. She dressed Yaakov in goat's hair so that he would feel and smell like Eisav. She prepared meat that would taste like Eisav's food. And since Yitzchak couldn't see, the only sense left for Yaakov to work on was the sense of sound. Surely Rivkah instructed her son to make every attempt to *sound* like Eisav. Yet Yaakov failed to do so.

While *Ibn Ezra* claims it was the sound of the voice itself that tipped Yitzchak off,[1] *Rashi* maintains that it was the *content* of the voice that made Yitzchak ask for verification of being in Eisav's presence.[2] If it was the sound itself, *Rashi* may argue, then Yitzchak should have asked

---

1   See *Ibn Ezra, Bereishis* 27:40, ד"ה ופרקת. See also *Ramban*, v. 21.
2   *Bereishis* 27:21–22.

earlier to feel Yaakov's arms. It was only after Yaakov invoked the name of God that Yitzchak was tipped off to a possible mix-up.

On this issue, *Rashi* leads us to a curious point. At first he informs us that Yitzchak grew skeptical of being before Eisav because Yaakov used the word "please," when he said "קום נא שבה." Then *Rashi* suggests that it was Yaakov's use of God's name that made Yitzchak ask to feel his arms. Which is it, the נא or God's name?[3]

The answer is that it must be both. Even as Yaakov is nervously running through the motions of his mother's directions, he uses the language of spirituality. It's very easy to invoke God's name at every turn. Many people use *"baruch Hashem," "im yirtzeh Hashem,"* etc., all the time and this is a good thing. Many other people use the language of courtesy at every turn, saying "please," "thank you," and "excuse me"—and this is also a good thing. The challenge is to be both—to be involved in the hustle and bustle of service to God by running from minyan to a *shiur* to a *chessed*, without stepping on any toes in the rush of the performance of the above.

Yitzchak recognizes both of these characteristics in Yaakov and together, they tipped him off that the son in his presence could not be Eisav. And this is precisely the point. Even when circumstances require us to wear the garments of Eisav and we must feel and smell like him, there is no case when we can justify *sounding* like Eisav. Our קול יעקב must never be diminished at any cost for it is only that which can contend with the hands of Eisav. Let us always be sure that Yaakov's voice has the trappings of courtesy as well as spirituality.

---

3   *Rashi* mentions the use of God's name first (v. 21) then the use of נא (v. 22), although Yaakov's use of these two were inverted. Perhaps *Rashi* means to say that Yitzchak was ready to overlook the use of נא, mentioned first, but when Yaakov then mentioned God, Yitzchak's curiosity was piqued to ask which son stood before him, and the present question—the reference to God—is mentioned first.

— 2 —
Introduction to the Torah
ישמח משה במתנת חלקו

Ancient man harbored many irrational fears and superstitions. They fabricated reasons to explain natural phenomena such as thunder, lightning, solar and lunar eclipses, volcanoes, earthquakes, shooting stars, and more. The one natural phenomenon that confounded them most of all was death. They were obsessed with cheating death, and with communicating with those who had crossed the divide between this world and the next. The Torah strongly prohibits such acts under pain of death. A short *parashah* of only sixty-four verses, *parashas Kedoshim*, which is dedicated to living a life of holiness, lists the prohibition against communicating with the dead no less than three times.[4] That *parashah* concludes by encapsulating the first twenty chapters of *Vayikra*:

> והייתם לי קדושים כי קדוש אני ה׳ ואבדיל אתכם מן העמים להיות לי.
>
> *You shall be holy to Me for I the Lord am holy and have separated you from the nations to be Mine. (Vayikra 20:26)*

But then the *parashah* inexplicably concludes by repeating the prohibition of necromancy:

> ואיש או אשה כי יהיה בהם אוב או ידעני מות יומת באבן ירגמו אותם
> דמיהם בם.
>
> *A man or a woman that is a medium or a necromancer shall surely be put to death. They shall be pelted with stones; their blood shall be upon them. (Vayikra 20:27)*

It seems the Torah wants to connect to the very next verse, which begins *parashas Emor*, and prohibits death defilement to our religious functionaries.[5] *Kohanim* may not approach the death defilement that

---

4   *Vayikra* 19:31; 20:6; 20:27.
5   *Vayikra* 21:1–6.

so obsessed the idolatrous priests of the ancient world. The Torah wants us to concentrate on life, not death.

Eisav lived every day for the moment and faced death so regularly that it is no wonder that he would say,

הנה אנכי הולך למות ולמה זה לי בכורה.

I constantly approach death so of what use is a birthright to me? (Bereishis 25:32)

Eisav saw the color red and was so obsessed by it that he had to have the red food he saw immediately. The blood of the hunt, the slaughter of the game, became part of his very essence until it defined him, and he became known as Edom. To Eisav, red is the color of death, but for us red is the color of life. It is a reminder that death is supposed to remain a mystery. Our reaction to death is to purify it with a mitzvah that is as mystifying as death itself, *parah adumah*, the red heifer. The purification of the *parah adumah* offsets the inevitable despair and desperation of a life lived for the moment.

— 3 —
Introduction to the Haftarah

Malachi is the very last prophet God sent to His people.[6] His parting messages are to remember the Torah of Moshe (as if he anticipated that Jews would branch off into a rejection of Torah), and to announce the mission of Eliyahu HaNavi, who will herald the Messianic arrival. He begins his message with a delineation of the contrasts between Yaakov and Eisav, as if to say that only with the vanquishing of Eisav can our redemptive aspirations be realized. Malachi speaks to his people after the Second Temple had been built, and he expresses God's profound disappointment at the lack of enthusiasm in the Temple service.

Their lethargy and disillusionment in the Temple's rebuilding prevented the return of the second commonwealth from reaching

---

6   According to *Targum Yonasan*, *Malachi* 1:1, Malachi was Ezra.

the grandeur that was predicted by prophets such as Yirmiyahu[7] or Chaggai.[8] This element of the haftarah parallels Eisav's rejection of the birthright, which at that time, entailed Divine service.[9] The Jews in Malachi's day were behaving like Eisav. This aspect of Malachi's prophecy turns the rebukements of most of our prophets on their heads. The likes of Hoshea, Yeshayahu, Amos, Michah, Yirmiyahu, and others railed against the nation's scrupulous attention to the ritualistic detail of the Temple service, while ignoring the interpersonal laws, and the tears of widows and orphans.

Malachi does the opposite. He does not rebuke the people for any social decay but does castigate them for improper Temple service, akin to Eisav spurning the Temple service, which was his birthright. Then Malachi rails against intermarriage, which was so rampant at this time that Ezra and Nechemiah both made lists of intermarried men,[10] which incredibly included the sons of the Kohen Gadol![11] This parallels Eisav's marriage to Chittite women, which so aggrieved his parents.[12]

The vanquishing of Eisav, as it turns out, would require a sensitivity to the ritual aspect of Torah observance, a rejection of assimilation, and remembering the Torah of Moshe. The last prophet God sent us has a lot to teach us about our own day. The pendulum of the earlier prophets has swung in the opposite direction. If Yeshayahu, Amos, and the others would see us today, they would marvel at the incredible array of *chessed* organizations, Tomchei Shabbos, *gemachim*, Hatzolah, free burial societies, and hundreds of others dedicated to the messages they delivered. Our challenge today is to live up to Malachi's expectations and curb the tendencies of Eisav that have attached themselves to us. It is understandable that this would be so because Yaakov wore Eisav's garments for a short while. Let Malachi also marvel at our efforts in spurning Eisav's rejection of his birthright.

---

7   Chap. 31.
8   Chaps. 1 and 2.
9   See *Rashi, Bereishis* 25:32, 34.
10   *Ezra* 10, *Nechemia* 13.
11   *Ezra* 10:18.
12   *Bereishis* 26: 34–35.

— 4 —
Derashah
ושם נעשה לפניך את קרבנות חובותינו

So far, the women of *Sefer Bereishis* have had their way with the most important family decisions. God first told Avraham to obey Sarah's wishes regarding his two sons,[13] and then entrusted the destiny of Yitzchak's two sons to Rivkah by revealing to her the nature of their relationship with three Hebrew words "ורב יעבוד צעיר."[14]

The meaning of these words seems to be the source of the dispute between Yitzchak and Rivkah regarding their sons. Rivkah perhaps understood, as do most commentaries and translators, that these words indicated the older (Eisav) would serve the younger (Yaakov). However, Yitzchak could have claimed, as does the *Daas Zekenim*,[15] that if the word *tza'ir* means "younger," then the word *rav* is not a parallel word for "older," and is therefore not referring to Eisav. The word should have been "*ha'bechor*" or "*ha'gadol yaavod tza'ir*." As such, Yitzchak always understood that something great, *rav*, would work its way to his younger son.

Yet Yitzchak favored the older one. At first glance, there seems to be a natural explanation: why wouldn't the man of the house, responsible for putting food on the table by the sweat of his brow, favor the son who helps him with this task? Rivkah, on the other hand, favored the son who was pure and resided close to home. It seems that Rivkah favored the one who fit more with Yitzchak's background of wholesome purity and simplicity, while Yitzchak favored the one who fit more with Rivkah's Aramean background of hustle and bustle and interacting with the world at large.

Each son in his youth had positive qualities with possible drawbacks. Yaakov was a worthy son of Yitzchak but lacked the drive of an Avraham. Eisav proved indispensable to the support of the family but

---

13   *Bereishis* 21:12.
14   *Bereishis* 25:23.
15   *Bereishis* 25:23.

lacked the spiritual underpinnings necessary for a patriarch. Rivkah felt Yaakov could be driven to a more aggressive pursuit of the ideals of Avraham, while Yitzchak felt Eisav could be brought into a spiritual framework to direct his actions.

The one who bore the two knew better. She couldn't tell this to Yitzchak at this point because they had discussed their sons' destinies and knew they disagreed. (Simple logic would indicate that Rivkah shared her oracle from God with Yitzchak the day she heard it, and only then did they have the above debate.) Yitzchak felt that Eisav deserved the blessing of material benefits, while Yaakov would be perfectly satisfied with the blessing of Avraham (which he *did* receive at the end of the *parashah*, in addition to the one he took from Eisav).[16] Rivkah feels that Yaakov must be blessed with both, and if Jews do well whenever given equal opportunity, it is due to Rivkah's switch, which made us doubly blessed.

But the switch came at a price. It caused Eisav's enmity and made a fugitive of Yaakov. Yaakov seems to truly regret what he did as he seems to return the blessing and all the troubles in *parashas Vayishlach*.[17] If Yaakov thus receives his atonement, surely our takeaway is to have an impeccable reputation in business and in monetary dealings. The women in *Bereishis* who vouchsafed our destiny would stand for nothing less. Rivkah trusted that Yaakov's descendants would incorporate spiritual values alongside our material success, in a way that would benefit those around us. If the *rav* that comes to the younger one leads to material success, let us always use it for a *kiddush Hashem* in a way that would make Rivkah proud.

---

16   See *Bereishis* 28:3–4.
17   *Bereishis* 33:8–11.

— 5 —
Mussar Moments

What we keep, we temporarily have;
what we spent, we once had;
what we give away, we possess forever.

Comment

Yitzchak bestowed blessings upon his sons, not simply so they could enjoy material possessions, but so that they could become givers themselves. The best legacy we can give our children is to teach them to transform from takers to givers and one day, to teach their own children to do the same. Our Sages maintain that Yitzchak introduced the concept of regularly tithing his produce,[18] and he passed this legacy onto his descendants; the Torah contains a plethora of mitzvos that teach us to be magnanimous with our possessions.

The most important arithmetic to master
is the one that enables us to count our blessings.

— 6 —
Birth

New parents embark on the most important and sacred task they will encounter, to prepare the next generation for a productive life. It is crucial to give each child individual care because no two children are alike. Children are not cookies to be cut in a similar fashion. Even identical twins, who share the same genetic makeup and grow up in the same

---

18   See *Rambam, Hilchos Melachim* 9:1, based on *Bereishis* 26:12.

environment, need special individual attention. This is made clear by the master of pedagogy, Rabbi Shimshon Raphael Hirsch.

> *Our Sages, who never objected to drawing attention to the small and great mistakes and weaknesses in the history of our great forefathers—thereby making them all the more instructive for us[19]—here too, on* ויגדלו הנערים*, make a remark which is indeed a "signpost" for all of us. They point out that the striking contrast in the grandchildren of Avraham may have been due not so much to a difference in their temperaments as to mistakes in the way they were brought up. As long as they were young, little attention was paid to the slumbering differences in their natures (See Rashi, verse 24). Both had exactly the same teaching and educational treatment, and the great law of education,* "חנוך לנער על פי דרכו וגו'"*—bring up each child in accordance with his own way" (Mishlei 22:6), was forgotten; that each child must be treated differently, with an eye to the dormant tendencies of his nature, and out of them, be educated to develop his special characteristics for the one pure human and Jewish life. The great Jewish task in life is basically simple, one and the same for all, but its realization is as complicated and varied as human natures and tendencies are varied, and the manifold varieties of life that result from them. Had Yitzchak and Rivkah studied Eisav's nature and character early enough, and asked themselves how all the strength and energy, agility, and courage that lay slumbering in this child be won over to be used in the service of God, and the future* גבור *be trained to become not a* גבור ציד *but in truth a* גבור לפני ה', *then Yaakov and Eisav with their totally different natures could still have remained twin brothers in spirit and life. Quite early in life, Eisav's "sword" and Yaakov's "spirit" could have worked hand in hand, and who can say what a different aspect the*

---

19   See an elaboration that Rabbi Hirsch makes on this point in *Bereishis* 12:10 regarding Avraham leaving Canaan for Egypt.

whole history of the ages might have presented. However, as it was, ויגדלו הנערים, *only when the boys had grown into men, one was surprised to see that, out of one and the selfsame womb, having had exactly the same care, training, and schooling, two such contrasting persons emerge.*[20]

Let us not put any child in a box, and let us aim to treat each one according to his own individual needs, strengths and talents.

— 7 —
B'nei Mitzvah

Rav Moshe Isserles, known as the *Rama*, refers to a custom for a parent to say "ברוך שפטרני מעונשו של זה" as a public announcement when a child has reached the age of mitzvah obligation.[21] The blessing is an expression of gratitude and praise that the parent is no longer responsible for the punishment of the child.[22] Others have explained this to the contrary, since parents are not likely to be relieved that their adolescent children will now be punished for their own sins. Rather, the point of this blessing is to acknowledge the opposite. Parents make this blessing because the child is no longer held accountable for *their*—i.e., their parents'—sins. Since pre-*b'nei mitzvah* children are not obligated in mitzvos, and there is therefore no violation for which they can be punished, it must be that the only punishment they can incur is for the sins of their parents. Once they turn *b'nei mitzvah*, they are on their own. But if this would be the meaning of the *berachah*, perhaps the child should make the *berachah*![23]

The source of this *berachah* is not from the Talmud. As such, some have the custom to refrain from mentioning God's name, and to simply

---

20   Shimshon Raphael Hirsch, *Bereishis* 25:27, ד"ה ויגדלו הנערים. This passage was excerpted from the English translation of Rabbi Hirsch's commentary *Terumas Tzvi* (New York: Judaica Press, 1986), p. 121.

21   *Shulchan Aruch, Orach Chaim* 225:2.

22   This is the explanation of the *Mordechai* and the *Maharil*.

23   See *Magen Avraham, Orach Chaim* 225:5 from *Levush*.

say, "ברוך שפטרני מעונשו של זה."[24] The earliest source of this custom is *Bereishis Rabbah* 63:10, from the beginning of *parashas Toldos*. The Midrash cites this blessing in the context of the Torah's description of Yaakov and Eisav's growth to maturity, "ויגדלו הנערים."[25] In light of this Midrash, some do have the custom of reciting the full *berachah* with God's name.[26]

Perhaps we can expound a deeper meaning of this blessing. Attaining the age of adolescence tends to be a rebellious time in the life of a child. Authority is questioned, peer pressure is applied, hormones are raging, the body is changing. It's a very difficult time. Perhaps we can translate "פטרני" not that the parent is absolved, but in the framework of "פטר רחם—the opening of the womb." The parents acknowledge the need to be open to the rebelliousness of their child and be proactive in helping the child navigate this difficult period. The same DNA has the potential to create a Yaakov or an Eisav. The Talmud[27] admits that *mazal* is needed along with our best efforts to raise well-adjusted and productive children, but *mazal* never waits around for those who rely on *mazal* and nothing else.

—8—
Marriage

ויעתר יצחק לה׳ לנכח אשתו.

Yitzchak pleaded with God on behalf of his wife. (Bereishis 25:21)

This line is meant to correct a mistake of the past. When God introduced the chapter of *Bris Bein Habesarim* by telling Avraham, "שכרך הרבה מאד—Your reward will be very great,"[28] Avraham asked what God would give him seeing that "אנכי הולך ערירי—I am going [to my death]

---

24   See *Rama, Orach Chaim* 225:2.
25   *Bereishis* 25:27.
26   *Vilna Gaon, Orach Chaim* 225:2, *Biur HaGra*, ד"ה י"א מי וכו, *Chayei Adam* 66:3.
27   *Moed Katan* 28a.
28   *Bereishis* 15:1.

childless."²⁹ God assured Avraham that he would have his own son. Ten years later, Sarah selflessly suggested to Avraham that perhaps he was meant to be the father of a great nation with someone else and gave him Hagar to marry. The situation deteriorated and Sarah expressed indignation with Avraham for his insensitivity to her plight.³⁰ *Rashi* explains this indignation from the previous chapter. When Avraham questioned God's promise of great reward, he said, "I am childless." Sarah argued that Avraham should have said "*We* are childless." Had Avraham said that, God's response would have been to assure Avraham that he *and* Sarah would indeed bear a child together, and then Sarah would never have suggested that Avraham should marry another woman.

Yitzchak would not make this mistake. He prayed on behalf of Rivkah because he didn't want to confront infertility by marrying another woman as his father had done.

The lesson is to always place your beloved at the front line of all your dreams, visions, and pursuits. This was indeed Avraham's customary behavior with Sarah. When they traveled, the Torah says, "אהלה ויט—He pitched his tent,"³¹ spelling "his tent" as if it says, "her tent." *Rashi* explains that this teaches that Avraham always placed Sarah before himself. The one time he did not was the cause for much regret. Let Yitzchak's prayers remind us of who comes first in our lives.

— 9 —
Seudah Shelishis
אתה אחד ושמך אחד

Our Sages held our great Biblical heroes accountable for every small infraction and pain they caused others. Yaakov is held accountable for the anguished sobs of Eisav in reaction to losing his blessing. *Bereishis Rabbah* (67:4) connects the language of those sobs to a much later

29 *Bereishis* 15:2.
30 *Bereishis* 16:5.
31 *Bereishis* 12:8.

Biblical event as punishment to Yaakov. Eisav's reaction is described as follows:

ויצעק צעקה גדולה ומרה עד מאד.

He cried with a great and exceedingly bitter cry. (Bereishis 27:34)

The Midrash notes the similarity in the reaction of Yaakov's descendant Mordechai to Eisav's descendant Haman, and his decree to kill the Jews of Persia. Mordechai's reaction is described as follows:

ויזעק זעקה גדולה ומרה.

He cried with a great and bitter cry. (Esther 4:1)

The tears of Eisav were measured and requited, and for centuries caused anguish to our people.

One has to wonder why our billions of tears have not been able to nullify Eisav's two tears that were shed over his lost blessing.[32] The prophet Yoel speaks of the Kohanim crying over the sorry state of our land. They ask:

למה יאמרו בעמים איה אלקיהם.

Why should the nations say, "Where is their God?" (Yoel 2:17)

The very next verse refers to God being zealous for His land and that He pitied His people to return them to their previous glory. This is because their tears were for God's sake. But if our tears are merely for our *own* deficiencies and deprivations, then our tears are no different than Eisav's and won't be able to drown out Eisav's tears. This is known as "מין במינו אינו בטל—an item within the same item cannot be nullified." Only if our tears are *different* from Eisav's selfish tears will those tears have their full effect. Only if we cry like the Kohanim of *Sefer Yoel* will we be able to drown out and nullify the tears of Eisav.

---

32   See *Midrash Tehillim* 80; *Tanchuma Yashan, Toldos* 24. Some sources say Eisav shed two tears, and some say three.

—10—
Word of the Parashah

ויקרא שמה שטנה—He called it [the well] **Sitnah**
Bereishis 26:21

Ramban describes the story of Yitzchak digging three wells in Philistia.

> *He called the first well Esek ("Contention"), which is an allusion
> to the First Temple, concerning which the nations contended
> with us and instigated quarrels and wars with us until they
> destroyed it. The second well he called Sitnah ("Enmity"),
> a name harsher than the first. This alludes to the Second
> Temple, which has indeed been referred to by this very name,
> "In the beginning of his reign, they wrote a 'sitnah' against the
> inhabitants of Judah and Jerusalem" (Ezra 4:6). And during
> its entire existence they were a source of enmity unto us until
> they destroyed it and drove us from it into bitter exile. The
> third well he called Rechovos ("Spacious"). This is a reference to
> the Future Temple, which will be speedily built in our days, and
> it will be done without quarrel and feud, and God will enlarge
> our borders.*[33]

This follows *Ramban*'s theme, often cited in *Sefer Bereishis*, of "*maaseh
avos siman l'banim*—the actions of previous generations serve as omens
for their descendants."[34]

The first and third wells are named and explained, but the second well
is simply named with no explanation offered. For this reason, *Ramban*
connects it to the שטנה instigated by the Persian anti-Semites who were
jealous that the Jews wanted to rebuild Jerusalem. These people were
called "צרי יהודה—the enemies of the Jews,"[35] and it is not a stretch

---

33 *Ramban, Bereishis* 26:20.
34 See *Ramban, Bereishis* 12:6.
35 *Ezra* 4:1.

to consider that a man called, "צורר היהודים—the enemy of the Jews," Haman,[36] led this group.

The name of the second well is related to the word שטן, a being who stands among God's angels.[37] The word appears quite often in the Bible as one who attempts to thwart or ruin the plans or goals of an adversary.[38] In Chazal, the שטן can be figurative, as in, "הוא שטן הוא יצר הרע הוא מלאך המות,"[39] which equates the שטן with the evil inclination and the angel of death. More often, as in *Iyov*, the שטן is a being with great powers of persuasion to bring out the worst in man.

This very *parashah* has a related word, "וישטם עשו את יעקב—Eisav despised his brother"[40] over the blessing he lost.[41] Perhaps the word for the wayward woman, סוטה is also etymologically connected.[42] This word in the Torah is spelled with the letter *sin* and Chazal expound the word as if it is a *shin*, which means that a man doesn't accuse his wife of such wayward behavior unless a spirit of שטות, "insanity," enters his mind.[43] If so, perhaps there is another explanation of שטן. When God asks שטן in *Iyov* what he's been doing, שטן answers,

משוט בארץ ומתהלך בו.

*I have been **roaming** all over the earth. (Iyov 2:1)*

Perhaps that is the job of שטן. If we exchange the *sin* of שטן to a *shin*, his job changes from an adversary to one who roams the earth looking to report all of man's deficiencies to God.

Perhaps Yitzchak named the second well שטנה because he too saw that he was beginning to roam around too much in the land of the Philistines in his search for water, and he was hoping to be able to take root in one

---

36 *Esther* 3:10; 8:1; 9:10.

37 *Iyov* 1–2.

38 *Shmuel I* 29:4; *Shmuel II* 19:23; *Melachim I* 11:14.

39 *Bava Basra* 16a.

40 *Bereishis* 27:41.

41 "לו ישטמנו יוסף," in *Bereishis* 50:15, has a similar meaning.

42 See *Tehillim* 101:3 and *Hoshea* 5:2 for similar usages.

43 See *Bamidbar* 5.

place. The realization of these hopes became manifest in the name of the third well, Rechovos:

כִּי עַתָּה הִרְחִיב ה׳ לָנוּ וּפָרִינוּ בָאָרֶץ.

Now at last God has granted us ample space to increase in the land. (Bereshis 26:22)

Parashas Vayeitzei

Insofar as the events of *parashas Vayeitzei* took place as a direct result of the end of *parashas Toldos*, some of the *divrei Torah* of *Vayeitzei* relate to the events of *Toldos*.

—1—
Friday Night
תכלית מעשה שמים וארץ

ויצא יעקב מבאר שבע וילך חרנה.

And Yaakov went out from Be'er Sheva and went toward Charan. (Bereishis 28:10)

The first verse in this week's *parashah* lists two verbs describing Yaakov's journey to Charan, because he has two reasons for leaving home. One, ויצא, is to fulfill his mother's charge to escape the wrath of his brother, and the other, וילך, to fulfill his father's charge to find a wife. If not for this second consideration, perhaps Lavan's daughter could have been brought to Canaan for Yaakov, just as Lavan's sister had been brought to Canaan for Yitzchak. Outside of Eisav's reaction, last week's *parashah* draws no evaluation regarding what Yaakov did. Yitzchak himself addresses Yaakov as if nothing had happened. And God speaks glowingly to Yaakov in the beginning of this week's *parashah* to assure him that his aspirations to fulfill the family legacy will not be diminished due to his sudden flight from his home.

However, the events facing Yaakov upon his arrival in Charan serve as ironic reminders that will atone for what he did. He falls in love with a younger sister, but ends up marrying the older one, and when confronting the source of the subterfuge, he is told, "It is not the practice in our place to marry off the younger before the older."[1] The additional phrase, "in our place," is a reminder of what Yaakov had done in his place. Chazal say that when Yaakov realized he had been with Leah, he asked her how she could do such a thing to her sister, and Leah's response was, "And you didn't do the same thing to your brother?"[2] *Rashi* says that Leah's eyes were weak because she cried when she learned that the older son of Rivkah, Eisav, would marry Lavan's older daughter, while the younger sister, Rachel, would get to marry Yaakov.[3] By this design, as soon as Yaakov said the words, "I am Eisav, your firstborn,"[4] he set in motion the events that would make Leah his wife.

What was Yaakov to do? His mother had insisted he do this! Hadn't his grandmother prevailed with his grandfather when it came to decisions for their progeny? Why shouldn't his mother similarly prevail with her children? And, furthermore, he had purchased the birthright.

But it was still wrong to deceive a father. And if he had gotten caught, he would have received a curse instead of a blessing. It was only when Rivkah offered to accept the curse in the event that Yaakov would get caught that he agreed to his mother's request. *Rashbam* asks: What kind of a son fears doing something because of the risk of a curse but is then convinced to do that thing with the understanding that his mother will be cursed instead? *Rashbam* answers that Rivkah then told Yaakov what God had told her when she was pregnant, "The older shall serve the younger,"[5] and therefore convinced Yaakov that this was his destiny.

---

1   *Bereishis* 29:26.
2   *Tanchuma* (Buber), *Vayeitzei* 11:1.
3   *Bereishis* 29:17, ד״ה רכות.
4   *Bereishis* 27:19.
5   *Bereishis* 25:23. This is an implied question based on *Rashbam* to *Bereishis* 27:13, ד״ה עלי קללתך.

Perhaps so, but we can also wonder why Yaakov didn't press further, saying, "Mom, if receiving the blessing that Dad wants to give Eisav is my destiny, then I believe it will come to me in some way, and if it isn't my destiny, I certainly don't want to come to it through subterfuge. Eisav himself told me long ago that he doesn't expect to outlive Daddy, which shows that the birthright means nothing to him. I feel very uncomfortable tricking Daddy." But he was still convinced to do so. The word that Yitzchak uses to describe what Yaakov did, "מרמה,"[6] has the same root as the word that Yaakov uses when challenging Lavan when marrying the wrong woman.[7]

The *Zohar* explains that Yaakov was right in taking the blessing from his brother, but he was also wrong. It's just that it was more right than wrong.[8] Not everything we do is one hundred percent right. In fact, very little is. Life is a balancing act of many different considerations working simultaneously. Some commentaries understand the following verse to make this very point: "There is not one good person on earth who does only good and doesn't err."[9] Life is complicated. We have imperfections, and Yaakov's decision to heed his mother's advice had consequences that emerge in the storyline and narratives that follow. What remains is why Rivkah saw the need to resort to tricking her husband. Why didn't she tell Yitzchak what God had told her when she was pregnant? Sarah was able to convince Avraham about his sons; why did Rivkah feel unequal to the task of convincing Yitzchak about his sons? These questions will be answered in the next section.

---

6   *Bereishis* 27:35.

7   *Bereishis* 29:25.

8   See *Zohar*, *Toldos* 61a–64a, where the point is stressed again and again that what Yaakov did was ordained from above, yet he was punished for deceiving his father.

9   *Koheles* 7:20, see *Alshich*.

—2—
Introduction to the Torah
ישמח משה במתנת חלקו

Why did Rivkah have to resort to subterfuge to ensure that Yaakov would receive the blessing reserved for Eisav? Why didn't she just tell Yitzchak what God had told her when she was pregnant, "ורב יעבד צעיר—the older shall serve the younger"[10]? In light of the blessing Yitzchak thought he was giving Eisav, it seems Yitzchak never knew about this. This blessing in full is:

> ויתן לך האלקים מטל השמים ומשמני הארץ ורב דגן ותירוש. יעבדוך
> עמים וישתחוו לך לאומים הוה גביר לאחיך וישתחוו לך בני אמך. אורריך
> ארור ומברכיך ברוך.
>
> *May God give you of the dew of heaven and the fat of the*
> *earth, abundance of grain and wine. Let peoples serve you and*
> *nations bow to you. Be master over your brothers, and let your*
> *mother's sons bow to you. Cursed be they who curse you and*
> *blessed, they who bless you. (Bereishis 27:28–29)*

Let us consider that Yitzchak was aware of God's oracle to Rivkah and fully accepted the prediction of ורב יעבד צעיר. He just disagreed about its meaning. If these words mean that the older shall serve the younger, then the word for "older" is misplaced. The oracle should have informed Rivkah that the "*bechor*" shall serve the younger. "*V'rav*," Yitzchak argued, means that something great, or greatness in general, will work its way to the younger one, and Yitzchak was determined to ensure that this would be so.[11] That greatness would manifest itself in the legacy of Avraham, in inheriting the land that God promised Avraham, and in receiving the Divine revelation and promises of the *Bris Bein Habesarim*.[12] At the same time, Eisav, with all his energies, vitality, and support of the family, would deserve the material blessings that Yitzchak could

---

10   *Bereishis* 25:23.
11   See *Daas Zekeinim, Bereishis* 25:23, cited above, *Toldos* 4.
12   *Bereishis* 15.

offer. Yitzchak wanted his two sons to work hand in hand to bring Avraham's Divine message to the world, in a partnership later known as a Yissachar-Zevulun relationship, whereby Zevulun is blessed with material wealth and supports Yissachar's spiritual aspirations.[13] In both versions of their blessings,[14] Zevulun precedes Yissachar, for the same reason that Yitzchak wants to make Eisav master over Yaakov. His mission would be to protect and support Yaakov and ensure that he is free of any impediments to his spiritual aspirations.

Needless to say, Rivkah disagreed. She didn't love Eisav any less than she loved Yaakov, but she knew her sons. She bore them. She remembered what their struggle had been inside her, even before they were born. Yitzchak grew up in a home of truth and integrity and was more naive in his expectations of what Eisav would do for Yaakov. Rivkah grew up with Lavan and Besuel and wanted Yaakov to have the material means to contend with their likes in the world. As is the case until now in *Bereishis*, the women decide in such matters; Rivkah vouchsafes Yaakov's material blessing, and Yitzchak seems to agree. When Eisav declares that this is the second time Yaakov has tricked him, he confesses to his father that Yaakov purchased the birthright when they were younger. Yitzchak's reaction is not to invalidate the blessing, given under false pretenses, but to accept his wife's wisdom.

When Yaakov leaves home to escape his brother's wrath and to find a wife, Yitzchak blesses him again:

וא-ל ש-ד-י יברך אותך ויפרך וירבך והיית לקהל עמים ויתן לך את ברכת אברהם לך ולזרעך אתך לרשתך את ארץ מגורך אשר נתן אלקים לאברהם.

May God Almighty bless you and make you fertile and numerous, so that you become an assembly of peoples. May He grant you the blessing of Avraham to you and to your offspring,

---

13   Zevulun was blessed with material wealth and supported the spiritual pursuits of Yissachar. See *Bereishis Rabbah* 72:5, 98:6. See also *Rashi, Bereishis* 49:13, ד"ה לחוף ימים.

14   *Bereishis* 49:13–14, *Devarim* 33:18.

that you may possess the land of your sojourning, which God assigned to Avraham. (Bereishis 28:3–4)

This is the blessing Yaakov was always meant to receive. Rivkah's actions gave Yaakov the material blessings with which our people have been blessed. Many of our prophets railed against our ancestors for not using that material wealth in the way that Rivkah envisioned. Let us consider how we spend our wealth so we may justify Rivkah's foresight and efforts in procuring it for us.

This wealth comes at a price, though. It necessitated our wearing the garments of Eisav, it caused longlasting enmity between Eisav and ourselves, and it forced us to flee. Let our resources be used, Rivkah would say, to sow seeds of love, charity, and justice, even to the sons of Eisav. At the end of the story, the last time Rivkah is mentioned, she is referred to as the mother of Yaakov and Eisav.[15] *Rashi* on this verse says that he does not know why the text refers to this again. Perhaps to indicate that for all Rivkah did, she still loved Eisav and hoped for the best for both her children ultimately desiring them to find common ground. See "(4) *Derashah*" below.

—3—
Introduction to the Haftarah

מה שהיה הוא שיהיה.

Whatever has been, is what will be. (Koheles 1:9)

The haftarah of *Vayeitzei* is a lesson in history that is also found in the narratives of the books of *Melachim II*[16] and *Divrei Hayamim II*,[17] in addition to the seventh chapter of *Yeshayahu*. The year is approximately 750 BCE and history is at a precarious crossroads, with the rising power of Ashur mounting a threat against the entire Ancient Near East. Aram joined a coalition with the Northern Kingdom of Ephraim (called

---

15   *Bereishis* 28:5.
16   Chaps. 16–18.
17   Chaps. 28–31.

this because the kings were from the tribe of Ephraim), and wanted the Southern Kingdom of Yehudah to join. Yeshayahu declared that salvation from Ashur would not come from alliances with evil nations but with the people's religious revival and renewed morality. Yehudah listened, declining to join the coalition, and in the year 732 BCE Aram was destroyed and scattered.

Hoshea employs an ingenious method of instilling faith into the hearts of his people. He addressed the Northern Kingdom of Ephraim, and at the beginning of the haftarah, he reminds them of Yaakov's trials in working for Lavan the Aramean, which take place in *parashas Vayeitzei*. Through so much hardship, contending with Lavan's chicanery and wiles, Yaakov still managed to escape with his soul, his family, and his fortune intact.

Our tradition teaches, as the Haggadah declares, that Lavan had lethal plans for Yaakov. "בקש לבן לעקור את הכל," says the Haggadah,[18] based on the midrashic rendition of "ארמי אבד אבי"—An Aramean [Lavan] tried to destroy my father."[19] Lavan himself declared such an intention of what he could have done to Yaakov, had God not intervened.[20]

Hoshea tries to assure his people that focusing on morality will save them from their enemies. Indeed, the Northern Kingdom of the ten tribes outlasted Aram, and the Southern Kingdom outlasted Ashur. However, Hoshea's calls for repentance were not heeded by the ten tribes the way Yeshayahu's message was heard by Yehudah. (This is not to compare the efficacy of the two prophets. Yeshayahu had the privilege of addressing a far more receptive audience.) Hoshea's people fell to Ashur in 722 BCE, and to this day we are still hoping to locate their descendants. Ashur surrounded Jerusalem in 701 BCE but could not conquer the city, and Yehudah outlasted the Assyrians. Many other nations besieged, fought, and conquered Jerusalem, and we have outlasted them all.

---

18   This is in the section of *Maggid* beginning with "צא ולמד."

19   *Devarim* 26:5, see *Targum Onkelos* and *Rashi*, ד"ה ארמי אבד אבי.

20   *Bereishis* 31:29, "I have it in my power to do you harm."

Victory always happened when we maintained our morality. The Babylonians, Persians, Greeks, and Romans could rule over us, but as long as we framed that misfortune as an outcome of our behavior, we knew that a change of that behavior could lead to our salvation. The Talmud doesn't attribute the destruction of the Second Temple to that which any historians would say—namely that an overwhelming force of Roman power overcame a weak and divided nation. Not so, says our tradition. We lost our Temple and our land because of *sin'as chinam*, baseless hatred. And if baseless hatred lost us our land, boundless love can get it back.

Let us recall Hoshea's injunction to focus on morality and remember that Aram today is Syria. Remember that Yeshayahu's similar words to the Jews of the Southern Kingdom, which were heeded, merited for them salvation from Ashur. Ashur comprised the land mass that today is called Iraq and Iran. These countries, which have had lethal intentions for us, cannot succeed in the face of the morality and love that the Torah and the prophets preached. Whatever has been, is what will be.

— 4 —
Derashah
ושם נעשה לפניך את קרבנות חובותינו

Some questions are left unanswered in the story that forced Yaakov to leave the family home and spend years in exile building his family. Why did Rivkah feel she had to resort to subterfuge in order to vouchsafe the birthright for Yaakov? Why didn't she talk this through with her husband the way Sarah did with Avraham? Is it conceivable that Rivkah and Yitzchak never discussed this? Is it conceivable that Rivkah didn't rush home to tell her husband they were having twins, along with the rest of the oracle she received that the younger would be greater? Why didn't Yitzchak bless Eisav on the spot? Why did he send him out to hunt venison first? Perhaps Yaakov and Eisav were indistinguishable at the age of fifteen, but surely by now, Yitzchak could detect the different directions they were taking in life—that the family legacy would be best protected under Yaakov and that such a legacy would be better served with a birthright. And surely Yitzchak can differentiate between goat hair and Eisav's hands! Each of these questions has a worthy answer, but taken as a whole, perhaps we can create the following scenario.[21]

Imagine a different picture from the one presented above; one in which Yitzchak and Rivkah are actually on the same page as far as which son should receive the birthright. But this needed a plan. Had the parents called their sons together for a family conference with the news of Yaakov's preference, this would have created deep enmity in Eisav, not only for his brother, but for his parents as well. Let us consider that if anyone in this story was oblivious to the plan, it was Yaakov and Eisav! The mission to hunt venison bought time for Yaakov to receive the blessing before Eisav's return. Rivkah conveniently heard when to spring into action, and she had to work from scratch so as not to tip off Yaakov that he was bringing his father prepared food. She knew Yaakov would have his doubts and had all the answers ready so as to have everything in place before Eisav's return. Yitzchak played along and knew that Eisav would not take well to this. The point was that these events should not cause Eisav to be bereft of his one redeeming quality: the honor he demonstrated to his father. Yaakov mentions God and speaks with courtesy, but Eisav speaks in third person. His *kibud av* is legendary, and his parents did not want to deny him this characteristic. Better he express anger at his brother than at his father.

If Eisav is treated harshly in the book of *Malachi*[22] and in Rabbinic literature, it is because of who his descendants became. Edom and Amalek became our fiercest enemies in *Tanach*, so that the treatment of Eisav resembles "*maaseh banim siman l'avos*—the deeds of the children serve as an omen for their parents." (Perhaps this explains the harsh treatment of Lot as well, in light of the deeds of his descendants, Amon and Moav.) If Eisav ever had a claim on Yaakov, that ended with the redemption from Egypt, because the legacy of Yitzchak surely included

---

21   I am indebted to my friends, Reuven Rosenthal and Howard Gootkin for their input on what follows.

22   See *Malachi* 1:2–5. Embedded in these verses is the statement that God Himself hates Eisav.

all the promises and predictions that God made to Avraham, including a long stay in Egypt, which Eisav's descendants never experienced. This is why Moshe's opening words to Pharaoh speak about Israel being God's firstborn.[23] The *p'shat*, the simple meaning of this declaration, is that God's cherished nation is Israel and not Egypt. *Rashi*[24] suggests this explanation first, and then renders the *d'rash*, a deeper meaning, that acknowledges that Israel, meaning Yaakov, is truly the firstborn, and not Eisav. With the redemption from Egypt, the Revelation at Sinai, and the entry into the land promised to Avraham, the nation named after Yaakov fulfilled all the patriarchal blessings that Eisav was all too glad to forego from his youth.

— 5 —
Mussar Moments

Whether you think you can or you can't, you're right.

Comment

The Torah describes seven years that Yaakov worked for Rachel:

ויהי בעיניו כימים אחדים באהבתו אותה.

They seemed to him but a few days because of his love for her.
(Bereishis 29:20)

Normally the opposite would be true; the days would seem to last longer in anticipation of the marriage at the end of seven years. The object of Yaakov's love is left as a pronoun at the end of the verse. Of course, the *p'shat* is that it refers to Rachel, who is mentioned in the beginning of the verse. However, since a feminine pronoun can refer to

---

23 *Shemos* 4:22.
24 *Shemos* 4:22, ד״ה בני בכורי.

objects as well as people, perhaps we can say that "באהבתו אותה" refers to the work Yaakov was given. This was essentially his first job, and he enjoyed it. It was surely no picnic to work for Lavan, as Yaakov declares at the end of this *parashah*.[25] Yet Yaakov persevered. Another person may have quit early on, saying, "I can't do this anymore."

When Yaakov awoke the morning after his wedding and saw that he had married under false pretense, he wanted to divorce Leah immediately.[26] Leah pleaded with him to consider that she may be carrying his child, and if so, to remain with her and not have her raise their child alone. She did indeed conceive that night and Yaakov remained with her and created half of the tribes of Israel with her. Yaakov was tempted to say, "I can't do this, I never wanted to." But he was convinced to say, "I can." Yaakov constantly confronts challenges by avoiding the easy way out.

He could also have tried to sneak home past Eisav in *parashas Vayishlach*, but then, too, he didn't take the easy way out; Yaakov takes the road of integrity and confronts his challenges head-on.

Fortunate is the person who can turn stumbling blocks into stepping-stones.

— 6 —
Birth

Our first utterance in the morning is an expression of gratitude for another day. "*Modeh Ani*" is an admission that our lives are filled with Heavenly gifts. The very name of our people—Yehudim—stems from our matriarch Leah, who thanked God for her bounty and named her fourth child Yehudah. This week's *parashah* reveals that Leah's life

---

25   See *Bereishis* 31:38–42.

26   See *Bereishis Rabbah* 71:2.

had its share of challenges and disappointments. Yet she declared her gratitude and gave us our name.

Actually, all of Yaakov's children can connect, either in their names or in the destiny of their tribes, to the values we as a people cherish. These values are encapsulated in the thirteen requests we present before God in the middle of the daily *Amidah*. They are:

1. אתה חונן לאדם דעת—Knowledge and understanding
2. השיבנו אבינו לתורתך—Repentance
3. סלח לנו—Forgiveness
4. ראה נא בעניינו—Personal redemption
5. רפאינו—Healing
6. ברך עלינו—Sustenance
7. תקע בשופר—National redemption
8. השיבה שופטינו—Judgment
9. ולמלשינים—Against heretics
10. על הצדיקים—For the righteous
11. ולירושלים עירך—Rebuilding of Jerusalem
12. את צמח—The kingdom of David
13. שמע קולינו—Hearing our prayers

Yaakov had thirteen children, and the names, lives, and values they and their descendants espoused connect to these thirteen values as follows:

1. **Reuven** was named with the hope that God would see Leah's pain and affliction. This corresponds to #4, ראה נא בעניינו, where God would see to our personal salvation.
2. **Shimon** was named with the hope that God would hear Leah's plight and struggles. This corresponds to #13, שמע קולינו, where God would hear our prayers.
3. **Levi** was named with the expectation that with three children, Yaakov would have to accompany Leah as a third hand to carry all the children together. This corresponds to #11, ולירושלים עירך, as Levi is the tribe that "accompanies" the Divine in their service in Jerusalem.

4. **Yehudah**, as explained above, was named to express gratitude that Leah received more than she had expected.[27] This corresponds to #12, את צמח, when the kingdom of David descended from Yehudah will be renewed, and the Jewish people will receive their reward beyond expectation.[28]

5. **Yissachar** was considered a reward for Leah, and our Sages maintain that his tribe produced the majority of the wise men of the generations.[29] This corresponds to #1, אתה חונן לאדם דעת.

6. **Zevulun** was named with the expectation that Yaakov would consider Leah to be the mainstay of his home. He became known in Chazal as a master of business and commerce.[30] This corresponds to #6, ברך עלינו.

7. **Dan** was named for Rachel's sentiment that she was being judged by God. This corresponds to #8, השיבה שופטינו.

8. **Naftali** was named because Rachel contended, joined, or acted in a foolish or crafty manner with her sister.[31] This can connect to #9, ולמלשינים, which is a blessing that was crafted against heretics.[32] *Tehillim* 14 and 53 both begin by saying that only a fool would deny what is plain to the eye, to become a heretic, "אמר נבל בלבו אין אלקים."

9. **Gad** was named for the good fortune that his birth portended. Gad came to be known as the fiercest of fighters,[33] who would protect our borders and help to initiate our salvation. This

---

27   See *Rashi, Bereishis* 29:35, from *Bereishis Rabbah* 71:4.

28   See *Zechariah* 3:8, *Yirmiyahu* 23:4–5, 33:14–16, for depictions of this reward, with the expression צמח.

29   This is based on *Divrei Hayamim I* 12:33, "Of the sons of Yissachar were men who knew how to interpret the signs of the times, to determine how the Israelites should act." See *Rashi, Bereishis* 49:13–14 and *Devarim* 33:18, from *Bereishis Rabbah* 99:9.

30   See *Bereishis Rabbah* 99:9.

31   *Rashi* renders these three interpretations, *Bereishis* 30:8, ד"ה נפתולי.

32   See *Berachos* 28b–29a for the origins of this blessing; *Yerushalmi, Berachos* 4:1, has a tradition that this blessing was originally part of the *Amidah*, and the nineteenth blessing came about when ולירושלים and את צמח, which were originally the same blessing, were separated.

33   See *Rashi, Devarim* 33:20, from *Sifri, Devarim* 355.

connects to #7,בשופר תקע , which is a blessing for our national redemption.

10. **Asher** was named for the happiness Leah felt when he was born. Asher lived in a very fertile area of Israel where olive oil flowed to the extent that it supported the rest of the country beyond his land.[34] This olive oil had many uses, in addition to serving medicinal purposes. This can connect to #5, רפאנו.

11. **Yosef** was named with Rachel's intention that God bless her with another child. Yosef is commonly known by our Sages as Yosef HaTzaddik,[35] which connects him to #10, על הצדיקים.

12. **Binyamin** was named by his father because he was born in Israel, south of where his siblings were born.[36] Binyamin settled in the part of the land where the Temple in Jerusalem was built. The *avodah* in the Temple was meant to draw a penitent closer to God. As such, Binyamin connects to #2, השיבנו אבינו לתורתיך.

13. **Dinah**—No reason is given for this name. According to our Sages, Leah used the conception of Dinah to entreat on behalf of her sister Rachel, in an expression of begging forgiveness for taking her husband.[37] This would connect to #3, סלח לנו, a blessing for forgiveness.

The name we bestow upon a child creates a destiny. The names and lives of all of Yaakov's children and their tribes created a destiny of values for the Jewish people for centuries.[38]

---

34   See *Sifri, Devarim* 355.

35   This is connected to the midrashic reference to Yosef in *Amos* 2:6, "על מכרם בכסף צדיק." See *Targum Yonasan, Bereishis* 37:28. *Megillah* 3a refers to *Targum Onkelos* to the Torah, and *Targum Yonasan ben Uziel* to Neviim. Onkelos generally follows the plain meaning of the text in its Aramaic translations while *Targum Yonasan* favors a translation that adds interpretation. There is a *Targum* to the Torah known as *Targum Yonasan* that follows this more liberal interpretive model, and since its origins are unknown, it tends to be called "Pseudo-Jonathan." In this work, I refer to it as *Targum Yonasan*, as it appears in the *Mikraos Gedolos*.

36   Directions in the Torah are from the standpoint of someone facing east, *kedem*. Therefore, *yamin*, "to the right," will point south. The left will point north, while west is often called *yamah*, "toward the sea," which is behind someone in Israel who is facing east.

37   See *Targum Yonasan, Bereishis* 30:21, *Tanchuma, Vayeitzei* 8, *Berachos* 60a.

38   The remaining six blessings of the *Amidah* can also connect to Torah personalities. The three patriarchs famously connect to the first three blessings, while Moshe, Aharon, and

—7—
B'nei Mitzvah

There is a mitzvah that presents itself the very moment our children become *b'nei mitzvah*. Since the Jewish day begins at night, the mitzvah of *k'rias Shema shel Arvis*, the nighttime *Shema*, arrives alongside the birthday. It is a worthwhile "first mitzvah" to perform, which begins with a declaration of God's uniqueness. Day has just turned to night, and this is the time that Yaakov was just leaving Israel and he stopped to pray, "כי בא השמש—as the sun was setting."[39] Our Sages say that this is where Yaakov established the nighttime prayer, *Maariv*.[40] Nighttime is called ערב, which connotes a "mixture"—it is murky and unclear. Yaakov was on a mission but the odds were against him. He was a fugitive, with no resources to gift a prospective bride as was done on behalf of his father. With these worries in the background, he brightened his horizons with the nighttime prayer. This was Yaakov's way of bringing light to the darkness. Yaakov, in next week's *parashah*, contends with an angel throughout the night and survives to the morning intact, with the blessing of a new name. He was given this name just as morning was breaking. Morning is בקר, which connotes "clarity." It is the opposite of ערב, just as the mission of *b'nei mitzvah* is to bring clarity to doubt and light to darkness. We do this with every mitzvah we perform. Up to the age of *b'nei mitzvah*, it was all for practice; now it's for credit. Yaakov showed us in *parashas Vayeitzei* how to transition to a new day and a new phase: a new identity starts with the first mitzvah of each day, *k'rias Shema* and *Maariv*.

Miriam connect to the last three. Many people experience difficulty in focusing on the middle thirteen blessings of the *Amidah*. Perhaps connecting each of the thirteen children of Yaakov—and what they represent—to the corresponding blessing may keep our thoughts on track.

39 *Bereishis* 28:11.
40 *Berachos* 26b.

—8—
Marriage

In the liturgy of the *Selichos* we say:

מי שענה לאברהם אבינו בהר המוריה הוא יעננו.

מי שענה ליצחק בנו כשנעקד על גבי המזבח הוא יעננו.

מי שענה ליעקב אבינו בבית אל הוא יעננו.

May the One who responded to Avraham at Mount Moriah, answer us.

May the One who responded to his son Yitzchak when he was bound atop the altar, answer us.

May the One who responded to Yaakov at Beis El, answer us.

In our own time of dire need, we remind ourselves of how God responded to others in similar circumstances and ask for a similar response. We can readily see the immediate need of Avraham and Yitzchak in their respective trials in the first two lines above, but we have to wonder, what was Yaakov's pressing need in the beginning of *parashas Vayeitzei* when he stopped at Beis El to warrant its juxtaposition to his father's and grandfather's life-threatening situations? Granted, he made a request of God, and God responded, but Yaakov's need at the time does not seem to be on the level of that of his father or grandfather in their respective moments of prayer.

Actually, Yaakov was in *great* need. He was seventy-seven years old, had no prospects for marriage at the moment, had no job or home of his own, and he was a fugitive! He was on a mission to find these things, but he had no money to impress anyone the way Eliezer impressed his mother's family a generation before. Now we have a sense of the urgency of Yaakov's prayer at Beis El. Yaakov emerged from God's words with the phrase, "וישא יעקב רגליו."[41] *Rashi* interprets these words as if

---

41   *Bereishis* 29:1.

Yaakov's legs lifted him off the ground, confident in his ability to turn his situation around.

His salvation came suddenly in the form of his beautiful cousin, Rachel. He seems to have fallen in love at first sight with Rachel, but in reality, there is no such thing as love at first sight. Love must be informed. Love takes time to mature and became a true indelible bond. Love at first sight is actually infatuation at first sight, and Yaakov spent seven years turning infatuation into love. *Rashi* points out that Yaakov's expression to Lavan at the end of seven years smacks of vulgarity.[42] In the very least, Yaakov expresses the fact that during those seven years he and Rachel remained chaste. They spent the time learning the true message of love, which is in getting to know one another before marriage without the distraction of physicality. With marriage can come true love and true knowledge, as in, "והאדם ידע את חוה את אשתו—Adam knew Chavah his wife."[43]

Yaakov significantly turned his life around in Charan. There were many bumps along the way and many challenges before him on the horizon. God's encouragement in *parashas Vayeitzei* uplifted Yaakov and gave him the strength to face his challenges head on.

— 9 —
Seudah Shelishis
אתה אחד ושמך אחד

"*Baruch Hashem*" is a common response to inquiries about our health, our jobs, our relationships, and anything of concern to us. Upon evaluating any situation we face, our religious sensitivity drives us to bless and thank God along the way. Six different people in the Torah said *Baruch Hashem*—and incredibly, all six were not of our people! The following is a full list of Torah characters who blessed God, one of them being Lavan.

---

42 See *Rashi, Bereishis* 29:21, from *Bereishis Rabbah* 70:18.

43 *Bereishis* 4:1.

1. **Noach:** "ברוך ה׳ אלקי שם—Blessed is the Lord, the God of Shem" (*Bereishis* 9:26).

2. **Malki-Tzedek:** "וברוך א-ל עליון אשר מגן צריך בידך—Blessed be God most high who has delivered your enemies to your hand" (*Bereishis* 14:20).

3. **Eliezer:** "ברוך ה׳ אלקי אדני אברהם—Blessed is the Lord the God of my master Avraham" (*Bereishis* 24:27).

4. **Lavan:** "בוא ברוך ה׳—Come in you blessed of the Lord" (*Bereishis* 24:31).

5. **Avimelech:** "אתה עתה ברוך ה׳—You are now blessed of the Lord" (*Bereishis* 26:29).

6. **Yisro:** "ברוך ה׳ אשר הציל אתכם מיד מצרים ומיד פרעה—Blessed be the Lord who has delivered you from the Egyptians and Pharaoh" (*Shemos* 18:10).

In each of these cases, God is being blessed in recognition of His special relationship with Avraham, Yitzchak, Yaakov, or someone in the performance of a mitzvah.

Yosef, at every turn when helping others, invokes the name of God as the source of that assistance, to the point where Pharaoh himself begins to do so. After evaluating Yosef's interpretation of his dreams, Pharaoh says:

> הנמצא כזה איש אשר רוח אלקים בו אחרי הודיע אלקים אותך את כל זאת אין נבון וחכם כמוך.
>
> *Can we find another like him, a man in whom is the spirit of God? Since God has made all this known to you, there is none so discerning and wise as you. (Bereishis 41:38–39)*

Yosef sanctifies God's name and when this happens, even the gentiles of the Torah notice. When Yosef revealed his true identity to his brothers, he said, "שמני אלקים לאדון לכל מצרים,"[44] which can be exegetically twisted to teach, "I have placed God as the Master of all of Egypt." This

---

44   *Bereishis* 45:9.

is what the Jew does when sanctifying God's name. Such actions bring blessings from God that can be recognized by all.

At some point above, the discerning reader will have a question. This should have been a *d'var Torah* in *parashas Chayei Sarah* when Lavan said *Baruch Hashem*. The reason I included this *d'var Torah* in *parashas Vayeitzei* is that Lavan's statement of *Baruch Hashem* in *Chayei Sarah* is in stark contrast to his attitude in *Vayeitzei*. He saw the match for his sister as a blessing because of all the gold and gifts that were showered on the family. Let the reader contrast this to Lavan's feelings about this match. Yaakov came empty-handed and so Lavan did not see his arrival as a blessing. In fact, Yaakov brought incredible blessings to Lavan's household.[45] Yaakov meets the difficult challenge of maintaining his moral stature even though Lavan fails to recognize the blessings from God that Yaakov procured for him.

—10—
Word of the Parashah

והנה **סולם** מוצב ארצה—A **ladder** was set on the ground
Bereishis 28:12

The word סולם is a common modern word and appears often in the Mishnah,[46] Talmud,[47] and Midrash.[48] It means "ladder" and is found only once in the entire Bible, in Yaakov's dream. Our commentaries referred to these lone words with phrases such as "אין לו" or "אין לו אח חבר," i.e., this word has no brother or no friend. As mentioned in *parashas Noach*, the technical term for this is "hapax legomenon," Greek for a word that appears only once in a particular body of literature. When a word appears once we can only infer its meaning from its own context. We can also infer the meaning of the word from similar usage in ancient Semitic languages such as Aramaic, Arabic, Akkadian, or Ugaritic. It is

---

45 See *Rashi, Bereishis* 30:27, ד"ה נחשתי, from *Tanchuma, Beshalach* 16, and *Rashi* to *Bereishis* 30:30, ד"ה לרגלי.

46 See *Bava Basra* 3:6; *Shabbos* 5:4.

47 See *Shabbos* 26a; *Eruvin* 77b; *Chullin* 142a.

48 See *Rus Rabbah* 4:21; *Bereishis Rabbah* 68:12.

also possible to determine the meaning from similar Hebrew cognates, which will be analyzed below. Rav Saadiah Gaon made the first attempt to collect examples of hapax legomena. He wrote the book in Arabic and he named the work, *The Book of Seventy Unique Words in the Bible*, but by the time he completed the work, he had collected ninety-five such examples. This work polemicized against Karaites who reject the Oral Tradition of *Torah She'baal Peh*. Rav Saadiah's list demonstrated the value of interpreting the written text of the Bible with Oral Tradition, often using Mishnaic, Talmudic, and midrashic texts in interpreting these unique words.

In Yaakov's dream, angels ascended and descended a סולם that was set in the ground. If סולם is a lone word, its root certainly isn't. There are numerous Biblical words beginning with סל that have the connotation of elevation or height. סוללות are ramps and mounds that a besieging army builds to scale a wall.[49] This root also defines a סלע, which is an elevated rock, as in "ושים בסלע קנך—You put your nest in a rock."[50] The connection of this root to the idea of elevation is also identified in words such as "עודך מסתולל בעמי—You still exult against my people,"[51] and "סלו לרוכב בערבות—Extol Him who rides upon the clouds."[52] It may also be why a מסילה is a "highway"[53] and why so many chapters and songs in *Tehillim* end with the high note of "סלה." It may even be why a long-necked locust is called a סלעם,[54] and why a large basket, often balanced on one's head, is called a סל. Finally, the word appears in a similar form in an Akkadian poem referring to something with which a king ascends to heaven.[55] The word in Akkadian is a metathesis of the Hebrew word, where the second and third letters are switched so that סלם becomes סמל. Incredibly, *Ibn Ezra* explains סלם as a סמל, a "symbol" of the connection between heaven and earth. The closest the earth ever came to

---

49   *Yirmiyahu* 32:24. See similar usage in *Yeshayahu* 37:33 and *Yechezkel* 4:2.
50   *Bamidbar* 24:21.
51   *Shemos* 9:17.
52   *Tehillim* 68:5.
53   *Bamidbar* 20:19.
54   *Vayikra* 11:22. See *Chullin* 66a and *Avodah Zarah* 37a.
55   Dr. Hayim ben Yosef Tawil, *An Akkadian Lexical Companion for Biblical Hebrew* (2009), p. 263.

this connection was at God's revelation at סיני, which happens to share a numerical value of 130 with סלם.[56] The סלם of Yaakov's dream is available to every one of us by learning and following what was revealed to us at סיני.

---

56   See *Bereishis Rabbah* 68:12.

Parashas Vayishlach

—1—
Friday Night
תכלית מעשה שמים וארץ

ויאמר שלחני כי עלה השחר ויאמר לא אשלחך כי אם ברכתני. ויאמר
אליו מה שמך ויאמר יעקב. ויאמר לא יעקב יאמר עוד שמך כי אם
ישראל כי שרית עם אלקים ועם אנשים ותוכל.

Then the man said, "Let me go, for it is daybreak." But Yaakov
replied, "I will not let you go until you bless me." The man
asked him, "What is your name?" He replied, "Yaakov." Then
the man said, "Your name will no longer be Yaakov, but Yisrael,
because you have struggled with God and with men and you
have prevailed." (Bereishis 32:27–29)

This is how a man, a people, and a land received their name. Yaakov's
original name, however, is not based on quite such a dramatic encounter. He was named not for a characteristic that could be discerned in
him as an infant, but for the manner in which he emerged from his
mother's womb: clinging to his twin brother's heel as if to pull back on
the firstborn and all that his destiny entailed. Yaakov's deeds during
the first half of his life all take place against the backdrop of the heel he
tried to pull back. From the day he purchased his brother's birthright

to the day he took Eisav's place under the outstretched hands of his father's blessing, Yaakov was figuratively consumed with pulling back his older brother's heel.

Yaakov is seventy-seven when he is forced to flee his brother's wrath. He has no prospects for marriage at the time, nor a job or a home of his own. But he is driven to find these things away from home, as he struggles to find himself. He has another lifetime of years in which to do so (Yaakov would live for seventy more years, the proverbial Biblical length of a lifetime), and he begins in earnest. That struggle peaks in *parashas Vayishlach* as—just before confronting Eisav after more than twenty years apart—he wrestles with a man. At that time, he has a family and is financially secure, but he still has no home.

As a result of this struggle, his name is changed from Yaakov to Yisrael. Until this long journey from home Yaakov only endeavored to pull back his brother's heel. Now, as he puts the earlier struggle behind him, he is struggling with God. This is a harbinger for things to come.

Yisrael is going to teach the world about the true religious model. Religion is not an "opium of the masses," as Karl Marx declared. Religion is not limited to the pursuit of ideals such as peace, tranquility, serenity, and eternal bliss, nor is it an escape from the challenges of life. Yisrael teaches that the true religious experience is born of struggle. Not a struggle against God but *with* God—on the same side as God, raising a megaphone to a deaf world, calling attention to the plight of the weak, and lifting the downtrodden, as Yisrael's descendants would do for hundreds of years. There is no rest from such a mission. It's a constant struggle and one that turned Yaakov's attention from the heel to the head, as the word ישראל can be transposed to spell "לי ראש—I have a head." No longer is Yaakov defined by his association with a heel. For the next seventy years Yaakov would struggle to create a new image so that he could create a people, "Yisrael," to inhabit a land of Yisrael.

Yaakov's struggle left him with a wrenched hip socket, and a similarly placed sciatic nerve on an animal is therefore forbidden to us. This nerve is called the "*gid ha'nasheh*,"[1] which connotes slipping away and

---

1　*Bereishis* 32:33.

forgetting.[2] Yaakov has begun putting the first part of his life behind him. He will soon return to his homeland, which will one day be named after him, as a sign that he had completed his mission.

—2—
Introduction to the Torah
ישמח משה במתנת חלקו

Yaakov was told by his mother to dodge Eisav's wrath by escaping to her brother in Charan. Rivkah assured Yaakov that Eisav's fury would settle in but a few days, and then she would send for him. When Rivkah expressed to Yitzchak the need for Yaakov to leave home, she gave a different reason, saying that Yaakov must leave home to find a wife. This deflected attention away from the reason for Eisav's fury, while stressing the importance of Yaakov turning away from Eisav's grief- inducing marriages to Hittite women.[3]

But Rivkah never sent for Yaakov, and considerably more than a few days passed. There are different opinions regarding why Yaakov left for home when he did. One opinion connects to the confidence Yaakov gained by the birth of Yosef, since Yaakov's decision to return immediately follows the birth of Yosef.[4] Another opinion has it that Rivkah sent her nursemaid Devorah to inform Yaakov that it was safe to return, and she died shortly after arriving at Yaakov's camp.[5]

Yaakov attempts to appease Eisav prior to their face-to-face encounter by sending messengers bearing gifts. Eisav, however, responds without words, marching toward Yaakov with four hundred men, leading Yaakov to imagine the worst. Incredibly, when the two brothers meet, it is only the second time so far in the Torah that brothers speak, the first being

---

2   Yosef similarly names a child Menasheh in order to forget the unpleasant parts of his past (*Bereishis* 41:51).

3   See *Bereishis* 27:42–46.

4   See *Bereishis Rabbah* 73:7; *Bava Basra* 123b.

5   This opinion does not appear in Chazal. *Rashi, Bereishis* 35:8, ד״ה ותמת דבורה, cites it from Rabbi Moshe HaDarshan. The verse says that this is when Devorah died, and *Bereishis Rabbah* 81:5 adds that Rivkah died then as well. See Menachem Kasher's *Torah Sheleimah, Bereishis* 35, *siman* 35.

the dialogue of these same two brothers at the sale of the birthright.[6] Kayin says something to Hevel but the text leaves the conversation unsaid.[7] Shem and Yefes share no textual dialogue while covering their father.[8] Yitzchak and Yishmael share no dialogue when burying their father.[9] But Yaakov and Eisav share significant dialogue. The next time the brothers talk they are indeed "שני לאומים—two nations," as God had told Rivkah.[10] And later in the wilderness, when the Israelites request passage through Edom, the descendants of Eisav refuse.[11]

Yaakov teaches us that we must always be prepared for dialogue. Chazal say that whenever Rabbi Yehudah HaNasi had political reasons to journey to Rome, he would read *parashas Vayishlach* for instruction and inspiration for constructive dialogue with the descendants of Eisav.[12]

—3—
Introduction to the Haftarah

Sefer Ovadiah was chosen as the haftarah of *Vayishlach* because of its clear connection to Eisav, the father of Edom. Ovadiah has a unique characteristic that sets him apart from all other prophets; our Sages say he was not born Jewish, but was an Edomite convert.[13] As such, he was singularly qualified to speak of Edom's profound cruelty against Israel.

Ovadiah calls his former people, "בזוי אתה מאד—greatly despised and disparaged."[14] Chazal relate this to a number of facts of their nationhood. For one, Edom produced no language of its own. Furthermore, their kings, listed at the end of *parashas Vayishlach*, are never sons of

---

6   *Bereishis* 25:30–33.
7   See *Bereishis* 4:8. The Septuagint adds a short dialogue to the unsaid text, but the Masoretic text omits the conversation.
8   *Bereishis* 9:23.
9   *Bereishis* 25:9.
10   *Bereishis* 25:23.
11   *Bamidbar* 20:14–21.
12   See *Bereishis Rabbah* 78:15. *Ramban* cites this in the name of Rabbi Yannai in a comment to *Bereishis* 33:15.
13   *Sanhedrin* 39b.
14   *Ovadiah* 1:2.

the previous king; rather, each king rose to the throne by killing the previous monarch.[15] It was a rogue nation that transferred power violently, not peacefully. Edom, on the whole, never presented much of an actual threat against the Israelite nation. Their greatest trespass was in joining other nations in their conquest of Israel. We see proof of their foreign policy of ineffective hatred in several Biblical sources. *Tehillim* 137, "*Al naharos Bavel*," bids God to visit the iniquity of Edom upon that nation for joining hands with Babylonia in the destruction of Jerusalem; *Eichah* 4:21 refers to the rejoicing of Edom at the fall of Jerusalem; and *Amos* 1:11 refers to the wrath of Edom against his brother, which knows no end and has no limit.

In general, we are not to abhor the Edomite, for he is our brother. But a small segment of Edom, the nation of Amalek, is quite different. They attacked us at a moment of weakness when we left Egypt. They breached our lines at their most vulnerable, attacking women and children. Similarly, Ovadiah accuses the entire nation of Edom of destroying every last grape on the vine, even the unripe ones.[16] This is a metaphor for killing men, women, and children.

But Amalek's greatest trespass against us is that because of their behavior, we are commanded in the Torah to do the same to them. The Torah is not commanding us to perpetrate a cycle of violence, but rather, is recognizing that part of the duty of a moral people is to identify evil and eradicate it. The hatred of Amalek, or Haman, Torquemada, Chmielnicki, or the Nazis is so irrational that it bears no explanation. Just as our rabbis maintain that love that is not dependent on anything will always last, so too, these peoples' baseless hatred will not change. We must always be vigilant in calling attention to such hatred.

One further lesson from this haftarah is crucial. If God's greatest enmity is reserved for Amalek because they attacked the weak and unprotected, then we understand why the Torah is so preoccupied with mitzvos that help to protect and support the weak. Let us turn the

---

15   See *Avodah Zarah* 10a; see also *Rashi, Yevamos* 91b, ד"ה כתב לשם מלכות שאינה הוגנת.
16   *Ovadiah* 1:7.

tables on Amalek and Edom and turn back their cruelty by supporting those who need help, those who need us most.

— 4 —

Derashah

ושם נעשה לפניך את קרבנות חובותינו

Rambam advises us to choose the "golden mean"—the middle-of-the-road path in all our characteristics. We should avoid the extremes of all types of behavior,[17] but *Rambam* makes two exceptions. He says that we must go to extremes to beat down our inclinations to anger as well as haughtiness. He says that anger is usually triggered by a sense of arrogance that we are not getting the attention, credit, or rewards we feel we deserve.[18] This is why he put these two characteristics together. They work hand in hand. If we consider everything in life as a gift, cultivate a constant sense of gratitude, and comport ourselves with humility, we will be happier, calmer, and more cheerful.

The Gemara[19] says we can have an eighth of an eighth of *gaavah*, "arrogance," and this cryptic allowance is understood in different ways. One is that it is such a small number—the first squared number that is above 60—that such a minute amount of *gaavah* is גס (a form of arrogance), which has the numerical value of 63. If we have 1/64 of *gaavah*, it will not emerge in any way. In general laws of mixtures, when something is mixed in a volume of sixtyfold, the smaller item is nullified and halachically ceases to exist. So too, *less than* one sixtieth of a measure of arrogance will be nullified by our other characteristics. The *Vilna Gaon* suggests that the beginning of our *parashah* offers another explanation of this number. *Vayishlach* is the eighth *parashah* of the Torah, and the eighth verse of this *parashah* is *Bereishis* 32:11. This verse expresses Yaakov's admission to God, even after hearing promises of protection and salvation, that "I am unworthy of all the kindness that You have

---

17   See chap. 1 of *Rambam's Hilchos De'os*.

18   *Rambam, Hilchos De'os* 2:3.

19   *Sotah* 5a.

so steadfastly shown Your servant." This, says the *Vilna Gaon*, is the amount of *gaavah* we are allowed to have.

The week of reading *parashas Vayishlach* always coincides with the fifteenth of Kislev, which is the yahrzeit of Rabbi Yehudah HaNasi, the editor of the Mishnah, the last body of Jewish jurisprudence whose authority is unequivocal.[20] And when he died, the Talmud says that humility died with him.[21] He taught this well to his students. The Talmud teaches that two of his students taught the same thing in his name in exactly opposite directions, each one swearing that the way they taught it was the way they had heard it from their Rebbe.[22] Upon hearing what the other teacher had said, each one returned to class, to explain the issue at hand in the way the other interpreted it. They learned well from Rabbi Yehudah HaNasi, when and how to defer to another opinion, or at least to let it be heard and understood. The man with the greatest authority taught his students well, and how to exert it. It makes perfect sense then, that the greatest man among us, Moshe,[23] was also the most humble.[24]

The question for Yaakov, though, is why didn't he rely on the promises of God's protection? How could he worry, in light of those promises that Eisav would upend his blessings and destiny? The Gemara says that Yaakov feared "שמא יגרום החטא—lest he had sinned and thereby ceased to be worthy of God's promise."[25] Even though God does not relent on good promises,[26] Yaakov felt that the promise may have been only for him and not for his descendants.[27] The takeaway for us is to be ever

---

20 There is only one version of the Mishnah, and it has been explained by two Talmudic versions, the *Yerushalmi* and the *Bavli*, which are often at odds with one another.

21 *Mishnah Sotah* 9:15, 49a. *Kesubos* 103a says that when he died, holiness also died with him, but that only lasted one day.

22 *Yevamos* 33a.

23 *Devarim* 34:10.

24 *Bamidbar* 12:3.

25 *Berachos* 4a.

26 This is a standard based on *Yirmiyahu* 29 in his words to Chanania Ben Azur, and the *Rambam* records this in his introduction to the Mishnah, chap. 7, citing the verses in the beginning of *parashas Vayishlach*.

27 According to *Megillah* 31b and *Bereishis Rabbah* 44:14, Avraham asked a similar question when he said "במה אדע כי אירשנה" in *Bereishis* 15:8. See *Rashi, Bereishis* 15:6, ד״ה ויחשבה לו צדקה.

vigilant to be deserving of God's graces and beneficence and to consider everything we receive from God a gift beyond what we deserve.

— 5 —

Mussar Moments

To have more, desire less.

Comment

Koheles teaches, "אוהב כסף לא ישבע כסף—A lover of money never has his fill of money, ומי אוהב בהמון לא תבואה—nor a lover of wealth, his fill of income."[28] Our Sages teach that wealth is relative. A pauper who is happy with his lot is wealthier than a rich man who doesn't stop striving for greater and greater wealth. This is what they meant by "איזהו עשיר השמח בחלקו—Who is wealthy? The one who is happy with his portion."[29] In short juxtaposition, Yaakov and Eisav both evaluate what they possess. Eisav says, "יש לי רב—I have plenty,"[30] and Yaakov says, "יש לי כל—I have everything [I need]."[31] *Rashi* takes note of the difference.[32] Yaakov speaks in the manner of our Sages: he doesn't need more than he has. Eisav speaks the language of haughtiness. His lot is plentiful and abundant. Rivkah was told "ורב יעבוד צעיר," so "רב" is the very word that describes what Yaakov's lot was destined to be. Yet here Eisav claims to possess such a portion, perhaps indicating that he never reconciled himself to losing that lot.[33]

Yaakov's lot of "כל" is the third blessing we reference at the end of *Birkas Hamazon* when we ask to be blessed as our patriarchs were, "בכל מכל כל." Avraham was blessed בכל: "וה' ברך את אברהם בכל—God

---

28   *Koheles* 5:9.
29   *Pirkei Avos* 4:1.
30   *Bereishis* 33:9.
31   *Bereishis* 33:11.
32   *Bereishis* 33:11, ד״ה יש לי כל.
33   *Bereishis* 25:23.

had blessed Avraham with all things."[34] Yitzchak was blessed מכל:
"ואכל מכל—I have eaten of all of it."[35] And Yaakov was blessed with כל
in our verse: "יש לי כל."[36] The Talmud says that Yaakov's possessions
encompassed everything in this world, and he still managed to have
everything in the next world as well.[37]

The best things in life aren't things.

— 6 —

Birth

Yaakov lined up his children to meet his estranged brother Eisav,
preparing for the worst. When they are all listed as a unit, the text
refers to his eleven sons.[38] *Rashi* notices the omission of Yaakov's
twelfth child, Dinah.[39] Dinah was not mentioned, *Rashi* says, because
she was hidden. Dinah was kept in a box and was therefore not counted.
Rashi explains that she was hidden, lest Eisav set his eyes on Dinah for
marriage, as the common practice in the ancient world was to marry
one's brother's daughter.[40]

The Midrash finds fault with Yaakov for preventing what may have
catalyzed Eisav's rehabilitation. The text itself passes judgment on
Yaakov hiding Dinah. Yaakov's concern of what could happen to Dinah

---

34   *Bereishis* 24:1.
35   *Bereishis* 27:33.
36   *Bereishis* 33:11.
37   *Bava Basra* 16b–17a.
38   *Bereishis* 32:23.
39   *Bereishis* 32:23, from *Bereishis Rabbah* 76:9.
40   Avraham, according to Chazal, married his brother Haran's daughter, Yiskah. See *Rashi*,
     Bereishis 11:29, ד"ה יסכה, from *Megillah* 14a. *Rashi* in *Bereishis* 32:23 omits the continuation
     of the Midrash regarding the irony that Yaakov refused to give Dinah to a circumcised male,
     Eisav, and she ended up being taken by an uncircumcised male, Shechem, in *Bereishis* 34.
     Perhaps *Rashi* felt that "lest Eisav set his eyes on her," did not mean for himself but for one
     of his sons or grandsons. Eisav is close to one hundred years old by now and Dinah couldn't
     have been more than six or seven. Surely Eisav was circumcised, but *Rashi* couldn't be sure
     that his sons and grandsons were.

if exposed to the likes of Eisav backfires on him as soon as she leaves her box. This is not to insinuate that she brought the events of chapter 34 upon herself, but her curiosity got the best of her. Unexposed to anything but the confines of being boxed in, when she finally took the opportunity to "go out to visit the daughters of the land,"[41] it led to tragic consequences.

Children at birth are profoundly dependent upon their parents. We humans may be the most helpless species on the planet in these terms. It also takes us much longer than any other species to mature and go out on our own. But at some point, we obviously must do so, in stages, and one of the greatest challenges of parenting is to balance when to hold on with when to let go. Most *Bereishis* heroes do not find their calling until they leave their familiar confines and surroundings. Like everything in life, we must strike a middle ground between "boxing in" our children and giving them opportunities to develop independence. That's the best protection we can extend to our children.

— 7 —

B'nei Mitzvah

As Yaakov feared the worst in his confrontation with Eisav, he told his brother, "To see your face is like seeing the face of God."[42] Some opinions among our Sages fault Yaakov for engaging in such stark flattery.[43] Others detect a strategy that warns Eisav that Yaakov had common experiences in seeing God, hoping that this would impress his brother and restrain Eisav from causing harm.[44] However we understand this, we have a daily opportunity to "stand before the King."[45] This is what we do in our daily prayers. The Gemara tells a parable of a pauper who makes his way to the outer gate of a king's palace to beg for food, to

---

41   *Bereishis* 34:1.
42   *Bereishis* 33:10.
43   See *Bereishis Rabbah* 76:2–3.
44   See *Sotah* 41b.
45   This is the sentiment of *Mishnah Berachos* 5:1, and is a concept found often in *Shulchan Aruch, Orach Chaim, siman* 93–99.

no avail.[46] He then makes his way to the king's ballroom where a lavish feast is in progress, and he begs the king directly for food. The parable seems absurd. If the pauper couldn't get anyone to meet him at the king's fence, how did he get into the ballroom? The answer is, by saying *Shemoneh Esreh* and by asking for what we need as if we really mean it. Based on our core Jewish values, our daily liturgy places thirteen requests before God that mention health, knowledge, forgiveness, redemption, material support, and more, and we can ask for anything in the last of these thirteen blessings (*Shema Koleinu*). These are things that are important to us, and we can stand before the King and request them, each and every day. The ones who ignored the pauper at the gate are insensitive people who don't answer the cries of the needy. However, even when people don't answer us, we always have direct entry to God.

In *Tehillim*, King David expresses the difficulty he experienced in standing before God. He says:

לך אמר לבי בקשו פני את פני ה׳ אבקש.

On your behalf my heart says, "Seek my face." Then Your face, Lord, I will seek. (Tehillim 27:8)

The Dubner Maggid, Rav Yaakov Kranz, explains that David knew that when we stand before God in prayer, we should imagine ourselves, "כעומד לפני המלך," as if we are standing before the king. The awe we exhibit in the presence of the human king exemplifies how we should stand before God. David's problem is that there is no one before whom he could stand to experience these feelings. For this reason, he said to the people, "Seek my face." Fully cognizant of the awe in their faces, David was then prepared to seek God's face.

The Dubner Maggid speaks of the countenance of awe of the true believer who stands before God. Observe the face of recent *b'nei mitzvah*. Observe the excitement of performing mitzvos for the first time. See the meticulous care of the tefillin, the winding of the straps and the covering of the *batim*. See the wonderment on a girl's face the first

---

46   *Berachos* 31b.

time she separates challah. This enthusiasm is a blessing, and it is like standing before the King in His service. In that same chapter, David asks to reside in the house of the Lord every day of his life, to behold the beauty of the Lord and to visit His Temple.[47] David was asking to do something on a daily basis, but for it to remain as exciting as if he was doing it on occasion, as a visit. Our blessing for *b'nei mitzvah* is that their observance of mitzvos should always remain as exciting as it was when they performed them for the first time.

—8—
Marriage

If Yaakov's twenty years with Lavan weren't difficult enough, his two-year journey home was fraught with misfortune upon tragedy. His fear of the worst in Eisav's intentions in meeting him with four hundred men caused Yaakov great distress.[48] Then Yaakov is faced with the violation of his daughter, Dinah,[49] and the subsequent fear that his sons' reaction would cause the inhabitants of the area to attack him.[50] A report of Devorah's death follows,[51] and Chazal say this is actually the news that Yaakov's mother, Rivkah, had died.[52] Yaakov continues his travels, and finally a bit of good news comes in the birth of a second child to his beloved Rachel, but tragedy ensues as she dies in childbirth.[53] The misfortunes of *parashas Vayishlach* close with Reuven's trespass regarding Rachel's handmaid, Bilhah. The text reads:

---

47   *Tehillim* 27:4.
48   Eisav and Yaakov's messengers share no words in the text. The fact the messenger refers to precisely four hundred men implies that Eisav *did* address the messengers, but without revealing his intentions. Eisav must have told the messengers how many men were with him. Otherwise, the messengers would have said, "כארבע מאות איש—*about* four hundred men were with him." The number four hundred may be a rounded-off number to point to some kind of dialogue.
49   *Bereishis* 34:2.
50   *Bereishis* 34:30. According to *Ramban, Bereishis* 34:30, they were attacked, and Yaakov repelled the attack, as he mentions in *Bereishis* 48:22.
51   *Bereishis* 35:8.
52   *Bereishis Rabbah* 81:5.
53   *Bereishis* 35:16–19.

וילך ראובן וישכב את בלהה פלגש אביו.

Reuven went and lay with Bilhah, his father's concubine.
(Bereishis 35:22)

The text is plain and clear, yet our Sages maintain that Reuven actually did not touch Bilhah. Reuven was very pained, says the Midrash, to see his father's actions in the wake of Rachel's death. Reuven accepted that his mother, Leah, had taken a back seat to Rachel in his father's eyes, but he had expected that with Rachel's death, Leah would take her prominent role as Yaakov's favorite. When Yaakov moved his couch to Bilhah's room, Reuven couldn't stand it. He would not allow his mother's honor to take a back seat to Rachel's handmaid! He took it upon himself to send a message to his father by violating his father's privacy by bringing his father's couch to his mother's tent. So egregious was this rebellion that the text considers it as if Reuven violated Bilhah herself.[54] By denying Yaakov of his conjugal connection to Bilhah, Reuven is considered to have violated Bilhah.[55] Rabbi Yehudah HaChassid considers that the word וילך is referring to Reuven who went out to teach his father a lesson,[56] but it was for naught because Yaakov nonetheless slept with Bilhah, as וישכב is referring to *Yaakov*.[57]

It seems that our Sages were willing to judge Reuven favorably in spite of the plain meaning of "וישכב את בלהה," because his intentions for his mother's welfare were honorable. But this is part of Reuven's problem. He always has good intentions, but he is not always aware of the consequences of not judiciously acting on those good intentions.

---

54 See *Rashi, Bereishis* 35:22, ד"ה וישכב, from *Shabbos* 55b.

55 A similar reckoning is extended to the sons of Eli in the same Gemara (*Shabbos* 55b). By keeping women from returning to their husbands after giving birth, the sons of Eli are considered as if they violated the women (*Shmuel I* 2:22).

56 *Bereishis* 35:22.

57 In the apocryphal works of the Book of Jubilees 33:1–17 as well as the Testament of the Twelve Tribes 1:1–15, Reuven acts as the plain meaning of the text indicates, but achieved his goal according to both sources, that Yaakov now moved his couch to be with Leah and dropped any connection to Bilhah.

He means to save Yosef,[58] he means to return Binyamin home,[59] and He means to protect his mother, but he is "פחז כמים—he is unstable,"[60] and that is his undoing.

A successful marriage is founded on stability. The stability of love, of devotion, of shared values, and of respect. If one spouse continuously lets the other one down, expressing remorse and making excuses will wear down the relationship. The one causing the hurt needs to focus less on the intentions and more on the consequences of their actions. Good intentions are of course crucial, but Reuven loses his birthright because his intentions rarely translated to a successful end when it mattered most. In a successful marriage, this always matters.

—— 9 ——
Seudah Shelishis
אתה אחד ושמך אחד

Rav Yaakov, the son of Rabbeinu Asher (known as the *Rosh*), wrote three great works. His most famous work is called the *Arbaah Turim*, the "Four Columns," which laid the foundation for the *Shulchan Aruch*, which adopted its format. He has another work called *HaTur Al HaTorah* (known as *HaTur Ha'aroch*, "The Long Column"), a *p'shat*-based commentary, as well as a second Torah commentary called *Baal Haturim* (known as *HaTur Ha'katzar*, "The Short Column"). This work was included in the canon of *Mikraos Gedolos* commentaries and is the furthest thing from *p'shat*. Practically every comment is a *gematria* (numerical value) or *notrikon* (acronym), or Masoretic detail connecting verses that share a word or any other Masoretic phenomenon. The *Baal Haturim* loved numbers. It could not have been merely a coincidence that he chose the four names of his four columns as he did, with the relevant numbers of *simanim* in each book. They are distributed as follows:

---

58   *Bereishis* 37:22.
59   *Bereishis* 42:37.
60   *Bereishis* 49:4.

- אורח חיים—697 *simanim*
- יורה דעה—403 *simanim*
- אבן העזר—178 *simanim*
- חשן משפט—427 *simanim*

Altogether, the entire *Arbaah Turim* has 1,705 *simanim*, which is the exact *gematria* of the names of the four books.[61]

In *parashas Vayishlach*, the *Baal Haturim* connects an incredible mathematical calculation to a Masoretic anomaly with another *parashah*, *Pinchas*. He points to the fact that *Bereishis* 32:15, which begins to describe Yaakov's gift to Eisav, ends every word in the verse with the final *mem*.

עזים מאתים ותישים עשרים רחלים מאתים ואילים עשרים.

Two hundred she goats and twenty he goats, two hundred ewes and twenty rams.

The next two verses complete the list of animals for a total of 550 animals. The *Baal Haturim* points to the only other verse in the Torah that ends every verse with the final *mem*, and it too is related to animals:

ומנחתם ונסכיהם לפרים לאילם ולכבשים במספרם כמשפטם.

And their meal offerings and libations for the bulls, the rams, the lambs, according to their number after their ordinance. (Bamidbar 29:33)

The *Baal Haturim* demonstrates that if we add up all the *Musaf* offerings listed up to that point we find:

- Shabbos and Rosh Chodesh: 236
- Pesach and Omer: 78
- Shavuos: 24
- Rosh Hashanah: 10
- Yom Kippur: 13
- Sukkos with 70 bulls: 189

---

61   This is found in the book *Mekor Baruch* by Baruch HaLevi Epstein, vol. 1, p. 631.

The list also adds up to 550. The Midrash says that if the nations of the world knew how they harmed themselves by destroying the Temple, they would have left it untouched.[62] The sacrificial order of the Temple gave order to the world and set it right. The *gematria* of 550 spells תקן, referring to fixing the world, just as Yaakov tried to fix his relationship with his estranged brother.

— 10 —
Word of the Parashah

והנה רחבת ידים לפניהם—It is large enough for them
Bereishis 34:21

The word ידים here is idiomatic. It refers to a large place that can sustain Yaakov's clan alongside the inhabitants of Shechem.[63] The Torah uses this word again when commanding clean hygiene in a military camp: "ויד תהיה לך מחוץ למחנה."[64] יד is translated by *Onkelos* as אתר, a "place," and the *Sifri* on this verse says so explicitly: "אין יד אלא מקום."[65] This also explains the idiom, "על יד," which means "next to," as in, "איש על ידו לדגליהם—Every man *in his place*,"[66] by their standards.

In some cases, the word יד draws attention to a place of special significance, such as a monument—as in the pillar that King Saul set up as a memorial to his achievements. The text refers to it as, "והנה מציב לו יד."[67] Similarly, Avshalom erected a pillar as a memorial to himself called "*Yad Avshalom*" because he had no children to remember him.[68] The word יד also euphemistically refers to that which produces progeny, for example:

---

62   *Bamidbar Rabbah* 1:3.

63   See *Ibn Ezra*, *Bereishis* 34:21, ד"ה רחבת ידים.

64   *Devarim* 23:13.

65   *Sifri*, *Devarim* 257:1.

66   *Bamidbar* 2:17.

67   *Shmuel I* 15:12.

68   *Shmuel II* 18:18. That Avshalom erected this pillar because he had no children to remember his name is difficult in light of *Shmuel II* 14:27, which states that he had three sons and a daughter. See *Sotah* 11a.

בְּבֹּקֶר זְרַע אֶת זַרְעֶךָ וְלָעֶרֶב אַל תַּנַּח יָדֶךָ.

In the morning [in your youth] sow your seeds, and in the evening [even in advanced age] do not withhold your hand. (Koheles 11:6)[69]

Perhaps in the most well-known usage of this idiom, Yeshayahu consoles childless men that they will have a memorial even better than that which can be offered by sons and daughters. He calls this memorial "יָד וָשֵׁם."[70] It is an everlasting name that cannot be cut off, as Yeshayahu declares. It was only fitting to memorialize our nation's greatest tragedy with a place called יָד וָשֵׁם, Yad Vashem. Those who were murdered in the Holocaust would have a place, a יָד to ensure that the world would not forget what was done to them. This יָד is an everlasting place for the remembrance of their name.

69　In *Yevamos* 62b this is understood to mean continuing to have children even at an advanced age.

70　*Yeshayahu* 56:5.

Parashas Vayeishev

—1—
Friday Night
תכלית מעשה שמים וארץ

All of Yaakov's trials in the latter part of *Bereishis* can be traced to the fifth *aliyah* of *parashas Toldos*, when he stood in for his brother's blessing. That set a string of events in motion that began with Yitzchak's instructions for Yaakov to leave home to marry a daughter of his uncle Lavan in Aram. The more pressing reason for Yaakov to leave home was actually to escape his brother's wrath. If not for that, surely a marriage could have been arranged for Yaakov the way it was arranged for Yitzchak. When Yaakov at first balked at the suggestion to deceive his father, he expressed reservations that such deceit would cause him to be cursed. Rivkah volunteered that the brunt of such a curse should be "עלי—upon me,"[1] so Yaakov had nothing to fear.

The *Vilna Gaon* says that this word, עלי, would haunt Yaakov for more than fifty years. It is a three-letter Hebrew word that is an acronym for three people who gave Yaakov much grief. The first letter is *ayin* and stands for Eisav. The second letter is *lamed* and stands for Lavan. Eisav is also known as Edom, and together, Edom and Lavan represent

---

1   *Bereishis* 27:13.

two different types of threats to Yaakov. Edom is red and Lavan is white. One is stark and noticeable, and the other tries to do its harm surreptitiously, but make no mistake—both are dangerous to Yaakov's survival. Yaakov and his descendants survived both Edom and Aram, where Lavan lived, and the most harm to Yaakov came in the form of the third letter. That letter is *yud* and is represented by all the inner turmoil caused by the Yosef saga.

Parashas Vayeishev midrashically represents Yaakov's desire to finally settle, rest, and relax[2] from all his struggles from the *ayin* (Eisav) and the *lamed* (Lavan). It was not to be. The word עלי has three letters. One might surmise that the turmoil in Yaakov's life, caused by the *yud* (Yosef), was worse than the other two combined, because if we have internal peace, we can contend with any external threat. By the time *Bereishis* ends, this turmoil will be resolved, but there will still be growing pains for our young nation. In *parashas Mikeitz*, Yaakov suffers additional turmoil and assesses all his suffering by repeating, "עלי היו כלנה—All this has come upon me."[3] The third letter once again is the source of the most pain for Yaakov but will yet be the source of unburdening his pain.

— 2 —

Introduction to the Torah
ישמח משה במתנת חלקו

Yosef, at seventeen, exhibits curious behavior in our *parashah*. Perhaps he couldn't help being his father's favorite, but the bad reports about his brothers—and the nerve of sharing his dreams with them—was taking things too far. These were not only dreams in the eyes of Yosef's brothers; they were aspirations. In fact, they were prophecies. The haftarah for this Shabbos ends with the prophet Amos declaring, "God has spoken, who can but prophecy?"[4] If an individual truly believes that

---

2   See *Bereishis Rabbah* 84:3.

3   *Bereishis* 42:36.

4   *Amos* 3:8.

a Divine message has been extended, it must be shared. The question remains, why would a member of a Hebrew family of shepherds dream about preoccupations more common to the Egyptians, such as farming and astronomy? Yosef's dreams should have been about sheep, shepherds, or staffs bowing to him, not bundles of grain and celestial bodies.

Yosef understood that there was about to be an upheaval of the family. Theirs was the generation that would descend to the strange land that God foretold to Avraham. Yosef suggested they prepare for this. Yosef was a dreamer, and he had a lot to dream about. The brothers were shepherds like their father, but Yosef wore a *kesones pasim*.[5] This can mean a coat of stripes, and somehow has evolved to be a coat of many colors. It more likely means a long-sleeved cloak, as a *pas* is a "wrist" in Hebrew, so that a *kesones pasim* covers the entire arm to the wrist. The other brothers wore short sleeves as they worked in the pastures, while Yosef studied indoors. As his story unfolds through the rest of *Sefer Bereishis*, we see how proficient he is in interpreting the dreams of others. We can imagine how he interpreted his own dreams. We must be ready for the exile, and we need not be frightened by the prospect of learning the wisdom that exists beyond our own family traditions.

Yosef proved that he was correct. The beginning of *Sefer Shemos* describes how Yosef remained in Egypt as he always was, a man who would constantly invoke the name of God, a man who would refuse an immoral act at all costs, and a man who would not let immense power affect him.[6] He raised two boys, born in Egypt, who both rose to become prominent tribes in Israel along with their uncles.

---

5   *Bereishis* 37:3.

6   This is based on *Shemos* 1:5, "ויוסף היה במצרים." *Rashi* cites *Sifri, Devarim* 334, which understands the word היה to refer to the fact that Yosef remained the same throughout all his experiences. Rabbi David Pardo, in his commentary to *Rashi, Maskil L'David*, explains that the name Yosef here means to contrast the Egyptian name צפנת פענח that was given to him by Pharaoh (*Bereishis* 41:45). Yosef may have had a name change, but he always remained Yosef.

—3—
Introduction to the Haftarah

כה אמר ה' על שלשה פשעי ישראל ועל ארבעה לא אשיבנו על מכרם
בכסף צדיק ואביון בעבור נעלים.

Thus said the Lord: For three transgressions of Israel, for four,
I will not revoke it because they have sold the righteous and the
needy for a pair of sandals. (Amos 2:6)

At first glance, the narrative of the sale of Yosef in *parashas Vayeishev*
is connected to the very first verse of this haftarah, a reference to a *tzad-dik* being sold for a pair of shoes. The connection between Yosef, who
came to be known as Yosef HaTzaddik, and the *tzaddik* in this verse, is
pervasive throughout Chazal, and a tradition arose that Yosef was sold
for a pair of shoes, even though the Torah never says so explicitly.[7] Most
commentaries, however, understand this verse in *Amos* differently. The
tzaddik in the verse, according to *Rashi, Ibn Ezra, Radak,* and *Metzudos,*
is an innocent man who is sold into slavery because he could not repay
a debt on a pair of shoes. Regardless, in Amos's words, this is the sin
that seals the fate of the kingdom of Israel.

There is precedent in *Tanach* for the despicable practice mentioned in
this verse. In *Melachim II,*[8] a woman complains that creditors are com-ing to take her children as slaves because she can't pay her debt. There is
a fascinating Aggadah that juxtaposes the opening verse of our haftarah
to a verse in *Hoshea,* the prophet who was a contemporary of Amos.

חבור עצבים אפרים הנה לו.

Ephraim is attached to idolatrous images. Let him be.
(Hoshea 4:17)

---

7   See *Targum Yonasan* to *Bereishis* 37:28.

8   Beginning of chap. 4. This is read as part of the haftarah of *Vayeira;* see "*Vayeira,* (3) Intro-duction to the Haftarah."

Chazal understood the attachment denoted by the word חבור to refer to a unification of the people in their pursuit of idolatrous services. Chazal present a reinterpretation of this verse as an incredible dialogue between God and the angels. The angels protest Ephraim's behavior, "Ephraim is united in idolatry!" And God answers, "הנח לו—Let him be," which could be understood to mean, "At least he is united. Come back to Me when he is not; when there is social decay, I will react accordingly."

Some time later, the angels return with a report of the events described in *Amos* 2:6. When this behavior comes to light, Ephraim's fate is sealed. God could forgive idolatry, but He would not forgive consigning debtors to slavery.[9]

God's reaction to Ephraim's behavior seems to be consistent with a parent's reaction to children's misbehavior. Just as God set rules for His people in the Torah, every parent has household rules by which to abide. Like the laws set out in the Torah, parental rules are often particular to each specific family, and sometimes each specific child, depending on his or her situation and needs. Generally, however, the parents lay down two different types of rules; one pertaining to how the children relate to their parents and the other how the children relate to each other. The first set of rules may include curfew times, how one is dressed at the family table, attendance at family gatherings, as well as household chores. The second set of rules asks all the children to be civil to each other, to care for each other, and occasionally to selflessly sacrifice for each other. This must be deftly orchestrated by parents who make all children feel equally treated and loved.

A parent is likely to be more hurt when a child fails at the second task than at the first. A parent can live with a child who fails to mow the lawn or clean the basement or do the shopping. But parents are more seriously hurt if their children are cruel to one another. This is why God says to let Ephraim be, even in disobedience. At least they are united. But the specter of children selling one another into slavery is too much to bear. Such cruelty to the weak is what lost the ten tribes.

---

9   See *Bereishis Rabbah* 38:6 in a comment about the Tower of Bavel. See also *Tanchuma*, *Tzav* 10.

The bulk of the book of *Amos* is dedicated to improving the morality of his people to avoid the impending exile of the ten tribes at the hands of the Assyrians. The message of *Amos* rings true for us even today. If immorality lost the tribes, then surely caring for the less fortunate is an excellent step toward finding them. God is our loving parent, and we need to treat our siblings well to deserve His good graces.

This is surely the main connection to *parashas Vayeishev*. The sale of Yosef is a stain on our collective history that needs constant atonement. Rabbi Meir Simcha of Dvinsk explains that this is why on Yom Kippur we read about the ten martyrs who atoned for Yosef's ten brothers.[10] It constantly needs atonement until boundless love replaces baseless hatred.

The haftarah has additional connections to *Vayeishev*. It refers to a father and a son being with the same woman,[11] which parallels the saga of Yehudah and Tamar. It refers to violence done through garments,[12] which parallels Yosef's tunic being dipped in blood, or the garment Potiphar's wife grabbed from Yosef. The haftarah refers to Nazirite lads,[13] which can connect to Yosef, who is referred to in the Torah as "נְזִיר אֶחָיו—separated from his brothers."[14] Amos refers to the selection of the Israelites as God's chosen,[15] even as Yosef was the favored child in his family.[16] Finally, the haftarah concludes with Amos professing that he must not remain unspoken.[17] Perhaps this is why Yosef had to reveal his dreams. He saw them as prophecies. His brothers unwittingly catalyzed the realization of his dreams even while professing that they felt they were quashing them.[18]

Amos's strategy is to compare the unfortunate events of history to a famous ancient story of reprehensible behavior. God has spoken,

---

10   *Meshech Chochmah, Vayikra* 16:30.
11   *Amos* 2:7.
12   *Amos* 2:8.
13   *Amos* 2:11.
14   *Devarim* 33:16.
15   *Amos* 3:2.
16   *Bereishis* 32:3.
17   *Amos* 3:8.
18   *Bereishis* 37:20, "We shall see what will become of his dreams."

Amos has transmitted the message. The message went unheeded and the Northern Kingdom that Amos addressed was destroyed. But Amos's message lives on. If immorality exiled us, morality can redeem us.

— 4 —
Derashah

ושם נעשה לפניך את קרבנות חובותינו

There are twenty-four books of the Hebrew Bible, and the Gemara considers eighteen of them to be *"b'dieved,"* meaning "after the fact," or "of necessity." That fact is that we are sinners and these books help bring us back to the straight path. "If not for the sinning of the Israelites, the only Biblical books revealed to them would have been the Five Books of Moses and the Book of Yehoshua."[19] The workings of the prophets have been called that which gives comfort to the uncomfortable, and that which makes the comfortable uncomfortable. A prophet's job is to place God's case before the people, and also to place the people's case before God. Simply put, the prophet's job is to drive his listeners to repentance and a better life. With this in mind, it must be of interest to learn which prophet is chosen to rebuke us on the Shabbos between Rosh Hashanah and Yom Kippur, known as Shabbos Shuvah. There are approximately forty prophets in *Neviim* and *Kesuvim*, so when the prophet Hoshea gets the call for such a mission, we might wonder why such prophets as Yeshayahu, Yirmiyahu, or Yechezkel were overlooked for the more minor prophet, Hoshea?

Chazal state that Hoshea was chosen for Shabbos Shuvah because he was descended from the tribe of Reuven,[20] and the Midrash continues that since Reuven was the first person ever to perform *teshuvah*, the prophet for Shabbos Shuvah should be descended from him. This is problematic. Where do we see that Reuven repented, and for which sin? Also, there are numerous midrashim about Adam's repentance,[21]

---

19 *Nedarim* 22b.

20 *Bereishis Rabbah* 84:19.

21 See *Eruvin* 18b and *Zohar*, vol. 1, 253b.

and Kayin's repentance,[22] as well as others[23] before Reuven (the reader may recognize some references to these cases in the *Selichos* of the *Yamim Nora'im*).[24] Does this Midrash disagree with those references? The Kotzker Rebbe points to two verses in this week's *parashah* that refer to two reasons for Reuven's repentance: one is for his sin regarding Bilhah, and the other is in not protecting Yosef.

When Reuven *returned* to the pit and saw that Yosef was not in there, he rent his clothes. He *returned* to his brothers and said, "The boy is gone, now what am I to do?"[25] The Kotzker Rebbe says that Reuven repented for two sins. What he did regarding Bilhah surely needed repentance, but he was the only one who had wanted to save Yosef,[26] so why did he need to repent for that? The answer is that Reuven teaches us a powerful message of repentance that transcends the *teshuvah* of anyone who preceded him.

Reuven didn't make excuses. The most common reaction to being confronted with wrongdoing is the initial reaction of Adam and Kayin, which is to shirk responsibility.[27] Reuven repents because he knows he could have done better. The Midrash teaches that if Reuven would have known that the Torah would record his intentions, he would have put Yosef on his shoulders and carried him home.[28] His plan was to leave Yosef in the pit and return later to take him home, but in between, the Midianites pulled him out of the pit and sold him.[29] The truth is that everything we do is also being recorded and will be played back for us one day.

---

22   See *Tanchuma, Bereishis* 9, *Zohar*, Vol.1, 254a.

23   See *Bereishis Rabbah* 38:12 and *Tanchuma, Shemos* 18, regarding Terach, and *Bava Basra* 16b, regarding Yishmael.

24   The refrain for this prayer is recited before the open *aron* and is called "דרך תשובה הוראת לעם השובבה."

25   *Bereishis* 37:29–30.

26   *Bereishis* 37:22.

27   God's questions to both Adam in *Bereishis* 3:9 and Kayin in 4:9 were meant to open them up to repentance for their sins, and both at first made excuses. See *Rashi, Bereishis* 3:9, ד"ה איכה; *Bereishis* 4:9, ד"ה אי הבל אחיך.

28   *Rus Rabbah* 5:6.

29   See *Rashbam, Bereishis* 37:28.

Reuven's descendant is chosen for Shabbos Shuvah because we are all Reuven, time and again. Let's all do our best, exert patience and understanding when others slide, give comfort to the uncomfortable, and not be comfortable ourselves until we've tried our hardest.

— 5 —
Mussar Moments

Things seem to turn out best for those who make the best of the way things turn out.

Comment

At the age of seventeen, Yosef was uprooted from his home and family and spent the next thirteen years navigating trials and tribulations in many forms. He was sold numerous times, accused, convicted, and jailed. But at every turn he charged ahead to success and favor. He never surrendered to the ignominious fate that seemed to follow him, as he turned every stumbling block into a stepping-stone. Everything that happened to Yosef is a learning experience and whoever can live that way is always a winner.

We never lose. We either win or we learn.

— 6 —
Birth

Our Sages, in both the Talmud and Midrash, generally presented the deeds of our patriarchs in a positive light. Since their actions often served as omens for the future,[30] it served our better interests to shine

---

30   This is known as "*maaseh avos siman l'banim.*" See *Sotah* 34a. See also *Bereishis Rabbah* 40:8, "אמר הקב״ה לאברהם אבינו צא וכבוש את הדרך לפני בניך." See also *Ramban, Bereishis* 12:6.

a beam of positivity on all their actions, as this beam would reflect upon us.[31] *Radak* and *Ramban*, however, stand out in their commentaries on *Bereishis* for their willingness to be critical of the patriarchs and matriarchs,[32] even in cases justified by midrashim.[33]

It is quite significant that commentaries that exert an extraordinary effort to justify everything Yaakov does with the birthright, the blessings, his dealings with Lavan and Eisav, and more, nonetheless find a serious problem with his favoritism of Yosef in *parashas Vayeishev*. *Rambam* cites the Gemara that finds fault with Yaakov's favoritism,[34] and codifies it into law:

צוו חכמים שלא ישנה אדם בין הבנים בחייו אפילו בדבר מועט שלא יבוא לידי תחרות וקנאה כאחי יוסף עם יוסף.

Our Sages commanded parents not to differentiate between their children even in a small way in order to avoid competition and jealousy, as was the case regarding Yosef's brothers with Yosef. (Rambam, Hilchos Nachalos 6:13)

Preferential treatment will always foster resentment, whether to a child, a student, or a worker. But in all fairness to Yaakov, God Himself has chosen a preferred and cherished nation as His *am segulah*.[35] Yaakov recognized extraordinary potential in Yosef[36] and favored him with a *kesones pasim*. This was a long-sleeved tunic that reached his wrist, *pas yad*, as a sign of an education that only he received. The other brothers worked in the fields to support the family, in short sleeves or no sleeves

---

31 See *Tanna D'bei Eliyahu*, beginning of chap. 25: "כל אחד ואחד מישראל חייב לומר מתי יגיעו מעשי
למעשה אבותי אברהם יצחק ויעקב—Each and every Israelite must say, 'When will my deeds resemble the deeds of my fathers, Avraham, Yitzchak and Yaakov?'"

32 See especially their treatment of Avraham and Sarah's behavior toward Hagar in *Bereishis* 16:6.

33 See Allen Schwartz, *Conflict and Resolution in the Early Prophets* (Kodesh Press, 2020), p. 146, n. 195, for a list of questionable actions of the patriarchs and matriarchs found in *Bereishis Rabbah*.

34 *Shabbos* 10b.

35 *Shemos* 19:5.

36 See *Bereishis Rabbah* 84:8 and *Targum Onkelos* to *Bereishis* 37:3, where "בן זקונים" is rendered "בר חכים—a wise son."

at all. We can imagine a family of many sons where all but the youngest work in the coal mines with their father; the youngest, who demonstrates signs of great intellectual prowess, is the only one who gets to go to college and graduate school. We could imagine the older brothers feeling proud of their youngest sibling, without bearing any grudge for the opportunity presented to him that eluded them. But this would be less likely if the youngest sibling would capitalize on his favored status to their detriment.

This is the challenge of a chosen nation as well. We are called "ממלכת כהנים—a nation of Kohanim,"[37] and just as Kohanim serve the religious needs of the rest of their people, a nation of Kohanim is tasked by God to teach the entire world to find the Divine spirit of humanity that will affect their thoughts, speech, and actions. Even if the haters among them choose to deny the benefits this small chosen nation renders to the entire world, it doesn't change our mission. Yosef tried to be helpful to his brothers. Yaakov taught Yosef everything he knew, including his incredible prowess of shepherding.[38] According to *Seforno*,[39] Yosef in turn tried to share this information with his brothers because he always wanted to be helpful.

New parents are faced with many challenges. There is an incredibly helpless human being in our care who can be cold, hot, wet, dirty, hungry, or thirsty, and they have only one way to express any of these feelings. Add to that the care of other siblings and juggling this with so many other tasks, and maybe we'll reserve judgment on Yaakov. Our challenge is to raise our children to feel that they are part of a team where each member of the family is raised to reach their highest potential. Yaakov's favoritism of Yosef set in motion a series of events that fulfilled a Divine plan of how our nationhood would begin. It ends well because of Yosef's relentless desire to be helpful wherever he goes, and the unfolding story of how his brothers learned from their mistakes. In this light, we as a family helped Egypt survive the famine, and we

---

37   *Shemos* 19:6.

38   Cf. *Bereishis* 30:25–43.

39   *Bereishis* 37:2, ד"ה רועה את אחיו בצאן.

remained a family unit throughout the story. Thus Yaakov succeeded where Avraham and Yitzchak did not, whereby every one of his children carried on the family legacy that we continue to embrace many centuries later.

—7—
B'nei Mitzvah

וישב יעקב בארץ מגורי אביו.

Yaakov settled in the land of his fathers' sojourning. (Bereishis 37:1)

Notice the contrast in the words for "residence" in this verse. Yaakov's fathers were sojourners in the land, while Yaakov sought to *settle* in the land. Our Sages captured this point with the observation:

בקש יעקב לישב בשלוה.

Yaakov attempted to settle in tranquility. (Bereishis Rabbah 84:1)

He had struggled enough. He had fled enough. It was time to relax and retire. Not so fast. Our Sages continue:

קפץ עליו רוגזו של יוסף.

Peace would elude Yaakov, for the anger of Yosef's situation would overcome him. (Bereishis Rabbah 84:1)[40]

What message is being conveyed to Yaakov? In what way will the situation of Yosef be instructive to Yaakov that he was mistaken in desiring tranquility and peace? What is wrong with wanting to be settled?

The answer is in Yosef's life itself. *Seforno* explains "היה רועה את אחיו בצאן" as an attempt on Yosef's part to be helpful to his brothers. Chazal say Yaakov shared all his wisdom with Yosef,[41] and this must

---

40   See *Rashi, Bereishis* 37:2.
41   *Bereishis Rabbah* 84:8.

have included the intricate shepherding knowledge that Yaakov demonstrated at the end of *parashas Vayeitzei*. Yosef just wanted to share his knowledge with his brothers, but this didn't sit well with them; they resented the superiority his behavior engendered.

Yosef continued to try to be helpful to others. Pharaoh's butler and baker surely would not have come to him for dream interpretations as a matter of course. They only did so because Yosef opened up and offered to be helpful. This desire to assist manifests itself in Yosef's advice to Pharaoh. Yosef was called upon to interpret dreams, not offer advice. Yet, he couldn't help but direct his words to the implementation of a plan of maximum benefit.

This is why Yosef is known as Yosef the *tzaddik*. A *tzaddik* enhances and inspires all that is around him. Noach started off that way. At first he was called "איש צדיק,"[42] but because he didn't change anyone outside of his own family he ended up being "איש האדמה."[43]

Yaakov too began this way. Our Sages say that he established a marketplace, a system of coinage, and a series of bathhouses to maintain cleanliness and personal hygiene.[44] Yaakov, like the Jewish nation named after him, wanted to help enhance the quality of the life of anyone in his vicinity. The Jew must never rest. We must always make things around us better. That is to ease pain and tribulation, and to realize as Yosef did, that there is purpose to our struggles, "להחיות עם רב—to bring about the survival of many people,"[45] and to feed others or to help the weaker among us. This is what Yaakov came to learn about in his premature attempt at attaining "וישב." There is a world to shape, and we as a people have always been at the forefront of doing so, with our minds, hearts, deeds, and most of all, our indomitable spirit. There is no rest from this. Not everyone can be a Yaakov or a Yosef, but everyone can play a supporting role.

---

42   *Bereishis* 6:9.
43   *Bereishis* 9:20.
44   This is expounded from *Bereishis* 33:18, "ויחן את פני העיר" in *Shabbos* 33a.
45   *Bereishis* 50:20.

When children attain the age of mitzvos, they became part of Yaakov and Yosef's team. They can now fulfill obligations for others. Their supporting role can gradually turn to a leading role and even a starring role. For today we are celebrating a special birthday for a future star. Mazel Tov!

— 8 —
Marriage

A question was presented to the *Rashba* about publicizing the performance of a mitzvah.[46] The one who asked felt it might be untoward to engage in such a breach of humility, and that it might smack of a violation of the Mishnah that exhorts us to perform mitzvos without expectation of reward.[47] The *Rashba* responded to the contrary. Publicizing the performance of a mitzvah is not only allowed, it is praiseworthy, and he proved his point from *parashas Vayeishev*.

When Yosef's brothers suggested killing him,[48] Reuven quickly rose to Yosef's rescue and suggested that they not kill him themselves but leave him to die in a pit. The text reveals that Reuven had every intention of saving Yosef and bringing him home.[49] Perhaps this would be Reuven's way of getting back in his father's good graces for what he had done regarding Bilhah.[50] Regardless of his motivation, we see that Reuven's suggestion to leave Yosef in a pit was merely a stalling tactic for him to return and save Yosef. This never happened because before Reuven had a chance to return, the Midianites sold Yosef.[51] Chazal say that had Reuven known that the Torah would record his good intentions, he would have taken Yosef home on his own shoulders.[52] Just as the

---

46   *Teshuvos HaRashba* 981.

47   *Pirkei Avos* 1:2.

48   *Bereishis* 37:20.

49   *Bereishis* 37:21–22.

50   See *Bechor Shor, Bereishis* 37:22. Reuven felt unequal to the task of confronting his brothers away from their father. But if he could bring Yosef home and warn Yaakov not to expose Yosef again to such danger, Reuven could make his way back to his father's good graces.

51   *Bereishis* 37:28.

52   *Rus Rabbah* 5:6. This Midrash says the same regarding Aharon: had he known that the Torah

Torah records Reuven's intentions for posterity, so too we may record our mitzvos in a similar vein.[53]

There is also a mitzvah to publicize miracles. This is known as *pirsumei nisa* and is a significant element in our Chanukah observance. The halachah maintains that while we need not expend ourselves beyond 20 percent of our assets in the performance of any positive command,[54] when it comes to lighting the menorah, we must expend ourselves even beyond 20 percent.[55] We must even sell the shirt off our back if necessary to do the mitzvah. The *Avnei Nezer* asks why we are more stringent for the menorah, which is a Rabbinic mitzvah, than we are for Torah laws.[56] He answers that when a Jew truly wants to perform a mitzvah but can't afford it, God looks into his heart and rewards him as if he performed the mitzvah. But this doesn't work if the point of a mitzvah is *pirsumei nisa*, to publicize the miracle. Good intentions can suffice for *lulav* and *esrog* or tefillin but not for menorah. That is because my good intentions to light the menorah don't do anything for the person in the street who won't see my menorah. *Pirsumei nisa* needs more than just good intentions. It needs action.

Our Sages consider a successful match in marriage to be as miraculous as the parting of the Red Sea. Surely such a success requires us to publicize the miracle. Not to others but to one another, as a demonstration of gratitude to God for putting us together. The *kesubah* even contains the expression of the miracle. The groom declares that he will fulfill his obligations even to the point of selling the shirt off his back! He can't settle for 20 percent because there is a miracle to publicize.

---

would record his happiness for Moshe's appointment (*Shemos* 4:14), he would have met Moshe with musical accompaniment. A third case is cited by the Midrash, that had Boaz known that the text would record the amount of food he gave Rus, he would have given her more than a pinch (*Rus* 2:14).

53 See *Torah Temimah*, *Bereishis* 37:22 (ט) for another possible proof for such publicity.

54 *Kesubos* 50a.

55 See *Rambam, Hilchos Chanukah* 4:12–13.

56 *Avnei Nezer* to *Rambam, Hilchos Chanukah* 4:12.

— 9 —
Seudah Shelishis
אתה אחד ושמך אחד

There are two Masoretic points regarding the amount and format of verses in *parashas Vayeishev*. The first is that the number of verses in the *parashah*, 112, coincides with the number of words in *Tehillim* 92, known as "מזמור שיר ליום השבת—A song to the Shabbos day." Just as the first Shabbos was originally the culmination of the six days of Creation for God, every Shabbos is now the culmination for all of our acts of creativity over the previous six days. In the same vein, *parashas Vayeishev* begins the story that is the culmination of *Sefer Bereishis*. At first, man is consumed with his own self-aggrandizement. Man wants to attain divinity,[57] achieve fame through achievement,[58] increase his might,[59] become renowned,[60] rule over others,[61] and make a name for himself.[62] All of this stands in sharp contrast to Avraham, who calls out in God's name to spread His fame throughout the world.[63]

One of the blessings God bestows upon Avraham is "ואגדלה שמך—I will make your name great,"[64] which demonstrates that Avraham achieved what everyone before him sought, through God. Avraham's mission as the father of a covenantal nation begins to form in *parashas Vayeishev* as the culmination of *Sefer Bereishis* begins to take shape.

But there is still much that needs correction in *Bereishis*. Sibling rivalry, a constant in this book, is about to result in the sale of Yosef, which will put the patriarch Yaakov in such a state of depression, he will no longer be a conduit to attract the Divine spark. From the beginning of *parashas Vayeishev*, the Torah by far extends the largest stretch in

---

57   *Bereishis* 3:5.
58   *Bereishis* 4:20–22.
59   *Bereishis*: 6:1–2.
60   *Bereishis* 6:4.
61   *Bereishis* 10:8–10.
62   *Bereishis* 11:1–4.
63   *Bereishis* 12:8.
64   *Bereishis* 12:2.

which the active voice of God is absent. Since our Sages teach that the Divine Presence does not rest upon a depressed person,[65] Yaakov was in no position to serve as a receptacle for any Godly message.[66] God reveals Himself to Yaakov for the first time after twenty-two years, right after he learns that Yosef is alive.[67]

There is an attempt on the part of Yehudah to teach brotherhood among his sons as he instructs Onan to bear seed for his dead childless brother Er. Instead of providing offspring for Er, Onan wasted his seed on the ground, "ושחת ארצה,"[68] and Yehudah became bereft of a second son. In the end, after Tamar takes the initiative, two new sons are born to Yehudah to make up for his earlier losses.[69] This birth is mentioned in another Biblical narrative that shares the second Masoretic point with *parashas Vayeishev*. The book is *Megillas Rus* and the Masoretic connection is, amazingly, that both *Megillas Rus* and *parashas Vayeishev* begin every verse but eight with the letter *vav*. This letter is a connector, and it shows that there is a continuum of events in both stories that connect throughout the book. Each event hooks into the next, until the story is complete.[70] *Megillas Rus*, like *parashas Vayeishev* tells of two sons dying and also has a component of perpetuating the name of a childless dead man. In *Rus*, Ploni Almoni goes unnamed because he refuses to perpetuate the name of Machlon, and the reason he gives uses the same root that describes Onan's refusal, "פן אשחית את נחלתי—Lest I **waste** my estate."[71] Boaz takes the responsibility shirked by others, and with Rus creates the first sprouts of the Davidic dynasty. *Megillas Rus* also compensates for the missing names of God in *parashas*

---

65 "אין שכינה שורה מתוך עצבות," *Shabbos* 30b.

66 See *Bereishis Rabbah* 47:8, "האבות הן הן המרכבה—Our patriarchs were the 'chariot' that connected to God," a reference to the mystical prophecy of *Yechezkel*, chap. 1. Yaakov failed to live up to this model during the years he mourned for Yosef.

67 *Bereishis* 46:2.

68 *Bereishis* 38:8–9.

69 *Bereishis* 38:27–30.

70 The word *vav* in Hebrew is actually a "hook," mentioned many times (*Shemos* 26–38). There is only one other *parashah* that comes close to this incidence of verses beginning with a *vav* and that is *Vayeitzei*. It too contains chains of events that are "hooked" to each other.

71 *Rus* 4:6.

Vayeishev and *Mikeitz*. Practically every event in the story is attributed to God or Divine guidance. *Parashas Vayeishev*, with a little Masoretic help from *Tehillim* 92 and *Megillas Rus*, sets the stage for a successful transition from family to nation.

— 10 —
Word of the Parashah

ולא ידע אתו מאומה כי אם **הלחם** אשר הוא אוכל—He paid attention to nothing save for the **bread** that he eats.
Bereishis 39:6

Yosef excels in Potiphar's house and is left in charge of all Potiphar's affairs except for the bread that he eats.[72] *Rashi*[73] understands the word for bread, לחם, to euphemistically refer to Potiphar's wife.[74] Thus in the parallel verse, when Yosef refuses Potiphar's wife's advances, he tells her:

לא חשך ממני מאומה כי אם אותך באשר את אשתו.

He has withheld nothing from me except yourself, since you are his wife. (Bereishis 39:9)

Yosef seems to specify that the earlier reference to bread is actually Potiphar's wife.

Rashi comments similarly when Yisro tells his daughters to call upon Moshe so that he can break bread, maintaining that Yisro was hoping that Moshe would marry one of them.[75]

Ibn Ezra disagrees in both cases.[76] Yisro was offering Moshe food. It would be untoward to offer a daughter to a total stranger. And Yosef was indeed in charge of the entire household except for the food. לחם means more than just bread, as in "נותן לחם לכל בשר כי לעולם חסדו"—Who gives

---

72   *Bereishis* 39:6.
73   *Bereishis* 39:6, ד"ה כי אם הלחם.
74   See *Bereishis Rabbah* 86:6. *Targum Yonasan* renders לחם as Potiphar's wife as well.
75   *Shemos* 2:20, ד"ה ויאכל לחם.
76   *Bereishis* 39:6, "כי אם הלחם."

food to all flesh, His steadfast love is eternal.[77] Since "all flesh" includes animals, לחם cannot be limited to bread, which needs planting, seeding, and harvesting—things only humans do. לחם also often refers to what goes on God's altar, and this surely encompasses more than bread.[78] *Ibn Ezra* explains that Yosef was not put in charge of the food because the Egyptian dietary code prohibited the consumption of meat, so Potiphar would not put a Hebrew in charge of his kitchen. This also explains why it was abhorrent for an Egyptian to dine alongside Hebrews, and why Yosef set his brothers to sit separately from the Egyptians.[79]

Chazal understood an additional case of food or eating similarly euphemistic. *Mishlei* speaks of a sinner in denial:

כן דרך אשה מנאפת אכלה ומחתה פיה ואמרה לא פעלתי און.

Such is the way of the adulterous woman; she eats and wipes her mouth, and says, "I have done nothing wrong." (Mishlei 30:20)

The Gemara understands the eating in itself as the act of adultery and the wiping of her mouth, a cover-up of her treacherous ways.[80]

Perhaps we can also posit that the word for "war," מלחמה, is related to לחם. Basing himself on various scholars, Mitchell First explains that the root ל-ח-ם means to be pressed together[81] (which would equally apply to war when armies are pressed together, and the making of bread when dough is pressed together). Interestingly, this would explain the poetic quality of *Yeshayahu* (2:4) and *Michah* (4:3), where the prophet

---

77   *Tehillim* 136:25.

78   See *Bamidbar* 28:2, *Malachi* 1:7, and many others.

79   *Bereishis* 43:32. See Ibn Ezra, *Shemos* 8:22.

80   *Kesubos* 13a. This is in explanation of the Mishnah ad loc., which refers to adultery as "מדברת—speaking." It's also possible that washing of the feet in *Shmuel I* 25:41, as well as *Shmuel II* 11:8, are similar euphemisms. This is not to say that "washing of the feet" always denotes such a euphemism any more than bread does. The two cases above, like *Rashi's* two cases of bread, are cases where a good argument can be made for the euphemistic interpretation.

81   Mitchell First, *Roots and Rituals: Insights into Hebrew, Holidays and History*, p. 114.

speaks of a time when the weapons are pressed together for the sake of sustenance, rather than used in the act of fighting together in war.[82]

Many an ancient battle was fought over control of scarce food resources. In addition, control of our eating habits is a constant battle. This explains why so much of our halachic observance surrounds eating.

Perhaps Yeshayahu[83] and Michah[84] had these very connections in mind when they said, "They shall beat their swords into plowshares and their spears into pruning hooks."

Tools of war (מלחמה) are being beaten into tools of food production (לחם).[85]

This etymological similarity renders a double meaning in Moshe's assurance to the Israelites as they were cornered by the Egyptians against the sea. Moshe told them:

ה' ילחם לכם ואתם תחרישון.

God will fight for you and you shall hold your peace. (Shemos 14:14)

This can also be rendered: "God will make bread for you, but you have to plow."

---

82   I thank Rabbi Johnny Solomon for pointing this out to me.

83   *Yeshayahu* 2:4.

84   *Michah* 4:3.

85   Basing himself on various scholars, Mitchell First explains that the root ל-ח-ם means "to be pressed together" (which would apply equally to war, when armies are pressed together, and the making of bread, when dough is pressed together). Interestingly, this would explain the poetic quality of *Yeshayahu* 2:4 and *Michah* 4:3, where the prophet speaks of a time when the weapons will be pressed together for the sake of sustenance, rather than for the act of fighting together in war.

Parashas Mikeitz

— 1 —
Friday Night
תכלית מעשה שמים וארץ

וייקץ פרעה: וייׁשן ויחלם שנית...וייקץ פרעה והנה חלום.

Pharaoh was stirred from his sleep. He fell back asleep, and he dreamt again...Pharaoh was stirred from his sleep and realized he was dreaming. (Bereishis 41:4–5,7)

Daas Zekeinim explains that dreams of cows eating other cows, while strange, are not strange enough to make the dreamer realize he is not in a state of reality.[1] Cows after all, do eat. However, when Pharaoh dreams of stalks of corn devouring other stalks, he realizes he must be experiencing a dream.

Yosef explained that the repetition of the dream represents the immediacy of the interpretation. "As for Pharaoh having the same dream twice, it means that the matter has been determined by God, and that God will shortly bring it to pass."[2] Also, the seven years of famine are described by Yosef as years "אשר אין חריש וקציר—in which there shall be

---

1   *Bereishis* 41:7.
2   *Bereishis* 41:32.

no plowing nor harvest."[3] The first dream represents the חריש as cattle used for plowing,[4] and the stalks of corn represent the קציר.

We know the dreams refer to seven years of plenty followed by financial disaster, years with no worthwhile land for cows to plow and no grain to harvest, years that will consume the previous years of plenty. And the Nile—which in Pharaoh's dream spawned the symbolic images[5]—will not be able to stave off the famine. Pharaoh appreciates this valuable inside information and accepts Yosef's advice toward preparing for the lean years.

One curious point needs comment. Pharaoh pursued many avenues of interpretation before appealing to a Hebrew prisoner.[6] What was so novel about Yosef's interpretation that no one else could have divined?

The answer lies in the message of Chanukah, which always coincides with the Torah reading of the saga of Yosef and his brothers. Pharaoh *should* have dreamed about the strong devouring the weak. This makes sense in relation to his life experience and to the world's natural order; what baffles him the most about his dream is that the exact opposite took place. Yosef's interpretation was so unique because only a Hebrew could have told the most powerful world leader why his subconscious might be preoccupied with the weak overcoming the strong instead. True Jewish survival makes no sense to the natural order. However, it makes sense in a prophecy of Zechariah in the haftarah of Shabbos Chanukah, "לא בחיל ולא בכח כי אם ברוחי—Not with might nor with strength but in My spirit [i.e., of God]."[7]

This is the secret of Jewish survival, and Pharaoh's dreams are about the Hebrews as much as they are about what would bring them from Canaan to Egypt.

---

3   *Bereishis* 45:6.
4   See *Iyov* 1:14.
5   *Bereishis* 41:2–3.
6   *Bereishis* 41:8;15.
7   *Zechariah* 4:6.

—2—
Introduction to the Torah
ישמח משה במתנת חלקו

The story that immediately follows the sale of Yosef relates that Yehudah left his home and family. The verb that describes his departure is "וירד—he went down."[8] *Rashi*[9] cites the Midrash that this indicates "שהורידוהו אחיו—that his brothers lowered his standing."[10] They blamed him for Yosef's sale. We can understand this, because Yehudah was the one who suggested selling him.[11] According to the Midrash, the brothers claimed:

אלו אמרת להשיבו היינו שומעים לך.

Had you said to return him we would have listened to you.

This guilt was too much to bear for Yehudah and he left the source of it behind.

In our *parashah*, Yehudah again is persuasive as he convinces Yaakov to entrust Binyamin in his hands. Reuven tries to assure Yaakov that he can be entrusted with Binyamin. Reuven is so sure that Yaakov would not lose a second son that he absurdly offers his own sons as ransom for the safe return of Binyamin.[12] Yehudah takes a different approach. He offers himself as the guarantor for Binyamin's return. Perhaps we can imagine Yehudah making the following argument to his father: I can't be as sure as Reuven that I will succeed in this mission. But I *do* know what you feel like. I will not allow you to lose a second son. I have already lost two sons, and I will not allow this to happen to you. This convinces Yaakov, and Binyamin is released. Yehudah is convincing because of his empathy. Yehudah also begins the healing process of *Sefer Bereishis*.

---

8   *Bereishis* 38:1.
9   *Bereishis* 38:1, ד"ה ויהי בעת ההיא.
10   *Bereishis Rabbah* 85:2; *Tanchuma, Ki Sisa* 22.
11   *Bereishis* 37:26–27.
12   *Bereishis* 42:37.

He mentions that Yosef is their brother when he suggests selling him: "Let our hands not be upon him for he is our brother and our flesh."[13]

Yehudah also attempts to teach brotherhood to his own son, when he tells Onan:

בא אל אשת אחיך ויבם אותה והקם זרע לאחיך.

*Join with your **brother's** wife and do your duty by her as a brother-in-law and provide offspring for your **brother**. (Bereishis 38:8)*

The responsibility Yehudah takes in *parashas Mikeitz* is part of a healing process for brotherhood in the latter part of *Bereishis* that had already begun in last week's *parashah*, and will continue into the next. In order for Israel to succeed as a nation, we must first succeed as a family, and the first elements of that success have begun to sprout.

— 3 —
Introduction to the Haftarah

The haftarah of *Mikeitz* is rarely read since the haftarah of Chanukah usually preempts it. When *Mikeitz* is not during Chanukah, we read a haftarah whose connection seems to be that both the *parashah*[14] and the haftarah begin with a dream.[15] Besides a series of dreams of the prophet Zechariah in the beginning of his book, the only other detailed dream in *Neviim* is in the story of Gideon.[16] Pharaoh's dream and all these cases of dreams in *Neviim* are so remote as to warrant an additional connection for the haftarah of *Mikeitz*. The main part of the story is to showcase Shlomo's wisdom as it manifests through his determination of the true mother in a dispute over a baby. Shlomo perceived that one woman didn't care about having the baby; she wanted to keep the baby from the other woman. Indeed, even *after* the true mother offered the

---

13 *Bereishis* 37:27.
14 *Bereishis* 41:1.
15 *Melachim I* 3:5.
16 *Shoftim* 7:13. There are some additional dreams in some of the books of *Kesuvim*, but a haftarah is taken only from the books of *Neviim*, not *Kesuvim*.

baby to the other woman so long as the baby would live, this impostor insisted that the baby be cut in half. It is clear then that she came to court that day, not because she wanted the baby, but because she didn't want the other woman to have it.

There is a hint in the Midrash that explains why the impostor didn't want the real mother to have her baby.[17] The Midrash says that these two women were mother-in-law and daughter-in-law. The mother-in-law had two sons: one was married to the second woman in our story and the second son was the baby Shlomo threatened to cut in half. The daughter-in-law suffocated her baby just before her husband died, and she was therefore in need of *yibum* or *chalitzah*[18] from her husband's baby brother. Rather than wait for the baby to grow older, her plan was to claim the baby as her own as a proof that she was really not in need of *yibum* or *chalitzah*. Whatever the reason, Shlomo perceived who the real mother was, and of course never intended to actually kill the baby.

Nonetheless, this same Midrash finds fault even with Shlomo's suggestion to cut a baby in half. That a room full of incredulous onlookers could even think that a king of Israel could exercise such power is a breach that goes a step too far. And this may be our connection to the *parashah*. Whether Yosef's motivation in his treatment of his brothers was to fully realize the prophecy of his dreams,[19] or to vouchsafe a full degree of repentance for his brothers,[20] it seems that Yosef went too far in his plan. He had spent nine years in power without easing his father's pain. It should have been clear to him that the brothers had repented for what they had done to him.[21] They had already bowed to him, and the essence of his dreams had already been realized. Yosef lost ten years of life for hearing "עבדְּךָ אָבִינוּ—our father your slave" five times and then

---

17   *Koheles Rabbah* 10:16.

18   Cf. *Devarim* 25:5–10. A woman whose husband died childless is either to be taken in marriage by her dead husband's brother, called *yibum*, or freed from the family connection by *chalitzah*. If the man left a living child before dying, his widow is freed from both rituals.

19   *Ramban, Bereishis* 42:9.

20   *Abarbanel, Bereishis* 41:54, questions 4–7.

21   See *Bereishis* 42:21–22.

another five times in translation.[22] These sources agree that like Shlomo, Yosef abused his power when it came to his brothers, even if he did so for a lofty purpose. As such, the מלכות, "kingship," was not bestowed by Yaakov upon Yosef, who would have seemed the obvious choice because of his dominion over the brothers at that point. But because he took this dominion too far, the kingship was bestowed upon the one who challenged him, and that was Yehudah. And in the haftarah, when Shlomo acts similarly—by even considering cutting a baby in half—it ironically portends to a kingdom that will be split in the lifetime of Shlomo's son, Rechavam.[23] Thus the Torah and haftarah connection extend beyond a dream to include a powerful message of kingship and power.

— 4 —
Derashah
ושם נעשה לפניך את קרבנות חובותינו

A Roman Caesar was very impressed with Rabbi Yehoshua's intelligence and challenged the Rabbi to predict what he would dream that night. Rabbi Yehoshua told him that he would dream of being pressed into the service of the Persian king and he would be forced to pasture pigs with a golden staff. The king thought this foolish and mocked the Rabbi's ridiculous prediction. The Caesar became so consumed with the matter that he couldn't stop thinking about it all day. So consumed, as a matter of fact, that he ended up dreaming about just that sight.[24] An occurrence that would never normally enter his consciousness indeed ended up entering the Caesar's mind that night. Rabbi Yehoshua understood that our dreams reflect our deep-rooted thoughts, fears, and challenges.[25]

Perhaps Pharaoh, one of the world's most powerful men, deeply feared being devoured by a band of other lesser nations and thus dreamed

---

22 *Pirkei D'Rabi Eliezer* 39.
23 See *Melachim I* 12. Chazal draw a similar irony from King David's impetuous pronouncement for Tziva and Mefiboshes to split a field in *Shmuel II* 19:30. *Yoma* 22b says that at that very moment, a Heavenly voice proclaimed that the kingdom shall be split.
24 *Berachos* 56a.
25 The Gemara itself makes this point, *Berachos* 55b.

about the robust being devoured by the lean. How else could his dreams be understood? This may be what baffled his magicians, who could not offer a satisfactory interpretation.

Yosef too seems to dream out of his league when he envisions objects relating to farming and astrology. A Hebrew shepherd should have dreamed perhaps about a ram, a sheep, and eleven shepherd's staffs, or perhaps eleven wool bundles. Instead, Yosef envisions Egyptian preoccupations—heavenly bodies and grain harvests.

This reveals that Yosef knows the brothers will not remain in Canaan and that a long exile faces them. Yosef feels that preparation for our life in exile was necessary so that we could survive or even thrive there. The brothers disagreed. They felt that they could survive in the exile as a separate entity, not affected by, and not affecting, society at large. The brothers also felt that engaging Egyptian society would prove detrimental to maintaining their way of life. Yosef was thrust into exile against his will and ended up paving the way for his family's smooth transition into Egypt.

The Chanukah story and *Mikeitz* share a profound theme of the weak overpowering the strong (in *Mikeitz* this is manifest in Pharaoh's dreams). They also share themes regarding the Jew's ability to overcome the allure of assimilation. Let us always remember that the Chanukah story was not only about freedom from the oppression of a wickedly despotic king. Chanukah is also about freedom from the delights and temptations posed by the secular culture at large.

Yosef's moral equilibrium was sorely tested in *parashas Vayeishev*. He passes from challenge to challenge without losing his faith, as he declares to Potiphar's wife, to the butler and baker, and to Pharaoh himself, that God directs his every move.

Our Sages declare that if anyone ever attempted to excuse himself from his obligation to study Torah because of his powerful urges, or his good looks, he would have Yosef to answer to.[26] The Gemara goes on

---

26   *Yoma* 35b.

to elaborate about the extraordinary temptations posed by Potiphar's wife—yet Yosef withstood them.

Another Talmudic description of Yosef's temptation pits him against two other Biblical characters who were similarly tempted, only that their temptations were even greater.[27] The two characters are Boaz in the book of *Rus*, and Palti ben Layish in *Shmuel I*. The temptation of Boaz was greater than Yosef's because Rus was lying at his feet, alone at night,[28] and the temptation of Palti ben Layish was even greater than that of Boaz because being alone with Michal, an *eishes ish*, was a recurring situation.[29] One has to wonder then, why Palti ben Layish isn't the one to set up as a paradigm for the one overcome by urges. The answer is that Yosef had to do battle with urges well beyond the realm of Potiphar's wife. The test of fortitude for Boaz and Palti, to which Yosef is compared, is limited to a test regarding carnal temptations. Yosef, in addition to overcoming those urges, had to struggle with maintaining his moral stature in the face of the incredible power he wielded in a land not known for its morality. He literally held sway over life and death in Egypt for thousands of people. Rav Yehudah HaChassid says that Yosef inquired about everyone who came to Egypt for food. He asked about their families and their backgrounds because he would be more lenient with people who were unable to pay.[30] He'd put in extra food or extra money for poor families. He brought temporary morality to Egypt. Yosef proved that the Jew *can* engage secular society and not only not succumb to its allures, but to stamp an imprimatur of *yiras Shamayim* onto it. In next week's *parashah*, Yosef tells his brothers to tell their father:

שמני אלקים לאדון לכל מצרים.

God has made me lord of all of Egypt. (Bereishis 45:9)

---

27   See *Sanhedrin* 19b.

28   *Rus* 3:8.

29   See *Shmuel I* 25:44. The Gemara cited above says that Palti refrained from drawing near to Michal under the consideration that she was David's wife.

30   *Bereishis* 43:7.

This can also be read: "I have made God the Master of Egypt."

This was the ultimate fulfillment of his dreams, and our mission wherever we go, to place the stamp of *yiras Shamayim* and morality wherever we are.

— 5 —
Mussar Moments

If you want your dreams to come true, wake up.

Comment

Yosef's brothers hated him because of his dreams.[31] He was favored over them and took advantage of that favoritism with his evil reports[32] and his immature habit of relating his dreams of superiority to his brothers. They would do everything in their power to prevent his dreams from coming to fruition. When they saw him in a moment of unprotected vulnerability, they said, "Here comes that dreamer! Come now, let us kill him and throw him into one of the pits and we can say, 'A savage beast devoured him.' Then we will see what becomes of his dreams!"[33] These events unfolded, setting in motion a series of occurrences that would make Yosef's dreams come true! It was the brothers who made Yosef's dreams come true even as they attempted to thwart them.

As for Yosef, he doesn't begin to realize his dreams until he is removed from his familiar surroundings. It is only in the unfamiliar environs of Egyptian servitude that Yosef "wakes up" to find himself. It is precisely when Yosef is challenged that he finds his calling for leadership and accomplishment.

---

31   See *Bereishis* 37:8, 37:19–20, and 42:9.
32   *Bereishis* 37:2. This also refers to "דבריו—his words," referenced in *Bereishis* 37:8.
33   *Bereishis* 37:19–20.

It is never too late to become the person you might have been.

— 6 —

Birth

Parashas Mikeitz begins at the end of two years. If that sounds strange, it's because it is strange. These two years are at the end of an unknown period of time, as far as the verse itself is concerned. The last *Rashi* in *parashas Vayeishev* explains that the two years refers to the time Yosef spent in jail after interpreting the butler's dream.[34] The butler saw no gain in helping Yosef, so he conveniently forgot him. As soon as he saw some profit in mentioning Yosef, he conveniently remembered him. He references Yosef with all kinds of caveats just in case the referral doesn't bear fruit for Pharaoh.[35] He calls Yosef a נער, as if he's young and foolish. (Yosef was thirty years old at the time.) He also refers to Yosef as an עבד, who couldn't possibly rise to leadership. These derogatory references to Yosef are meant to protect the butler in case Yosef's interpretation is not favorable in Pharaoh's eyes.

As it turns out, the referral was a good one and Yosef did indeed impress the king. According to Chazal, Yosef was punished with spending these two extra years in jail because he placed his trust in the butler's hands.[36] This may have proven worthwhile had the butler not been so devious and conniving. He only helps Yosef when it is profitable for him to do so.

An analysis of the butler's behavior at the end of *Vayeishev* and the beginning of *Mikeitz* is instructive for new parents. Parents need to be many things for their children. They need to be empathetic, hardworking, sacrificing, and they need to set a good example for their

---

34   *Bereishis* 40:23.

35   *Bereishis* 41:12. See *Rashi*, ד"ה נער עבד עבר.

36   *Bereishis Rabbah* 89:3.

children. At the top of this list though, is that parents must be *dependable*. Humans depend on their parents more than any other species on the planet and for a longer time. The butler only becomes dependable when it suits him. This is not the model for parenting. As it turns out, of course, the butler forgetting Yosef is all part of the plan for Yosef to remain in place where Pharaoh would find him when he needed him. Had Pharaoh freed Yosef two years earlier under the recommendation of the butler, Yosef would have long been gone by the time of "מקץ שנתים ימים—the end of two years." The greatness of Yosef is that he turns every disappointment and setback into a positive development. There are bound to be setbacks in every endeavor, but caring parents know how to learn from Yosef to build such setbacks into learning experiences for their children. Parenting is the supreme act of giving to someone profoundly dependent on us. May the new parents rise to this exciting and rewarding challenge.

— 7 —
B'nei Mitzvah

As God's plan for Yaakov's family's descent to Egypt unfolds, we see a number of people playing starring roles, such as Yosef, Yehudah, and Pharaoh. Pharaoh's dream in the beginning of this week's *parashah* plays a crucial role in the continuum of our story. A dream usually represents a collection of random thoughts, memories, and experiences, some from long before, some recent, some from moments before. In Pharaoh's case, the dream is a prophecy, and Yosef is careful to explain this when he begins his interpretation by saying: "את אשר האלקים עושה הגיד לפרעה—God has told Pharaoh what he is about to do."[37] Prophecies are not random, but some of the supporting roles in our story are played out by actors in what might appear to be a random fashion. There are some supporting roles, like that of Reuven, the Midianite merchants, Potiphar, Potiphar's wife, the baker, and the butler. There are some passing roles as well. These roles were brief, but without them we can

---

37   *Bereishis* 40:25.

also say that the story would not have unfolded. This includes the man who informed Yosef where to find his brothers.[38] This apparently random encounter was so crucial to our story that *Rashi* identifies this man as an angel Gavriel.[39] *Ibn Ezra* insists that this was an ordinary man who happened to have known where Yosef's brothers had gone. He says this not only on *p'shat* grounds, since the verse refers to him as a man, but also on *hashkafic* grounds. It was all part of God's plan, and this man could have been anyone.

There is another unsung hero, a very tiny one who also helps this story along. Without this little character, Yosef would have remained in jail indefinitely. The hero is the fly that was found in Pharaoh's cup.[40]

The point is that in all great stories, great people do great things. But all great stories have supporting actors, and passing actors, as well.

B'nei mitzvah have all kinds of roles to play. On your special day of attaining the age of mitzvah obligation, you're the star, and there are many roles to play in the ensuing years. Some will be supporting roles, and some will be perhaps just to send someone else in the right direction.

A janitor at NASA was once asked what his job was, and he answered, "I'm helping put a man on the moon." Everyone has a role to play. Some as starters, some as pinch hitters, pinch runners, or defensive replacements. They are all on the same team with the same objective, and they are all ready for their calling.

— 8 —
Marriage

Yaakov's overprotective care of Binyamin comes at the expense of his other children and their families. The food has run out and Yaakov still balks at sending Binyamin, a requirement of the viceroy if they are to acquire food and gain Shimon's freedom. Yaakov explains why Binyamin receives this special treatment. It's not just that Binyamin

---

38   *Bereishis* 37:15.

39   See *Rashi, Bereishis* 37:15, ד"ה וימצאהו איש.

40   *Bereishis Rabbah* 88:2. See *Rashi* 40:1, ד"ה חטאו.

alone remains from his union with Rachel, but that since calamity came to both Rachel and Yosef, "בדרך—on the road," this meant that Binyamin would be naturally more vulnerable than his brothers on the journey to Egypt.[41]

Yehudah takes full responsibility for Binyamin's safety,[42] and for this reason he is the one who challenges Yosef in *parashas Vayigash*. Yehudah's argument there concentrates on how painful Binyamin's absence would be for his father. One has to wonder why Yehudah made no mention of the fact that Binyamin had ten young children. Surely, if Yehudah wanted to move the viceroy's sense of pity, a reference to ten children being raised without a father might have been useful. The reason Yehudah didn't mention them is because he didn't obligate himself to Binyamin's children. Yehudah's argument is that he has taken full responsibility for Binyamin's return and needed to do all he could to ensure his guarantee to his father is secured. Yehudah does not attempt to appeal for pity. This is a practical transaction, and he makes his best case: I'll take his place.[43]

There is an important message for couples in the formulation of Yehudah's case before Yosef. He is focused singularly on the one to whom he took responsibility: his father. Every person is pulled in numerous directions from family members, from friends and acquaintances, from employers and employees, and many others. From the moment the glass is broken under the bridal canopy, each of you must focus no less than Yehudah, first and foremost, on how your actions, decisions, speech, and gestures impact on the other.

The Torah says that a man must leave his father and mother and cling to his wife.[44] *Seforno* takes this as a message to parents to stay out of the way of their married children.[45] They must focus on pleasing each other unencumbered by pressures placed on them by parents or in-laws. Yehudah may have made a more convincing case by bringing

---

41   See *Bereishis* 42:38, where Yaakov specifically refers to calamity "בדרך—on the journey."
42   *Bereishis* 43:9.
43   *Bereishis* 44:18–33.
44   *Bereishis* 2:24.
45   *Bereishis* 2:24, ד"ה על כן.

up Binyamin's children but that was not his main focus. So too, no one should ever get between a loving husband and wife.

I close with a parable. May the new couple be like a pair of scissors, inextricably joined together, and even if, as they go about doing their jobs they momentarily move apart, they always rejoin, punishing anyone who dares get between them.

— 9 —

Seudah Shelishis
אתה אחד ושמך אחד

Yosef connects to three pairs of dreams, and his ability to turn them into reality and offer practical advice on their basis is uncanny. Our Sages placed great value on the ability to unravel the different layers of a dream's meaning. The *masechta* in the Talmud that is dedicated to demonstrating the blessedness of God's gifts, *Maseches Berachos*, includes a large tract of dream interpretation.[46]

Yosef's own pair of dreams relate to his superiority and his dreams of grandeur. He correctly predicts the fate of the baker and butler from their deepest thoughts as they are reflected in dreams they expressed to him. All of this was practice for the lifesaving interpretation and advice Yosef rendered to Pharaoh.

Each set of dreams is associated with a number. Pharaoh's number seven connects to seven years.[47] The baker and butler's number three connects to three days.[48] Yosef's first dream is associated with the number eleven and his second dream is associated with the number thirteen. If the other four dreams are connected to time frames, what do eleven and thirteen signify for Yosef?

Yosef was seventeen when he was sold into slavery,[49] and he was thirty when he became viceroy in Egypt.[50] Two years prior to this is when

---

46 *Berachos* 55a–57b.
47 *Bereishis* 41:26.
48 *Bereishis* 40:12,18.
49 *Bereishis* 37:2.
50 *Bereishis* 41:46.

Yosef interpreted the dreams of the baker and butler.[51] This means that the numbers in Yosef's dreams were also connected to a time frame, namely years. Eleven years after being sold, Yosef correctly rendered the dreams of the baker and butler and should have been freed then. But his second dream had a representation of the number thirteen, because he spent two more years in jail.[52] Thirteen years after being sold is when he would interpret the dreams that would change his life and the ancient world.[53]

— 10 —
Word of the Parashah

ותרעינה באחו—They grazed in the **marsh**
Bereishis 41:2

God sent a message to Pharaoh through his dreams and Pharaoh relates the dreams to Yosef for interpretation. The Torah then repeats the dreams in their entirety with subtle differences here and there. There are two general approaches to these differences. One says it is not worthy to consider the meaning of any of these differences. The initial report is the all-knowing narrative of the text; the second report is in Pharaoh's own words.[54] The other position holds that since the Torah could have simply related that Pharaoh told Yosef his dreams, there must be some significance to the differences in what was ultimately written.[55]

---

51   See *Rashi, Bereishis* 40:23, ד"ה וישכחהו. This is the plain meaning of "ויהי מקץ שנתים ימים." It was two years after the previous story of the baker and butler.

52   According to Chazal in *Bereishis Rabbah* 89:3, the extra two years were a punishment for Yosef having put too much faith in the butler for his salvation. They may also have been a punishment for the gall in including a representation of his parents—the sun and the moon—in what bowed to him in his own dream.

53   I am indebted to my son-in-law, Rabbi Yoni Zolty, for suggesting these number connections to Yosef's dream.

54   This is the approach of *Rashbam, Ibn Ezra,* and *Ramban.*

55   This is the approach of Chazal and *Rashi.* After all, even considering what comes from the mouth of Pharaoh, namely in the retelling of the dream, the precise way to record is the Torah's decision. Surely Pharaoh spoke to Yosef in Egyptian, and it had to be translated to Hebrew. See an interesting discussion on the divergence between what was spoken by

Moreover, Pharaoh's first dream itself contrasts a description of the seven fat cows with the seven lean cows. Only the fat cows were grazing. The lean cows didn't need to graze; they ate the other cows!

The description of the grazing uses a rare *Tanach* word, "ותרעינה באחו—they grazed in the *achu*." The Koren translation renders *achu* as "reed grass," as does the Jewish Publication Society. ArtScroll translates as "marshland," as this is *Rashi's* rendition in French. Sinai renders the word, "meadow," and Robert Alter translates as "rushes." All these interpretations seem to fit with the occurrence of the word in *Iyov* 8:11:

היגאה גמא בלא בצה ישגה אחו בלי מים.

Can the rush shoot up without mire? Can the achu grow without water?

Any of the above words can fit with this verse. While *achu's* most common Hebrew cognate is the word "brother," we see its usage as a "fireplace" in *Yirmiyahu*,[56] while it seems to be onomatopoetic in *Yeshayahu*,[57] as if to say "*Ach!*"[58] Some scholars consider *achu* to be Egyptian in origin,[59] and there is a debate among some of the commentaries regarding *achu's* relationship to the Hebrew word for "brother," *ach*.

Ibn Ezra to our verse makes note of the verse in *Hoshea*: "כי הוא בין אחים יפריא—Though he be fertile among the *achim*."[60] He insists that the singular *achu* in our verse refers to a meadow or a type of plant, while the plural *achim* in Hoshea seems to refer to brethren. Yet in *Hoshea*, *Ibn Ezra* considers the two words *achu* and *achim* to be of similar origin. In reality, *Ibn Ezra* does not contradict himself. When he refers to brethren in our verse, he means to say that the two references are brethren,

a Torah personality and what ended up being written in the Torah in *Igros Moshe*, *Yoreh Deah*, vol. 1, *siman* 133, about the conversation between Moshe and Yehoshua regarding Eldad and Meidad in *Bamidbar* 11:28–29.

56   36:22.

57   44:16.

58   A similar usage of the word seems to appear in *Tehillim* 70:4, "האח האח."

59   Brown, Driver, and Briggs, *A Hebrew and English Lexicon of the Old Testament*, p. 28.

60   *Hoshea* 13:15.

namely that they share a common meaning.[61] *Ramban* attempts to connect all these words by drawing attention to the fact that all the separate grasses and rushes grow together in אחוה, in apparent "brotherhood," side by side, standing and swaying together in harmony.

The Midrash also notes this element of brotherhood.[62] As stated above, only the fat cows grazed "באחו," as a sign of how much easier it is to stand together when everyone is satisfied. When we level the playing field between the fortunate and less fortunate, as the Torah attempts to do with laws such as tithes, *shemittah*, *pe'ah*, *leket*, and charity, we increase brotherhood, where all grazing is done באחו, in the marsh, or in brotherhood.

---

61   This is the rendition of H. Norman Strickman and Arthur M. Silver's translation of *Ibn Ezra*, pp. 372–73.

62   *Bereishis Rabbah* 89:5.

Parashas Vayigash

—1—
Friday Night
תכלית מעשה שמים וארץ

I was once part of a group of approximately one hundred Jewish leaders given a three-minute test. We were brought into a room with a large screen and told to watch a video of six people, three wearing colored T-shirts and three wearing white T-shirts, pass basketballs to each other while moving in circles. We were told to count how many passes were made to and from those wearing white shirts only, which was not an easy task. After the time was up, we were asked for our observations. The observed numbers of passes ranged from fifteen to twenty-five.

We were then asked if we noticed anything unusual in the course of the video. About ten in the room had noticed something the rest couldn't believe. In the middle of the passes, a large gorilla walked out from one side of the room, stopped in the middle of the circle of the six passers, beat his chest a number of times, and then exited.

We were shown the video again, only this time with no directive to count passes. Then everyone saw the gorilla in the room, without a doubt. How could 90 percent of us have been oblivious to a gorilla? It's very simple—when we focus on only one issue, we tend to close our minds to everything on the periphery. Ninety percent of those of us in the study were so focused on one thing that we couldn't see anything else. (Not even one person who guessed the correct amount of passes saw the gorilla.)

Until *parashas Vayigash*, this human fallacy has been a major problem in the entire saga of Yosef. Yosef was so focused on his dreams, he failed to realize how his immature behavior was affecting his family. The brothers were so focused on their jealousies and hatred, they failed to see the ramifications of their actions. The brothers make a statement that implies they have begun to repent their earlier actions. When the brothers recall Yosef in the pit, they remember how they looked at his anguish and paid no heed as he pleaded with them. This is curious, because nowhere in the sale of Yosef is it mentioned that Yosef pleaded with them.[1] This is for the simple reason that no one noticed it at the time. His cries fell silently on his brothers' ears. Even Reuven, who intended to return and remove Yosef from the pit, was not moved by his pleas, at least not enough to actually save him on the spot.[2]

Not until *parashas Vayigash*, when Yehudah says, "כי עבדך ערב את הנער—Your servant has pledged himself for the lad,"[3] does anyone take responsibility for another. Thus, the reconciliation of brothers can begin; the rift between Yaakov's children can be healed. Things that had gone unnoticed and unsaid for so long can now be shared. *Sefer Bereishis* itself is on the way to being mended.

— 2 —
Introduction to the Torah
ישמח משה במתנת חלקו

The Yom Kippur *Musaf* liturgy includes a description of ten rabbis who were martyred for continuing to teach and observe Torah against Roman decree.[4] We read a similar liturgy on Tishah B'Av,[5] but without

---

1   *Bereishis* 42:21.
2   See *Bechor Shor, Bereishis* 37:21.
3   *Bereishis* 44:32.
4   This is in a section of the liturgy known as אלה אזכרה.
5   Known as ארזי הלבנון.

the introductory detail that these ten rabbis died over a period of time as atonement for the ten brothers of Yosef, who escaped the Torah's death penalty for kidnapping and selling.[6] While it's true that we may not punish vicariously in our courts, for each person dies for his own sin,[7] God's court does punish in this way.[8] In fact, while in the Yom Kippur liturgy, the idea of punishing these ten rabbis for the sale of Yosef emanates from the cursed Roman emperor, in a Midrash it emerges as a Heavenly decree.[9] However, *Rashbam* points out that a careful reading of the original story indicates that Yosef was not sold by his brothers at all.[10] They had planned to sell him to the sons of Yishmael whom they had seen from afar but before they had a chance, the Midianites pulled him out of the pit and sold him.[11]

The tradition that the brothers sold Yosef for a pair of shoes stems from the opening line of the haftarah of *Vayeishev*: "For three transgressions of Israel I would forgive but for the fourth I would not revoke their sin, because they have sold a *tzaddik* for money and a needy one for a pair of sandals."[12] Yosef himself told his brothers, "I am Yosef, your brother, whom you sold to Egypt."[13] This doesn't necessarily mean they actually sold Yosef but that they were responsible for him having been sold.[14] Another proof that the brothers didn't sell Yosef can be derived from their reaction to the harsh treatment they received upon arrival in

---

6   *Shemos* 21:16.

7   *Devarim* 24:16.

8   Cf. *Shemos* 20:5, 34:7, *Vayikra* 26:39, *Bamidbar* 14:18.

9   See *Bereishis Rabbasi, Bereishis* 37 (Albeck edition), p. 176.

10   *Bereishis* 37:28.

11   *Ibn Ezra* considers Midianites and Yishmael to be synonymous. They are both sons of Avraham (see *Bereishis* 25:2) and they are also interchangeable in *Shoftim* 8:22–24. We see even a third son of Avraham involved because the מדנים (without the *yud*) sold Yosef to Egypt in *Bereishis* 37:36, and in 39:1, we are told that Yosef was sold to Egypt by Yishmael! All three were sons of Avraham (see *Bereishis* 25:2).

12   *Amos* 2:6; see *Targum Yonasan, Bereishis* 37:28. See above, "*Vayeishev*, (3) Introduction to the Haftarah."

13   *Bereishis* 45:4.

14   This is similar to the prophet Nassan rebuking King David that he killed Uriyah with the sword of the Amonites (*Shmuel II* 12:9). David takes the blame for being responsible for the death of Uriyah.

Egypt to obtain food. They saw this as just desserts for what they did to Yosef and said, "Truly we are guilty concerning our brother, because we looked on at his anguish, yet paid no heed as he pleaded with us. That is why this distress has come upon us."[15] Had they sold Yosef, surely they would have mentioned that as the cause of their distress!

We read about the ten martyrs on Tishah B'Av to elicit sadness. We read about them on Yom Kippur to inspire atonement.[16] Even if the brothers didn't actually sell Yosef, they were responsible for his sale. *Parashas Vayigash*, like Yom Kippur, is about atonement, and the introduction of elements of the Yosef saga into the Yom Kippur liturgy sends a message of owning up to responsibility and not making excuses.

— 3 —
Introduction to the Haftarah

The haftarah of *Vayigash* is the first haftarah of the year from *Yechezkel*. Yechezkel was exiled with Yechanyah eleven years before the Temple was destroyed, and he began his prophecies five years later.[17] He is known for his symbolic prophecies in which he would act out certain commands from God, and then explain what these actions represent.[18] The Sephardic commentaries such as *Radak* generally felt that Yechezkel did not actually perform these actions, he only visualized them,[19] while the Ashkenazic commentaries, such as *Rashi* generally understood these prophecies literally.[20] Our haftarah has one such prophecy in which Yechezkel wrote the names Yosef and Yehudah on two trees. These two trees represent the two monarchies that ruled through most of *Sefer Melachim*. A descendant of Yosef ruled over the ten tribes in the

---

15   *Bereishis* 42:21.

16   See *Meshech Chochmah*, *Vayikra* 16:30.

17   *Yechezkel* 1:2.

18   See *Yechezkel* 12:11, where the prophet describes himself explicitly as having this mission.

19   See *Radak*, *Yechezkel* 5:2, where Yechezkel is told to shave his entire head with a razor in violation of *Vayikra* 19:27, and *Yechezkel* 37:1, where he is told to stand in a valley filled with bones in violation of *Vayikra* 21:1.

20   *Rashi* understands these prophecies that violate Torah law as "הוראת שעה—temporary dispensations."

North of Israel, and a descendant of Yehudah ruled over the Southern part of Israel.

Yechezkel's two trees are similar in scope to the two trees of Zechariah that are called "שני בני יצהר—the two sons of oil."[21] These represent the two Messianic figures, Mashiach ben Yosef and Mashiach ben David. There were two kingdoms, so there will be two Mashiachs. Mashiach means "anointed with oil," so it's not surprising that a tree, especially an olive tree, would represent our Messianic figures.

Yeshayahu also refers to Mashiach in terms of the growth of a tree. He declares:

ויצא חטר מגזע ישי ונצר משרשיו יפרה.

There shall grow a shoot out of the stump of Yishai, and a branch shall sprout from his roots. (Yeshayahu 11:1)

Yirmiyahu twice refers to this savior as a branch: a "צמח צדיק—a righteous branch,"[22] and a "צמח צדקה—a branch of charity."[23]

Zechariah says outright that Mashiach's name is צמח because his arrival is a process of growth.[24]

For this reason, our daily prayers request:

את צמח דוד עבדך מהרה תצמיח.

May the offshoot of Your servant David soon sprout.

And we refer to Israel as:

ראשית צמיחת גאולתנו.

The first sprouting of our redemption.

Yechezkel is the prophet who taught us that we can survive in the exile without the Temple. He taught us that as long it was necessary, we could replace the Temple with a *mikdash me'at*, a smaller version of the

---

21   *Zechariah* 4:1–14.
22   *Yirmiyahu* 23:5.
23   *Yirmiyahu* 33:15.
24   *Zechariah* 3:8. See above, "*Lech Lecha*, (9) *Seudah Shelishis*," n. 39 and n. 40.

Temple, which would be our shuls and study halls.[25] We have seen these first sproutings, and we are encouraged by Yechezkel's words that the strife that encompassed the two kingdoms for much of *Sefer Melachim* will not exist in the future.

Yehudah and Yosef confront each other in the beginning of *parashas Vayigash* and eventually make their peace. The two kingdoms they created will do so as well.

— 4 —

Derashah

ושם נעשה לפניך את קרבנות חובותינו

There is phenomenal goodwill between Yosef and his brothers in *parashas Vayigash*. The sibling strife that permeates *Sefer Bereishis* is finally healed after the brothers' reunion. There is also goodwill between the Egyptian populace and Yosef's family. They have been received well by Pharaoh and are understandably treated with honors.

One has to wonder, then, why these two examples of goodwill are so short-lived. In *parashas Vayechi*, immediately upon Yaakov's death, the brothers express the fear that Yosef had not truly reconciled with them.[26] How could this be? Furthermore, we'll shortly read how the Egyptians quickly turned on us and forgot all that Yosef had done.[27] How is this possible?

In an attempt to answer these two questions, we should reflect on our own position in today's world. How is it that public opinion throughout the world is so one-sided against Israel? In many polls and opinion pages in our country and Europe—not to mention Islamic nations—the world largely sides against Israel. On so many issues, even as Israel goes out of her way to minimize human loss in any of her terrorist and

---

25 This designation is based on *Yechezkel* 11:16, "ואהי להם למקדש מעט בארצות אשר באו שם"—I will be for them a diminished sanctuary in the lands where they have gone." This verse is expounded to refer to the synagogue in *Megillah* 29a.

26 *Bereishis* 50:15.

27 *Shemos* 1:8.

military encounters, she is excoriated for the simple act of self-defense and protection of her citizens.

The answer may be the oldest rationale for Israel's public opinion problem—plain old anti-Semitism. No matter what Israel does, it will be accused by the world. Yet we must still look within to understand our predicaments, and perhaps then we may understand why the world judges us so unfavorably. This is because we do it to ourselves. Consider how secular Israelis speak of the settlers. Consider how *chilonim* and *chareidim* speak of one another. And the profound *chillul Hashem* inherent in the way the Neturei Karta portray all Zionists makes the blood boil.

Yosef and his brothers are not fully reconciled because Yosef doesn't appear to forgive his brothers, nor do they ask him for forgiveness. They may understand in retrospect why events played out the way they did, but they have not fully atoned, which is why we still reference the story on Yom Kippur.[28] The sale of Yosef still needs atonement, and the brothers subconsciously express as much through their fear in *parashas Vayechi*, that Yosef may have them killed after Yaakov's passing.[29]

The idyllic Egyptian relationship also was short-lived. It didn't take much for the Egyptians to forget the Israelites' contribution to their salvation. (This is a story that repeats itself again and again throughout history.) In the eyes of the average Egyptian, Yosef despoiled them, as he took full advantage of his information to work an economic miracle.

If the narratives of our patriarchs serve as markers for future generations, the Jew in the Diaspora must be ever vigilant in how he earns and spends his wealth. Recurring economic volatility should serve as a wake-up call to us about being productive. Earning great wealth can serve as a powerful mechanism for improving the quality of life across the societal board. Life expectancy in the US in the twentieth century rose dramatically precisely because of the infusion of wealth, which led to greater research and healthier living.[30] But we have seen this lead to

---

28 See *Meshech Chochmah*, *Vayikra* 16:30.

29 See *Bereishis*, 50:15–21.

30 Statistics based on records from Department of Commerce Bureau of the Census, Sam L. Rogers, Director (1900). See also Dianne Whitmore Schanzenbach, Ryan Nunn, Lauren Bauer, "The Changing Landscape of American Life Expectancy" (June 2016).

greed and grotesque overuse of resources, often causing profound collapses. In order to maintain the phenomenal goodwill with which we have been blessed in the contemporary Diaspora, we must start internally, by seeing each other in a good light, and by continuing to be the *kiddush Hashem* that is our mandate, improving the quality of life all around us.

If we as a people want to be judged favorably in the court of public opinion, we must start to deserve this in the eyes of God by judging one another favorably, as the following story indicates. The Talmud tells of a man who acted in a questionable manner, and because someone gave him the benefit of the doubt by judging his actions favorably,[31] the man blessed him that he should be judged favorably by God as well.[32] We may ask what it means for God to give us the benefit of doubt. Does God have any doubt? Perhaps the blessing was for God to inspire *others* to see this man's actions favorably. May we be worthy of a favorable judgment and outcome for all our difficulties, and while we may ask for help from Above, we must start the work here below.

— 5 —

Mussar Moments

To the world you may be only one person, but to one person, you can be the world.

Comment

Brotherhood has had its problems in *Sefer Bereishis*. Beginning with Kayin and Hevel through our own narratives, brothers cannot seem

---

31   This is known as "הוי דן את כל האדם לכף זכות" (*Avos* 1:6), which translates precisely as, "Judge the entire man favorably." It does not mean judge every man favorably. That would be "הוי דן את כל אדם לכף זכות," and not every person deserves to be given the benefit of the doubt. Rather, we are being told to judge the entire individual in our assessment of his actions. Since we can never really know the entirety of another person's essence (כל האדם), we are bidden to judge the person favorably by giving him the benefit of the doubt.

32   *Shabbos* 127b, "הדן חבירו לכף זכות דנין אותו לכף זכות."

to get along. In our story, if the ten brothers had behaved in typical fashion of *Sefer Bereishis*, Binyamin would have been left to his own devices for stealing the viceroy's cup. But one brother steps forward to alter the course of brotherhood in *Bereishis*.

The brothers could possibly have justified passively moving on from the incarceration of Binyamin, since the viceroy's cup was found in his sack. The brothers had been passively watching the years go by without atoning for the sale of Yosef. Passivity turns to activity in our *parashah*. Notice the proliferation of passive verbs in the first three chapters of *Megillas Esther*. The Jews had passively become loyal to Persian custom and norm, neglecting the task of rebuilding the land of Israel after the seventy-year exile. In the Purim story and our story, individuals are inspired into action and they change the course of our history.

If we do nothing wrong, we're probably doing nothing, and that's wrong.

— 6 —
Birth

"וַיִּגַּשׁ אֵלָיו יְהוּדָה"[33] describes Yehudah drawing near to Yosef to plead on Binyamin's behalf. These three words are midrashically connected to the final prophecy of the prophet Amos, which begins, "וְנִגַּשׁ חוֹרֵשׁ בַּקֹּצֵר—The plowman shall draw near to the reaper."[34] This is a blessing for such plenty that the plowman begins preparing for the beginning of the next planting before the reaper has even completed the current harvest.

In the fields, the plowman begins a process concluded by the reaper. Each reaper though, is in competition with the others for the choicest and most plentiful fruits. The plowman, in contrast, engages in no

---

33   *Bereishis* 44:18.
34   *Amos* 9:13.

competition with the other plowmen. They are all focused on exactly the same task. In our *parashah*, Yehudah draws near to Yosef, and in *Amos*, the plowman draws near to the reaper. Yosef is the reaper. His dreams denote competition. Yehudah is the plowman. He is good at being convincing. He is not as righteous as Yosef and struggles to attain what comes naturally to Yosef, but he plows on to ensure a worthwhile harvest.[35]

The great challenge of parenting is to inspire children to accomplishment and achievement and to gracefully view the success of others without jealousy or envy. All the efforts of the *choresh* are in vain if it does not lead to a *kotzer* and a harvest. In the end, it is the *choresh* and the *kotzer* together who set brotherhood on the right track in *Sefer Bereishis*.

—7—
B'nei Mitzvah

Immediately upon revealing himself to his brothers, Yosef says:

אני יוסף העוד אבי חי?

I am Yosef, is my father still alive? (Bereishis 45:3)

Abarbanel, in a series of questions on Yehudah's encounter with Yosef in the beginning of our *parashah*, includes the obvious problem with Yosef's question.[36] Yehudah's long plea mentioned his father over twenty times! In their earlier encounter, Yosef had asked about their father, "העודנו חי—Is he yet alive?" and they had answered in the affirmative.[37] Surely, as far as the brothers know, Yaakov is alive. What new information can this question possibly reveal? *Abarbanel* answers that Yosef felt it was possible that all this time the brothers had fabricated the information about their father to gain his mercies. In reality, Yosef feared, Yaakov may have already died, and his brothers had been hiding

---

35   See *Bereishis Rabbah* 93:5, *Yalkut Hamachiri*, *Amos* 9:13.
36   *Bereishis* 44:18.
37   See *Bereishis* 43:27.

this from him. Now that they know he is Yosef, he asks for them to reveal the truth without reservation. Some English translations render "העוד אבי חי—Is my father well?"[38] which assumes that he is indeed alive.

Chazal understand Yosef's question as a rebuke of his brothers. He was actually asking how Yaakov has lived all this time. Has the family strife subsided? Has their father gotten over his loss? Their reaction, according to the Midrash was:

אוי לנו מיום הדין אוי לנו מיום התוכחה.

Woe unto us from the day of judgment and from the day of rebuke. (Bereishis Rabbah 93:10)

Yosef was essentially telling the brothers to prepare a story to tell their father regarding what happened the day Yosef was sent to meet them, and that he would corroborate their story. Yosef realized that Yaakov must never learn about his sale, for such knowledge would turn him against his sons. This is part of Yosef's repentance as well, for his role in the favoritism he received in his youth.

B'nei mitzvah face a rite of passage. The passage is the beginning of a legacy one generation bequeaths to the next. We identify that passage as a time of mitzvah obligation because the performance of the mitzvos is what defines this child from this time on. This is how the previous generation assures continuity. Of course, *b'nei mitzvah* look to the future as new opportunities and experiences present themselves, but our tradition especially looks to the past at such a time. The past reminds *b'nei mitzvah* to always remember the days of old and consider the years of many generations. This begins Moshe's precious advice in his parting words to his people, "זכור ימות עולם בינו שנות דור ודור." He continues: "שאל אביך ויגדך זקניך ויאמרו לך—Ask your father and he will inform you; your elders and they will tell you."[39]

---

38 See New Jewish Publication Society rendition, *Bereishis* 45:3. The Sinai translation of the Torah renders, "Does my father yet live?" which may also be interpreted as a question of the quality of his life.

39 *Devarim* 32:7.

Entrusted in the hands of those who celebrate today's milestone, we are sure that we can always say, "עוד אבינו חי—Our father Yaakov is alive and well."[40]

— 8 —
Marriage

There are ten dreams in the entire *Tanach*, and eight of them are within a space of fourteen chapters in *Sefer Bereishis*. Yaakov dreams of angels[41] and sheep.[42] Yosef dreams about bundles of grain and celestial objects.[43] Pharaoh's imprisoned baker and butler dream about their service to their king.[44] Finally, Pharaoh dreams about thin stalks of grain and cows devouring their fat counterparts.[45] While these dreams are found in *Vayeitzei*, *Vayeishev*, and *Mikeitz*, the true fulfillment of all these messages comes after the family is reunited in *parashas Vayigash*.

We dream about what preoccupies our thoughts, our aspirations, and our deepest hopes and fears. They all find expression in our dreams. The most wonderful of dreamers are about to join their greatest aspirations. The grand dreams of a bride and groom before their wedding have much to derive from these fourteen chapters.

Yaakov's entire life was before him at the time of his first dream. He was on his way to Aram to find a wife and build a family. Yaakov knew that circumstance would present life with the proverbial "ups and downs," so he dreams of angels ascending and descending a ladder. In the ladder of life, may the bride and groom never ascend or descend alone, and may angels always accompany you on your journey of life together.

Remember also that even our patriarchs had to concern themselves with the material needs of everyday life. It would be wonderful for you

---

40   *Bereishis* 44:28.
41   *Bereishis* 28:12–15.
42   *Bereishis* 31:10–13.
43   *Bereishis* 37:7–9.
44   *Bereishis* 40:8–19.
45   *Bereishis* 41:1–7. The other two dreams are in the story of Gideon (*Shoftim* 7:13) and Nevuchadnetzar (*Daniel*, chap. 2). Other references to dreams in the Bible are actually prophecies like those of Zechariah (chaps. 1–5.)

to dream only about angels, but the practical elements of life sometimes make us dream about spotted and speckled sheep. Even as you soar into celestial spheres of dreams as Yosef did, it is important to remember that you first have to bundle grain for material support. This is known as, "תיקון הגוף קודם תיקון הנפש—We must preserve the body before we go about preserving the soul.[46] There will always be manifestations of successes and failures, because that's life. Let the work of your hands, the bread of your toil, be for each other, for your community, for God, and not for the birds. Let the wine you pour be as a libation before God's altar and may you be worthy to serve in His court; and if you do, don't forget Yosef's dreams, and never forget each other's dreams. Remember that big problems can be swallowed up and overcome with love and devotion. May you always face abundance and plenty, but if abundance is ravaged by famine or loss, you will always have each other so that you can say, "Without you, no matter what I have, I have nothing. With you, no matter what I lack, I have everything." Sweet dreams.

— 9 —
Seudah Shelishis
אתה אחד ושמך אחד

The three patriarchs lived to three different ages. Avraham lived to 175,[47] Yitzchak lived to 180,[48] and Yaakov lived to 147.[49] Chazal say that Avraham should have lived to 180 as well, but he died five years early so that he would be spared the ignominy of witnessing Eisav's descent to immorality.[50] Yaakov's passing is introduced with the words, "ויקרבו ימי ישראל למות—And the time approached for Israel to die."[51] The Midrash

---

46   This saying is based on the *Rambam's* contention that physical pains and afflictions will hamper our efforts to attain full spiritual growth. See *Hilchos De'os*, chap. 4:1 This particular saying is attributed to Rebbe Nachman of Breslov.

47   *Bereishis* 25:7.

48   *Bereishis* 35:28.

49   *Bereishis* 47:28.

50   See *Bereishis Rabbah* 63:12, and *Rashi, Bereishis* 25:30, ד"ה מן האדם האדם. See also *Bava Basra* 16b.

51   *Bereishis* 47:29.

teaches that this formula foretells the fact that the person so described will not live as long as his father.[52] A similar formula appears regarding Moshe[53] and David Hamelech.[54] The two of them also did not approach their father's ages.[55] The Midrash teaches that Yaakov was also meant to live to 180, but that he lost thirty-three years because of his conversation with Pharaoh about his age.[56] Yaakov complained bitterly that he had aged much more quickly than his elders, and is taken to task by Chazal for this ungracious gesture. After all, even with all his troubles, he survived intact his encounters with Lavan and Eisav, Dinah and Yosef were returned to him, and all his children followed in his path. Yaakov lost one year for each word in the two verses of his conversation with Pharaoh.[57] These two verses begin with Pharaoh's question, and Yaakov loses years for those words as well because his very comportment bespoke an existence hardened by tragedy, misfortune, and hardship. The very fact that Pharaoh was moved to ask Yaakov his age is held against Yaakov in this reckoning of thirty-three words.

The *Baal Haturim* adds that Yaakov lost thirty-three years because he erred in so quickly pronouncing death, "לא יחיה," upon the one who stole Lavan's idols, without realizing that Rachel had taken them.[58] "לא יחיה" means "shall not live", but is reframed by *Baal Haturim* to refer to a negation of the *gematria* of יחיה, which is thirty-three.[59] If not for these considerations, Yaakov would have lived to 180 like his father Yitzchak.[60] These sources teach us not only to feel thankful for God's gifts and generous mercies, but also to present ourselves with an

---

52 *Bereishis Rabbah* 96:4.

53 *Devarim* 31:14.

54 *Melachim I* 2:1.

55 Moshe lived to 120 and Amram lived to 137. David lived to 70 and Yishai lived to 80 or more. See *Bereishis Rabbah* 96:4.

56 See M. Kasher's *Torah Sheleimah*, *Bereishis* 47:8, n. כג, for a series of sources on Yaakov losing thirty-three years. See *Daas Zekeinim*, *Hadar Zekeinim*, and *Chizkuni*, *Bereishis* 47:8.

57 *Bereishis* 47:8–9.

58 *Bereishis* 31:30–32.

59 *Baal Haturim*, *Bereishis* 47:28, ד"ה שבע שנים וארבעים ומאת שנה.

60 *Yerushalmi*, *Shabbos* 16:1 and *Midrash Tehillim* 22, add an additional twist to Yaakov's 147 years in a connection to the chapters of *Tehillim*. See the introduction to this book, n. 7, in this regard.

air of cheerful gratitude for all we have. An attitude of gratitude will determine our altitude even more than our aptitude.

— 10 —
Word of the Parashah

רק אדמת הכהנים לא קנה—Only the land of **the priests,**
he did not take over
Bereishis 47:22

The word כהן has four different meanings in the Torah, and *Targum Onkelos* has a distinct translation for each one. The most common usage of the word is reserved for Aharon and his descendants. They are the ministers before God and serve the religious needs of their people. The word appears as a verb, for Aharon and his sons were chosen, "לכהנו—to minister," before God.[61] According to Rabbi Shimshon Raphael Hirsch,[62] the word כהן is related to the roots כנן "to direct"; כנה, a special name; or כון, which means "correct," as in נכון, "prepared" as in מוכן, or "well-founded," as in מכון לשבתך. When כהן refers to Aharon or his sons, the *Targum* is כהנא, a direct translation.

Originally this service was the province of the בכורים, the "firstborn," but Moshe rejected the firstborn service after the worship of the golden calf and sanctified the tribe of Levi, who answered his call of "מי לה׳ אלי—Who is on God's side, come to me."[63]

Accordingly, the כהנים who offer sacrifices before this at Har Sinai,[64] are actually firstborn males, as our Sages indicate.[65] *Onkelos* renders this word with an elaboration: "כהניא דקריבין לשמשא." The word לשמשא is consistent with *Targum*'s rendition of the description of Malki-Tzedek,

---

61   *Shemos* 28:1.

62   Matityahu Clark, *Etymological Dictionary of Biblical Hebrew: Based on the Commentaries of Samson Raphael Hirsch*, p. 116.

63   *Shemos* 32:26–29. The Torah makes this point as well in *Bamidbar* 3:12–13, "ואני הנה לקחתי את הלוים מתוך בני ישראל." See also *Bamidbar* 8:16, "כי נתנים נתנים המה לי מתוך בני ישראל תחת כל בכור פטר רחם." *Devarim* 10:8 also makes this point: "בעת ההיא הבדיל ה׳ את שבט הלוי לשאת את ארון ברית ה׳ לעמד לפני ה׳ לשרתו ולברך בשמו עד היום הזה."

64   *Shemos* 19:22.

65   *Zevachim* 115b and *Rashi, Shemos* 19:22, ד״ה וגם הכהנים.

who is called "כהן לא-ל עליון—a priest of God Most High."[66] This is the second rendition of כהן as שמש, an attendant to God's service.[67]

The third rendition of כהן is reserved for two specific Torah characters, the father-in-law of Yosef, "כהן און,"[68] and the father-in-law of Moshe, "כהן מדין."[69] The Torah does not avoid referring to these men as priests of foreign nations, but the *Targum* refrains from referring to them in the terms of their service. כהן in these two instances is rendered רבא דאון and רבא דמדין. They serve as leaders, not in any religious capacity. This is consistent with the inclusion of David's sons as Kohanim in a list of political leaders in Israel.[70] This reference to Kohanim is rendered רברבין by *Targum Yonasan*, similar to כהן און and כהן מדין in *Targum Onkelos*. Surely David's sons from the tribe of Yehudah could not be Kohanim.[71]

The fourth rendition is in our *parashah*, and it refers to the land of the Egyptian כהנים that Yosef did not purchase.[72] *Onkelos* renders this word as כומריא, which is the word that *Targum Yonasan* reserved in many cases in *Neviim* for idolatrous priests,[73] and is the modern Hebrew word for a gentile priest.

The כהן at the end of *Sefer Shoftim* is not a descendant of Aharon but is also not an idolatrous priest.[74] *Targum* renders this reference to כהן as כהין,[75] the only time this root appears in *Targum* for someone who is not a descendant of Aharon. Perhaps this is because his role was that

---

66   *Bereishis* 14:18.
67   When the root of כהן is used as a verb, *Targum* will use this word, as in *Shemos* 28:1 where "לכהנו לי" is translated as "לשמשא קדמי."
68   *Bereishis* 41:45,50.
69   *Shemos* 2:16, 3:1, 18:1.
70   *Shmuel II* 8:18.
71   Neither the Biblical text nor any Rabbinic source finds fault with David appointing his sons as Kohanim because they did not act as Kohanim, but as leaders. This is in contrast to Uzziyahu, king of Yehudah, who defiantly offered incense in the Temple, and he is roundly condemned by the text of *Divrei Hayamim II* 26:16–20.
72   *Bereishis* 47:22.
73   See *Shmuel I* 5:5, "כהני דגון"; *Sefer Melachim* has numerous references to כהן הבעל, כהני במות, and כהנים לבמות. These are all rendered כומרים like the כהנים in Egypt.
74   See *Shoftim* 17:8–12.
75   *Shoftim* 17:10.

of a teacher.[76] Another person who might have been rendered a כומר by *Targum* is Amatziah the Kohen, who warns Amos to stop predicting the end of the Northern Kingdom.[77] Amatziah was the Kohen of a rogue shrine where sacrifices were offered outside the precincts of the Temple in Jerusalem, in defiance of Torah law.[78] He is referred to by *Targum* as "רבא דבית אל,"[79] putting him in league with כהן און and כהן מדין. He was not a son of Aharon, but he was also not idolatrous.

Finally, there is one last rendition of כהנים as כהניא, even though the reference encompasses a group well beyond the sons of Aharon. It refers to the entire people of Israel as "ממלכת כהנים—a kingdom of Priests, וגוי קדוש—and a holy nation."[80] *Targum* renders כהנים here as if we *all* are ministers in the mold of the descendants of Aharon, כהניא. This means that what Aharon's descendants are to the rest of their people, the Israelite nation is to the rest of the world. That is, that our mission is to spread the light of God in pure and clear speech for the nations to understand, a "שפה ברורה," in the words of Tzefaniah, which can be accepted by all so that they all will call upon the name of the Lord to serve him with consent, not coercion.[81] Our mission, as the verse teaches, was to minister to the religious sensitivities of a pagan world and inspire them to stream to Jerusalem to learn of God's ways and to walk in His paths.[82] This would lead to world peace as "nations shall beat their swords into plowshares and their spears into pruning hooks. Nation shall not lift up sword against nation neither shall they learn war anymore."[83] This is precisely the role of the Kohen whose daily blessing to their people ends with the words, "וישם לך שלום—And he shall grant you peace."[84]

---

76   See *Metzudos David*, *Shoftim* 17:10, ד"ה לאבד.
77   See *Amos* 7:10–13.
78   *Devarim* 12:26–27
79   *Amos* 7:10.
80   *Shemos* 19:6.
81   *Tzefaniah* 3:9, See *Berachos* 57b on this prophecy.
82   *Yeshayahu* 2:1–3; *Michah* 4:1–2.
83   *Yeshayahu* 2:4; *Michah* 4:3.
84   *Bamidbar* 6:26.

Parashas Vayechi

—1—
Friday Night
תכלית מעשה שמים וארץ

Yaakov blessed five of his sons using imagery that reflects the nature of an animal. Yehudah is a lion,[1] Yissachar is a donkey,[2] Dan is a snake,[3] Naftali is a gazelle,[4] and Binyamin is a wolf.[5] When Yaakov called his sons together for these blessings, he told them he was rendering messages for them that would occur "באחרית הימים,"[6] terminology used in *Tanach* to denote Messianic times.[7]

The image of Dan as a snake connects to events of the future through the Messianic age. The *Targumim* and *Rashi* connect Dan's snake to Shimshon, who could, like a snake, take down a horse and its rider.[8] Just after Yaakov blessed Dan, he begged God for salvation and said,

---

1   *Bereishis* 49:9.
2   *Bereishis* 49:14.
3   *Bereishis* 49:17.
4   *Bereishis* 49:21.
5   *Bereishis* 49:27.
6   *Bereishis* 49:1.
7   See *Yeshayahu* 2:2, *Michah* 4:1, *Yechezkel* 38:16, *Daniel* 10:14.
8   See *Targum Onkelos*, *Targum Yonasan*, and *Rashi* to *Bereishis* 49:17, ד"ה הנושך עקבי סוס.

"לִישׁוּעָתְךָ קִוִּיתִי ה׳."[9] *Rashi* says that Yaakov interrupted the blessings this way out of disappointment when prophetically seeing Shimshon's failure.

Chazal say that the Messianic line flows from Yehudah through Nachshon because of the nature of the root of his name, *nachash*, meaning "snake."[10] Mashiach's mission is to turn the world to the innocence of Gan Eden before the sin, caused by the snake.[11] This is why Yeshayahu's vision of the Messianic world describes a child playing with snakes.[12] God punished the snake with the enmity of the human,[13] and Yeshayahu's vision is to atone for the sin of Gan Eden. The snake, which represents the *yetzer hara*, "evil inclination," will be conquered and it will be like child's play to resist its temptations.[14] This connection between the snake and the Messianic age is also manifest in the common *gematria* of מׁשיח and נחׁש, 358.

We normally consider the lion of Yehudah to represent the Messianic figure. After all, Mashiach is descended from Yehudah. Yet the snake of Dan plays a role as well because of a certain aspect of Shimshon's leadership. Although he fought alone and never rallied troops in fighting the Philistines, Shimshon's greatest quality was his love of his people. He never wavered from supporting them while avenging the Philistine's tyranny. When Yaakov saw Shimshon in his vision, he was enthused to describe his exploits, but when he saw his failings, he was moved to ask for salvation. The salvation begins with the *ahavas Yisrael*, the love of his people that Shimshon displayed.

---

9   *Bereishis* 49:18.

10   See *Bamidbar Rabbah* 11:11.

11   See *Ramban, Vayikra* 26:6, ד"ה והשבתי חיה רעה מן הארץ.

12   *Yeshayahu* 11:8. See also *Radak, Yeshayahu* 11:8.

13   *Bereishis* 3:15.

14   Chazal explain Zechariah's prophecy of that which will be amazing in the eyes of God (8:6), as referring to our defeat of the *yetzer hara*. See *Sukkah* 52a.

—2—
Introduction to the Torah
ישמח משה במתנת חלקו

Parashas Vayechi begins in a unique fashion. While every weekly Torah reading begins a new paragraph in the *Sefer Torah*, *parashas Vayechi* continues on the same line that ends the previous *parashah*.[15] Chazal say this is an indication of certain elements that were being concluded. The patriarchal era was drawing to a close, the exile was just beginning, and Yaakov's prophetic visions were shutting down.[16] All of this is hinted through the closed beginning of *Vayechi*.

The Torah text is not written in paragraph form. There are open spaces in most columns on many lines. *Shiras Ha'yam*[17] and *parashas Haazinu*[18] are written with continual spacing between words and lines, and they are all set by ancient tradition.

The Chafetz Chaim posits that these spacings afforded Moshe the opportunity to fully absorb the message he was receiving and to contemplate how to best deliver it. This is a sign of humility on Moshe's part to help him fully intellectually and emotionally digest his message. Contrast this with the columns that comprise the story and prophecies of Bilaam,[19] and we catch a glimpse of Bilaam's arrogance. There is no spacing whatsoever in the columns of *parashas Balak*, because Bilaam feels no need for such contemplation. Since speaking well of the Israelites is not something Bilaam wanted to do, he does not dwell on his prophecies.

The new paragraphs of the Torah, divided by open lines (*parashah pesuchah*) or closed lines (*parashah setumah*), originally delineated 156

---

15   See the introduction to this book on different terminologies used for the weekly Torah portion, and the different configurations of Torah paragraphs. See also *Shulchan Aruch, Yoreh Deah* 275:2 and *Rambam, Hilchos Sefer Torah* 8:1–2.

16   *Bereishis Rabbah* 96:1. See also *Rashi, Bereishis* 49:1.

17   *Shemos*, chap. 15.

18   *Devarim*, chap. 32.

19   *Bamidbar*, chaps. 22–24.

Torah readings divided into a three-year cycle.[20] *Rambam* indicates that the custom of reading the Torah this way was no longer widespread in his day (the twelfth century).[21] This was originally the custom of Torah reading in Israel, while in Bavel, the Torah was completed annually.[22]

It stands to reason then, that the average Torah reading in Israel was about a third of the length of the average Torah reading in Bavel. However, this is not the case toward the end of *Sefer Bereishis*. The last twenty columns of *Sefer Bereishis* have very few *parashah* breaks because the story line is so compelling, and the normally shorter weekly Torah portions could not be broken down going all the way back to *parashas Vayeitzei*. *Vayechi* fits in with this scheme and continues the trend of columns without *parashiyos*, until the blessings of Yaakov break them up again. Yaakov's lost prophecy or the storyline of the last *parashiyos* of *Bereishis* are two very different explanations for the breaks in the Torah columns, and of course, however we understand this phenomenon, the unique nature of *Vayechi* draws *Bereishis* and a generation to a close.

Of all *parashiyos*, it is *Vayechi* that bears this unique phenomenon as we stand on the threshold of exile. If the open paragraphs represent Moshe's prophetic input into the Torah, then the closed beginning of *Vayechi* represents an end to Divine inspiration until God appears to Moshe in the beginning of *Sefer Shemos*.

— 3 —
Introduction to the Haftarah

The death of an ancestor—a patriarch or a matriarch—is the main focus of two Torah portions in *Sefer Bereishis*: *Chayei Sarah* and *Vayechi*. Each *parashah* has the root word for "life" in its title "*chai*," and each of their haftaros focuses on the transition of kingship from King David to

---

20   See *Encyclopedia Judaica*, 1st ed., vol. 15, pp. 1386–89, "Triennial Cycle," for a full chart of these readings.

21   See *Hilchos Tefillah* 13:1.

22   See the beginning of this book's introduction for sources regarding these customs in the *Talmud Bavli* and *Yerushalmi*.

Shlomo in the beginning of *Sefer Melachim*.[23] David assures Shlomo that his success hinges upon his pursuit of the Torah and its mitzvos:

וּשְׁמַרְתָּ אֶת מִשְׁמֶרֶת ה׳ אֱלֹקֶיךָ לָלֶכֶת בִּדְרָכָיו לִשְׁמֹר חֻקֹּתָיו מִצְוֹתָיו
וּמִשְׁפָּטָיו וְעֵדְוֹתָיו כַּכָּתוּב בְּתוֹרַת מֹשֶׁה לְמַעַן תַּשְׂכִּיל אֵת כָּל אֲשֶׁר תַּעֲשֶׂה
וְאֵת כָּל אֲשֶׁר תִּפְנֶה שָׁם.

*Keep the charge of the Lord your God, walking in His ways, and
following in His laws, His commandments, His judgments, and
His testimonies, as recorded in the Torah of Moshe, that you
may prosper in all that you undertake and wherever you turn.
(Melachim I 2:3)*

The picture of David's final days in *Sefer Melachim* is told from a very different angle than the way it is described in *Divrei Hayamim*. Both angles can be understood by analyzing David's connection to the Temple in Jerusalem during his final days.

In *Sefer Melachim*, David's end is quite inglorious. In fact, he abdicates the throne to ensure that his son Shlomo, not Adoniyahu, would rule after him. He seems quite vindictive of his enemies in our haftarah,[24] and nothing whatsoever is said of his connection to the Temple. This is a far cry from what we read in *Divrei Hayamim* about David's final days. There, numerous chapters are dedicated to David's preparations of all the necessary raw materials for the building of the Temple, and his beautiful prayers in the aftermath of his collections comprise the beginning and ending of our daily *Pesukei D'zimrah* prayers.[25]

The two different angles can be understood by examining a crucial aspect of David's connection to the Temple, an aspect whose presentation, moreover, is crucially different in the earlier and later narratives. David's desire to build the Temple is rebuffed. Many people know why

---

23   Chapter 1 is the haftarah of *Chayei Sarah*, and chapter 2, where David advises Shlomo with his final words, parallels Yaakov's final words to his sons.

24   *Melachim II* 5: 8–9.

25   Ashkenazic custom immediately follows *Baruch She'amar* with David's opening prayer, *Divrei Hayamim I* 16:8–36, and draws to a close with David's concluding prayer in ibid., 29:10–13.

this is so, but the reason does not actually appear when he is rejected.[26] He is simply told it is not his destiny to build the Temple, and that his son will build it.[27] The reason most people know is recorded in *Divrei Hayamim*: David shed much blood, and the Temple must be built by a man of peace, a man whose very name means peace, and that would be Shlomo.[28]

The narratives of David's final days in *Shmuel II* and *Melachim* are written to record the conclusion of his sin with Batsheva, and thus present the story in inglorious terms. *Divrei Hayamim*, however, is told from a different angle and captures the true essence of David's final days.[29] After the sin of Batsheva, perhaps David thought he had ruined his chances so thoroughly that not even his son could merit to build the Temple. David's penance and *teshuvah* ensured that not only would *his* son do so, but it would specifically be Batsheva's son, which was a true sign of his forgiveness.[30]

Midrash Tehillim underscores the fact that David's long life delayed the Temple's building.[31] In fact, David lived longer than any other king of Yehudah or the ten tribes. Some people even expressed hopes of David's speedy demise to expedite the Temple's construction. Chazal express a beautiful point to contrast the Temple service with David's pursuit of Torah:

טוב לי יום אחד שאתה עוסק בתורה מאלף עולות שעתיד שלמה בנך להקריב לפני.

I prefer a single day in which you engage in the study of Torah over a thousand burnt offerings that your son Shlomo is destined to offer before me. (Shabbos 30a)

---

26 *Shmuel II*, chap. 7; *Divrei Hayamim I*, chap. 17.

27 *Shmuel II* 7:12–13; *Divrei Hayamim I* 17:11-12.

28 See *Divrei Hayamim I* 22:8, 28:4.

29 *Divrei Hayamim* omits the story of Batsheva altogether. Perhaps this is the fulfillment of David's request (*Sanhedrin* 107a) to remove the story from *Tanach*. God did not remove it from *Sefer Shmuel*, but it was removed from *Divrei Hayamim*.

30 This seems to be the overall message of a series of Aggados regarding King David's last days in *Shabbos* 30a, as well as *Midrash Tehillim* 122, which are both referenced here.

31 *Midrash Tehillim*, chap. 122.

David's life was extended precisely because the ideals of Torah and Torah study are more pleasing to God than the Temple service itself, and the Gemara and Midrash express this preference in the words of God himself![32] Just as Yaakov prepares a path for his descendants by predicting their future in his blessings, so too, David initiates a path for the Temple's surest success—to ensure that Torah is upheld and practiced throughout the land. God's holy presence is attracted to moral righteousness just as it is attracted to the Temple.

— 4 —

Derashah

ושם נעשה לפניך את קרבנות חובותינו

There is a lot of water under the bridge that connects the first brothers in *Sefer Bereishis*, Kayin and Hevel, with the last brothers mentioned in *Sefer Bereishis*, Ephraim and Menasheh. In between, the microcosm of family units in each generation of Torah narratives grows to become a nation, and that in itself is a bridge to the next book of the Torah, *Sefer Shemos*. The picture of brotherhood in *Sefer Bereishis* is not pretty, but it does evolve after the fratricide of the first story. The Torah reader has no information about the relationship between Noach's sons or between Avraham and his brothers. Yitzchak and Yishmael part ways without incident, while Yaakov and Eisav break new ground in the Torah as the first siblings in the Torah text who actually carry a dialogue. They part amicably, but while the brotherly relationship seems to evolve for the better for now, it will take a significant step back in the next generation, before Yaakov's children reconcile without parting, as the bridge between family and nation.

Perhaps, we can explain this first step back as a function of the fact that while Sarah protected her son Yitzchak, and Rivkah protected her son Yaakov, there was no one to protect Yosef, or to advise him on

---

32 The Gemara bases this Divine statement on *Tehillim* 84:11: "Better one day in your courts [the study halls of David] than a thousand offerings [to be brought in the Temple, built after David's passing]."

how to mitigate the poisonous feelings he was bringing upon himself. If brotherhood suffers a setback in the Yosef saga, his own children help to bolster it toward the end of *Bereishis*. At least in earlier generations, the Torah gives reasons for the favoritism of the younger sibling. His offering is better,[33] he is the son of the favored wife,[34] or a Heavenly oracle chooses him.[35] But in the case of Ephraim and Menasheh, no reason at all is given for the favoritism of the younger sibling in terms of what has already happened. Yaakov's favoritism of Ephraim over his older brother is a function of what *will* happen.[36] We might forgive Menasheh for saying what Kayin, Yishmael, Eisav, and Yosef's brothers probably all said at some point: "That's not fair."

In fact, someone did say that, but not Menasheh. His father, Yosef, did. Yosef insisted that his father correct the mistake of favoring the younger over the older, but Yaakov held firm. "ידעתי בני ידעתי," said Yaakov.[37]

Yaakov understands Yosef's concerns. Surely Yosef wants to avoid the ill will between brothers that this unexplained favoritism may engender. Yaakov says ידעתי twice because his actions in favoring Ephraim over Menasheh stem from two points. What he does is not only borne out by prophecy of what will become of Yosef's two sons, but it will also help heal the rifts between brothers until now in *Sefer Bereishis*. Ephraim completes the trend of younger siblings becoming greater than their older brothers, and Yosef's vocal objection—in light of the silence of Menasheh—implies that the older brother has made his peace with what looked like an arbitrary decision. In a sense, Menasheh saves *Sefer Bereishis* by his acceptance of Ephraim's status. This sets the stage for the next book, in which our salvation comes at the hands of a partnership between brothers. Once again, the younger brother reaches higher heights, and this time the older brother not only accepts that but is

---

33   *Bereishis* 4:3–5.
34   *Bereishis* 21:10–12.
35   *Bereishis* 25:23.
36   *Bereishis* 48:16–19.
37   *Bereishis* 48:19.

happy for his younger sibling.[38] For Moshe's part, his apprehension at the mission with which he is charged falls away as soon as God assures him of Aharon's joy. This demonstrates a reciprocal love between Moshe and Aharon that would enable them to become redeemers, teachers, and religious and spiritual leaders of their people.

It took many generations, but brotherhood, by the beginning of *Sefer Shemos*, is characterized by consideration, sensitivity, cooperation, and respect. It comes just in time for our redemption, and the message for us is that redemption cannot come without it.

— 5 —
Mussar Moments

When the caterpillar thinks the world is over it becomes a butterfly.

Comment

הָאָבוֹת הֵן הֵן הַמֶּרְכָּבָה.

The patriarchs were God's conduit to the world. (Bereishis Rabbah 47:8)

A stage of our history is about to end. The patriarchal era is drawing to a close. Chazal refer to Avraham, Yitzchak, and Yaakov as God's "מרכבה," a reference to the mystical chariot of *Sefer Yechezkel*.[39]

The Midrash continues to speak of the patriarchs as having the ability to quite literally harness the Heavenly Divine presence for the world below. The Midrash offers evidence of this from three verses:

---

38 *Shemos* 4:14.

39 *Yechezkel*, chap. 1. This is the haftarah of the first day of Shavuos and connects to the incredibly spiritual experience the entire nation experienced, in which for that moment, they shared the מרכבה-relationship with God that Avraham, Yitzchak, and Yaakov had. Their mission as a people would become the same as the patriarchs: to be a conduit for God's presence in the physical realms of the earth.

1. "וייעל אלקים מעל אברהם"—God rose up from Avraham" (*Bereishis* 17:22).

2. "והנה ה' נצב עליו"—And behold God stood above it"[40] (*Bereishis* 28:13).

3. "וייעל מעליו אלקים"—And God rose up from him [Yaakov]" (*Bereishis* 35:13).

All three verses indicate that God was "upon" Avraham and Yaakov, as they served as vehicles for the Divine presence. The first and third verse are the narratives in which Avraham's and Yaakov's names were changed. The second verse refers to Yaakov, but not to Yitzchak. Perhaps we can explain this as a function of the fact that Yaakov would need extra impetus to achieve his mission of being a מרכבה. He struggled with life's vicissitudes to a much greater degree than his grandfather Avraham and his father Yitzchak. This extra impetus may be the origin of the explanation of Yaakov's face being on the side of God's Heavenly throne,[41] the source of which emanates from the second verse. As for the absence of Yitzchak in this reference, his name was not changed by God because he was originally named by God Himself—at the very time that God changed Avraham's name in the first verse above.[42] God was not part of Avraham's entire life,[43] and God doesn't appear to Yaakov during the entire time of Yosef's absence.[44] On the other hand, Yitzchak's entire existence harnessed the Divine. This might explain why, of the three verses above, none refer directly to him. God was always with Yitzchak.

With the passing of Yaakov, we would need new ways to harness the Divine, and the next book of the Torah describes how this will be done. It took many years of exile and servitude for the next step

---

40   In the plain meaning of this verse, the "עליו," above which God stands, is the masculine noun סולם, the "ladder." According to this *d'rash*, עליו refers to Yaakov.

41   *Targum Yonasan, Bereishis* 28:12, which refers to Yaakov as "גברא חסידא דאיקונין דידיה בכורסי דיקרא—a righteous man whose image is on God's majestic throne."

42   *Bereishis* 17:19–21. *Yerushalmi, Berachos* 1:6, refers to this difference regarding the names of the Avos.

43   See "*Lech Lecha,* (4) *Derashah*" for different opinions of the age at which Avraham found God.

44   See "*Vayigash,* (9) *Seudah Shelishis.*"

in our relationship with God, but we did so by maintaining our distinctive names, language, and dress,[45] so that when the time would come, we would be ready—this time, as a people—to be a מרכבה for God's presence.

Diamonds are just chunks of coal that stuck to their jobs.

— 6 —
Birth

There are a number of customs associated with birth and children that emerge from *parashas Vayechi*. The custom of naming a child after a family member is based on Yaakov's charge to Yosef:

המלאך הגואל אותי מכל רע יברך את הנערים ויקרא בהם שמי ושם אבותי אברהם ויצחק.

The angel who has redeemed me from all harm—bless the lads. In them may my name be recalled, and the names of my fathers, Avraham and Yitzchak. (Bereishis 48:16)

Yaakov knew how essential it was that his descendants continue to name their children as Hebrews, not as Egyptians. This charge was especially given to Yosef because he was given an Egyptian name,[46] but the Torah assures us that it was Yosef who remained in Egypt all along,[47] and that he had not changed.

Our Sages attribute the adherence to this charge as one of the reasons we merited redemption ahead of its time. We maintained our distinctive dress, our language, and our names,[48] and thus we did not fully sink into Egyptian culture and norms over the years we spent there.

---

45 *Vayikra Rabbah* 32:5. See also *Pesikta Zutrasa, Shemos* 6:6.

46 *Tzafnas Pane'ach, Bereishis* 41:45.

47 See *Shemos* 1:5, with *Rashi* from *Sifri, Haazinu* 357, and *Shemos Rabbah* 1:7.

48 See *Vayikra Rabbah* 32:5. See *Targum Yonasan, Amos* 6:1, where the words "נקובי ראשית הגוים"

Ashkenazic and Sephardic custom differ as to the fulfillment of Yaakov's words. Sephardim consider it honorable to name a child after a living relative, as Yaakov was alive when he charged Yosef, "ויקרא בהם שמי—to call children by my name." Ashkenazim bristle at this prospect and consider that just as Avraham and Yitzchak were no longer alive, the name Yaakov was not to be given until he was no longer alive, as well.[49]

A second custom emerging from our *parashah* is the custom of giving someone the honor of holding the baby boy during his *bris*. The position of *sandek*, as it is called, is usually assigned to the grandfather or great-grandfather or to an honorable rabbi or teacher who serves as a mentor and guide for the family. It is worthwhile for every child to grow up knowing who held him during his *bris*, and to hopefully follow in his path. The origin of the word *sandek* is unclear,[50] but the source of the custom points to the end of *parashas Vayechi* where Yosef saw three generations of descendants. There we read:

גם בני מכיר בן מנשה יֻלדו על ברכי יוסף.

The children of Machir son of Menasheh were likewise born upon the knees of Yosef. (Bereishis 50:23)[51]

Targum Yonasan translates "ברכי יוסף" as "גזירנון יוסף," which is a reference to Yosef holding his great-grandson during his *bris milah*. This demonstrates that the generations following Yosef continued to look to him for guidance and inspirations, and that like Yosef, they remained as they always were.

---

are translated "מקימין שום שום בניהון כשום בני עממיא." Amos berates the people for assigning gentile names to their children. See a halachic treatment of this in *Igros Moshe, Orach Chaim*, vol. 4, *siman* 66. See also *Tosafos, Gittin* 34b, ד"ה והוא.

49   See *Sefer Chassidim, siman* 460 and responsa of *Chasan Sofer, siman* 84. A full comprehensive treatment of this issue can be found in Rav Ovadia Yosef's responsa, *Yabia Omer, Yoreh Deah*, vol. 5, *siman* 21.

50   Some consider its origin in Greek and some in Aramaic.

51   *Midrash Tehillim* 35:10 on the verse "כל עצמותי תאמרנה ה' מי כמוך"—All my bones shall say, "Lord who is like you?" After listing a series of body parts that are involved in mitzvos, the Midrash refers to the thighs (extended from the knees), which hold the baby during a *bris*. See *Rama, Yoreh Deah* 265:11, and *Biur HaGra* ibid., 44–45.

This leads to a third source in *parashas Vayechi* related to children, and perhaps the most famous: boys are blessed just before Kiddush on Friday night with a verse from our *parashah*:

ישימך אלקים כאפרים וכמנשה.

May God make you like Ephraim and Menasheh. (Bereishis 48:20)

Girls receive a blessing that stems from a verse that references our matriarchs Rachel and Leah,[52] and adds the previous two matriarchs as well:

ישימך אלקים כשרה רבקה רחל ולאה.

May God make you like Sarah, Rivkah, Rachel, and Leah.

Menasheh and Ephraim represent our ability to maintain our religious and spiritual connections to our traditions even in the exile. They are also the first brothers in *Sefer Bereishis* who do not experience the conflict of sibling rivalry, so rampant in previous generations. Menasheh is actually tested in this regard when Yaakov sidesteps him for his younger brother, and while the text records Yosef's displeasure with this arrangement, Menasheh's silence is a sign of his acceptance of his place in the family. This camaraderie on the part of the brothers is the sentiment of the blessing we confer just as Shabbos begins—to have peace and tranquility in the home, the way *Sefer Bereishis* ends.

The blessing that girls receive expresses the hope that they approach life's challenges with the same steadfast courage of conviction demonstrated by Sarah, Rivkah, Rachel, and Leah. They dealt with infertility, famines, internal struggles, and rootlessness without losing faith in the missions of their families, and they helped forge the destiny of our people.

---

52   *Rus* 4:11.

—7—
B'nei Mitzvah

Sefer Bereishis ends with the blessings of the sons of Yaakov. Some commentaries object to the reference of Yaakov's last words as blessings. *Chizkuni*[53] is famous for referring to these last statements of Yaakov as predictions, rather than blessings.[54] As it turned out, each son met the expectation placed upon him when he became a tribe in Israel. This is especially instructive for Shimon and Levi. They received the same prediction together, but it manifested itself in their destiny in profoundly different ways.

The brothers got the last word when explaining why they killed the people of Shechem,[55] but Yaakov gets the last word at his deathbed. He says, "I will divide them in Yaakov and scatter them in Israel."[56]

Resigned to such a destiny, Shimon sunk to the lowest level of all the tribes. Their numbers in *Sefer Bamidbar* are less than half of most other tribes.[57] They are not blessed by Moshe at all in his parting words to his people,[58] and they were indeed scattered in Israel. When the other tribes received their land, the verse indicates that the tribe of Shimon assimilated within the borders of Yehudah, receiving no identifiably marked area of their own.[59] Levi, on the other hand, turned their scattering into a blessing. Their mission was to live among all the tribes and serve as the religious guides and teachers of their brethren.[60]

No one should feel resigned to certain failure regardless of circumstance. The collective tribe of Levi, in the exercise of their own free will to succeed, turned their destiny to their betterment and to the advantage of all their brethren—and Shimon could have done the same.

---

53   *Chizkuni* is the name of the Torah commentary of Rav Chizkiya ben Manoach (b. 1240).

54   *Chizkuni, Bereishis* 49:1, ד"ה אשר יקרא אתכם.

55   See *Bereishis* 34:31.

56   *Bereishis* 49:7.

57   See *Bamidbar* 26:14 and the rest of the chapter.

58   *Devarim*, chap. 33.

59   *Yehoshua* 19:1.

60   See *Yehoshua*, chap. 21.

A teacher once received her attendance lists with a number next to each name. She saw numbers like 143, 176, 162, 138, 159, 181, and 197! *This is amazing*, she thought. *The IQs of my students are off the charts*. She planned to challenge them with high-level cognitive thinking and projects that would jar their considerably high intelligence. The class rose to the occasion and excelled well beyond expectation. It wasn't until early spring that the teacher discovered that those numbers were not the students' IQ numbers, but their locker numbers. It didn't matter. They had met the expectations placed before them. Obviously, expectations must be measured and realistic to guarantee success. At the same time, Shimon and Levi's destiny shows that nothing in the realm of expectation is etched in stone. Not even in Yaakov's parting words to his children. His predictions—as well as Biblical prophecies—can be manifest in multiple ways, depending on the exercise of our free will to act with morality and *yiras Shamayim*.

B'nei mitzvah begin to strike their own imprint on their surroundings. Expectations are always high in our community and opportunity knocks loudly and often. The Kotzker Rebbe gives a *chassidish* perspective on Shimon and Levi's lot. Yaakov felt that although Shimon and Levi were misguided, they—for the first time in *Sefer Bereishis*—exerted extraordinary efforts for a sibling. Yaakov wanted to spread at least this aspect of their behavior among his other sons by scattering the fervor of Shimon and Levi among them. May our *b'nei mitzvah* exercise their budding determination to reach their potential.

— 8 —
Marriage

The Midrash relates that on his return to Egypt, Yosef stopped at the pit into which he was thrown,[61] to recite the blessing[62] upon seeing the place where he miraculously survived a life-threatening situation.[63] The Midrash continues that the brothers mistakenly interpreted

---

61   *Bereishis Rabbah* 100:8.
62   See also *Tanchuma, Vayechi* 17.
63   *Mishnah Berachos* 9:1.

Yosef's actions as a sign that he still bore a grudge for what they had done to him.

The reason the brothers thought Yosef still harbored a grudge was that they never saw him recite such a blessing at any one of the other numerous places where miracles had likely been wrought for him. When Yosef recited this *berachah* only at the pit, they drew their erroneous conclusion. In reality, the reason Yosef never recognized so many other miraculous events in his life with a *berachah* was because that *berachah* is only said upon a miracle that defies nature.[64] All the other miracles were certainly consequential, but they occurred along the lines of a natural order. That Yosef survived his ordeal in the pit, surrounded by snakes and scorpions,[65] was nothing short of miraculous and deserved a *berachah*, and his gratitude to God.

Our Sages consider a successful match to be in the framework of the miraculous.[66] It is a miracle in the form of a natural order, so it doesn't warrant a daily blessing. But it does warrant daily gratitude. Our daily *Amidah* includes the words:

ועל נסיך שבכל יום עמנו ועל נפלאותיך וטובותיך שבכל עת ערב ובקר וצהרים.

Your miracles which are with us every day and for your wonders and favors at all times, evening, morning, and afternoon.

Out of all our miracles, the one for which we have the most gratitude is the miracle of love and we celebrate it today, naturally.

— 9 —
Seudah Shelishis
אתה אחד ושמך אחד

There are two hints in *parashas Vayechi* to *divrei Torah* regarding the number sixty. The first is the Gemara that visiting the infirmed removes

---

64   See *Orach Chaim* 218:9.
65   *Bereishis Rabbah* 84:16; *Shabbos* 22a.
66   See *Sotah* 2a. See also "*Vayeishev*, (8) Marriage."

1/60th of that person's sickness and pain.[67] This may not be sufficient to significantly alter the state of the sick person, but if enough people visit, it will. When Yosef visited Yaakov, who was ill, Yaakov strengthened himself to sit up in bed: "וישב על המטה."[68] The *gematria* of the word המטה is 59 because Yosef's visit removed 1/60th of Yaakov's illness and he was left with 59/60ths.

The first Mishnah in *Maseches Peah* points out that there is no set amount of *bikkurim*, "first fruits," that we must bring to the Temple. However, Chazal have assigned a designation of 1/60th to fulfill the obligation of *bikkurim*.[69] There is a hint to this as well from our *parashah*. Yehudah's blessing mentions, "ולשורקה בני אתונו," which literally means that the vines in Yehudah's land will be so thick that he'll be able to tether a donkey to its branches.[70] Chazal interpret this to mean that every single tree in the future will produce so much fruit, it will require two donkeys to carry it.[71] The Gemara informs us that a donkey, for the purposes of rentals and liability, is able to carry the volume of 15 *se'ah* (the volume of 2,160 eggs).[72] If so, two donkeys can carry 30 *se'ah*. The Torah says to put the *bikkurim* in a טנא, a "large basket."[73] The Mishnah indicates that a טנא carries half a *se'ah*.[74] If so, the ratio of the vessel carrying *bikkurim* is 1/2:30 or 1:60. And 60 happens to also be the *gematria* of טנא, the large basket in which the *bikkurim* are placed.

---

67   *Nedarim* 39b.
68   *Bereishis* 48:2.
69   *Mishnah Peah* 1:2.
70   *Bereishis* 49:11.
71   *Kesubos* 111a.
72   *Bava Metzia* 78b–79a.
73   *Devarim* 26:2.
74   *Mishnah Tamid* 3:6.

— 10 —
Word of the Parashah

חכלילי עינים מיין ולבן שנים מחלב—His eyes are red with wine
and his teeth, white with milk
Bereishis 49:12

Rashi translates חכלילי as "red" based on the rendition of *Targum Onkelos*, "יסמקון." *Rashi* offers a proof text from *Mishlei*, which describes the woe and travail caused by excessive wine: "למי חכללות עינים."[75] This refers to bleary eyes, the redness of which becomes noticeable in someone who has drunk an excess of wine.[76]

This verse is a description of the abundance of wine and milk that the land of Yehudah will produce. Rabbi Shimshon Raphael Hirsch considers the root of חכלילי to mean to "sparkle," "shine," or "emit color."[77] Hayim Tawil's Akkadian lexicon points to its similar usage in Akkadian poetry, in which *ekelu* means "dark."[78] As such, a number of English translations read "Eyes that are darker than wine and teeth that are whiter than milk."[79]

Ramban takes the word in a very different direction. He says, "הנראה בעיני שהוא הפוך—It seems to me to be overturned." What *Ramban* means by this is that the root of the word is not חכל but כהל. Many words in *Tanach* switch letters in this way, the most common examples being כבש and כשב as well as שמלה and שלמה. This is known as metathesis, and according to *Ramban*, means that in this case, the word connects to the eyes in a different way. *Ramban* explains the word in light of the verse, "כחלת עיניך—You paint your eyes."[80] This was done for cosmetic or medicinal purposes.

---

75 *Mishlei* 23:29.
76 *Pesikta Zutrasa, Vayechi* 49:12, applies this description to the Messianic era.
77 *Etymological Dictionary*, p. 80, "חכל."
78 *Akkadian Lexical Companion*, p. 106.
79 So translates Robert Alter, as well as the new JPS translation. Koren and ArtScroll translate as *Onkelos* and *Rashi*.
80 *Yechezkel* 23:40.

The effect, however, is essentially the same. The land of Yehudah will produce so much wine that people will have to paint their eyes due to the damaging effects of the alcohol. *Ramban* then suggests that the Arabic word *el cahol* shares a similar derivative with חכלילי, referring to alcohol.

A final *Tanach* connection to חכלילי is the name of Nechemiah's father. Nechemiah was the cupbearer for the Persian king Artaxerxes I. He is called התירשתא.[81] This is an honorific Persian title but is expounded nonetheless as a Hebrew word. The word תירש, meaning "wine" is embedded in the verse and *Rashi* explains that he is called התירשתא because he was given a היתר, "permission," for שתייה, to "drink" some wine before serving it to the king.[82] Nechemiah's father's name is among the two closest words in *Tanach* to the word of our *parashah*. Nechemiah ben Chachalyah served wine for a living, and חכלילי is the effect wine has on the inhabitants of Yehudah.

---

81   *Nechemiah* 7:65, 8:9, 10:2.

82   *Yerushalmi, Kiddushin* 4:1.

About the Author

RABBI ALLEN SCHWARTZ has served the Upper West Side of Manhattan since 1985 and has been the rabbi of the historic Congregation Ohab Zedek for the past thirty-three years. He has taught over three thousand students at Yeshiva University since 1983 and currently teaches at Manhattan Day School. His Bible curriculum is widely used in day schools and high schools in the New York area, and he has also served as camp rabbi and educational director at Camp Morasha and Camp Mesorah for many summers. He is the author of numerous articles on Biblical and Rabbinic themes and has published the commentary of Rabbi Elazar Rokeach to *Sefer Mishlei* (Book of Proverbs), *The 4 Sons Haggadah*, and *Conflict and Resolution in the Early Prophets*.

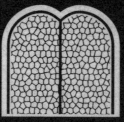

MOSAICA PRESS
BOOK PUBLISHERS

Elegant, Meaningful & Bold

info@MosaicaPress.com
www.MosaicaPress.com

The Mosaica Press team of
acclaimed editors and designers
is attracting some of the most
compelling thinkers and teachers
in the Jewish community today.
Our books are available around
the world.

HARAV YAACOV HABER
RABBI DORON KORNBLUTH